THE STATE OF THE NATION

THE STATE OF

THE NATION

PARLIAMENT

The three-part programme on Parliament which is the subject of this book is Granada Television's third excursion into examining a subject of major national importance in depth and in launching the subsequent television programmes prominently and at a greater length than is usually allotted to current affairs.

The first was a series of five programmes on Britain's economy, transmitted in April and May 1962 under the title *For Richer for Poorer, An Inquiry into the Business of Britain.*

The second was a series of five programmes on Britain's economy, transmitted in August and September 1966 under the title *The State of the Nation.*

The three-part programme on Parliament, lasting a total of

five hours, was transmitted at 10.30 pm on three consecutive nights: 23, 24 and 25 July 1973.

This book contains a transcript of this programme, together with an explanation of how the particular subjects were chosen and how they were treated, a selection of tables from the survey of public attitudes to Parliament that was conducted for the programme (the most extensive survey yet attempted on this subject) and excerpts from viewers' letters and press criticisms resulting from the programme.

The Editor of the programme on Parliament was Brian Lapping. Research for the programme was carried out by Norma Percy. For Part 1 the director was Roger Graef, parliamentary consultant Maureen Tomison, cameraman Charles Stewart, film editor Terence Twigg, sound recordist Iain Bruce. For Part 2 directors were Peter Mullings and Royston Morley, researcher David Kemp. For Part 3 directors were Eric Harrison and Peter Mullings. The narrator was Mike Scott. The Executive Producer was Jeremy Wallington. The book was edited by Duncan Crow.

Parliament

Published October 1973
Copyright © Granada Television Limited
36 Golden Square London WIR 4AH
Manchester M60 9EA

Designed by Alan Pinnock
Made and printed in Great Britain by
William Caple & Co Ltd Leicester
Set in Monotype Garamond

ISBN 0 904005 01 1

Contents

How it all happened

by Brian Lapping and Norma Percy

Granada spent something over a year and a half completing *The State of the Nation* on Parliament.

Parliament was chosen as the subject because it seemed to be at a moment of crucial change. Britain was about to enter the European Economic Community, with its enormous implications for Parliament: loss of total sovereignty over tax-raising and customs duties; senior decision-makers (in the Commission in Brussels) under no obligation to report to the House of Commons; a new and important body of business (EEC regulations and directives) to be handled; in all a challenge that seemed to call for significant adaptation of the way Parliament operates. At the same time Parliament awaited the report of the Royal Commission on the Constitution which seemed likely to recommend separate Parliaments for Scotland and Wales and possibly the regions of England. Thus the EEC might steal powers from above and new regional assemblies from below.

These challenges came at a time when the House of Commons had itself recently digested a series of reforms: Richard Crossman, when he was Leader of the House from 1966 to 1968, removed much of the procedural mumbo jumbo – such as the interruption of business by Black Rod, signifying the Royal Assent to bills – that impeded business on the floor of the House, got rid of some tedious summer late night sittings by sending part of the Finance Bill to Committee, increased the opportunity for back-benchers to raise topical issues on the floor of the House, and started an experiment in the use of specialist Select Committees. William Whitelaw, when he became Leader of the House in 1970, carried this last experiment a stage further: he created a permanent Select Committee on Public Expenditure, with a wide-ranging brief to probe many areas of Government policy. These committees marked a possible new path for the House of Commons: by means of them, back-bench Members might become much more expert and effective overseers of Government policy. Thus the door was ajar to further Parliamentary reform. Finally, when we began planning the television programmes, the admission of television cameras to the chamber seemed imminent: both William Whitelaw and his successor as Leader of the House of Commons, Robert Carr, promised a debate on televising the proceedings for an experimental period and that they would support this; had cameras been admitted, the consequences for many of the procedures of the House might have been considerable. In short, given that Parliament is an important institution and an admirable subject for an ambitious series of programmes, the time seemed particularly apt.

But what were we to say about Parliament? This chapter attempts to describe how we worked towards that decision.

Our starting point was Bernard Crick's book *The Reform of Parliament*, written in 1963, which had launched public interest in making MPs more informed critics of the Executive, primarily through the development of investigatory Select Committees. But 'the reform of the committee system' seemed an arid and mechanistic subject for a television programme. So we turned away from Crick, with his detailed concern about the workings of the machinery of the House of Commons, towards what seemed a wider canvas: the people and Parliament. We began with the thesis that the public is discontented with Parliament. The widespread complaints that Mr Heath's government, like Mr Wilson's before it, did the opposite of what it had promised; the allegedly menacing demands of Scottish and Welsh nationalists for more power to the regions; the marches, sit-ins and defiance of law by trade union militants, students and tenants; the fashionable talk of demands for 'participation' all pointed to the hypothesis that there is substantial dissatisfaction about the way big decisions get taken in Britain, with Parliament, presumably, high on the list of culprits. To assess the extent of this feeling, we commissioned the biggest survey of public attitudes to Parliament that has ever been attempted. In the early planning stages of our project this seemed likely to provide the starting point for our television programme.

At the same time we looked for ways to deal with this supposed dissatisfaction. Was there some way, for example, to develop the MP's constituency surgery work? The area of his activities in which the MP is most effective is in solving constituents' problems. And this is an area in which the demand for help is growing. Government services, nationalised industries, large companies, all put the individual at a disadvantage, and none of the organisations that try to help has a national standing equal to the job. The MP is the one figure people know they can turn to. Why not, therefore, greatly strengthen his ability to provide an efficient service? If every MP was given a local shop with a full-time social worker and secretary to assist him, he could provide a service for constituents much superior to anything now available. This would both make the job he does for them more visible, thus strengthening public confidence in the MP, and increase the amount of 'feedback' from constituents about where the shoe pinches. Our scheme was to provide increased service to constituents without substantially increasing the burden on the Member himself: his staff in the constituency shop would filter cases, dealing with the simple ones on the spot (thus relieving the MP of trivia and of cases for which he can be no more than a post-box), while increasing the number of difficult ones he could himself handle.

Several MPs with whom we discussed this idea were enthusiastic, and some were prepared to have the experiment tried in their own constituencies. Further support for the idea came from our survey of public attitudes to Parliament: most citizens seem to value the MP's constituency work above any other aspect of his duties, while only half are aware that their MPs run 'surgeries'.

But in the end we rejected this as a major theme for the programme. Changes, possibly along the lines described above, might help MPs perform their constituency role even better than most of them already do. However, the main duty of MPs is in their national, political role, and it is here that they appeared weakest. So we concentrated our efforts in this area.

Our attempts to tackle supposed popular dissatisfaction were not limited to the MP's constituency role. The political parties' methods of selecting parliamentary candidates had been criticised. In some 450 of the 630 parliamentary constituencies one party has a safe majority: in those seats the electorate as a whole does not choose the Member; a small group meeting in private, the party selection committee which chooses the candidate, takes the real decision. One suggestion that has been put forward is that primaries – in which candidates, including sitting MPs, were selected by a vote of all paid-up party members before each election – could increase public participation, particularly in safe seats; could give constituents a chance to pronounce on the cross-party issue of the moment (e.g. Britain's entry into the EEC) without going against their political party; could reward the efforts of a hard-working MP with greater security in his constituency, while allowing the electorate to replace a less hard-working MP without letting the opposition in. The case seemed strong, but we decided in the end against including primaries in the television programme because this theme would have involved immersing viewers in such complicated side-issues as the relations between the Labour Party and affiliated trade unions.

While we had been considering ideas for constituency surgery improvements and primaries – both designed to respond to supposed public discontent with Parliament and MPs – our survey was being put to the public. The results undermined our thinking. The majority of the public express a consistently high level of satisfaction with Parliament and their own MPs. Citizens in Scotland and Wales seem to be just as happy as those in England. Trade union members are just as happy with Parliament as the rest of the community. And while the public's answers to certain detailed questions about Parliament suggested that most citizens would not perform well in quiz programmes about the constitution, the general grasp of realities seemed surprisingly high: the power of Parliament was not overestimated but its value was recognised nonetheless. The only group to express serious disaffection was the young (those aged 18–24) and while we were at first inclined to think this a serious cause for concern, closer examination of the answers of young respondents suggested general youthful indifference rather than profound disaffection from Parliament itself. The survey suggests, though it cannot prove, that the young become more interested in Parliament, and more favourably disposed towards it, as they vote in elections and grow older.

The results of the Granada survey stopped us in our tracks. As one member of the team working on the programmes put it, 'Parliament is the people's voice and the people are satisfied with it; so why should we produce television programmes about reform?' The answer was that our talks with MPs, Clerks of the House of Commons, Civil Servants, academics and political journalists were clearly revealing a great deal that is wrong with Parliament, and if our survey showed that the public did not realise this, the obligation on us to inform them was all the greater.

What did the participants think was wrong? A surprisingly

large number of those we first spoke to agreed: a big job needs doing, Parliament is the obvious instrument to do it, yet doesn't. The frustration of MPs, particularly young ones, repeatedly focussed on Parliament's failure – and their own – adequately to serve as the people's watchdog over the Executive. Part of this job is performed by Ministers, the public's representatives at the head of civil service departments, who, when a decision has been proposed say 'I want to see the papers on this, I want to satisfy myself that all is well'. But the enormous growth in the size of government, and in the number and complexity of important decisions, has meant that Ministers perform this function over less and less of the area of responsibility of their departments. Inevitably, a growing proportion of medium-sized and even quite large decisions gets taken by Civil Servants without being carefully examined by a Minister at all. Yet, when MPs who are not Ministers try to shoulder some of this burden, Ministers have tended to reply in a mixture of pique and fear, not 'Keep out, it's none of your business to poke into sensitive areas', but, 'Look, old boy, I'll tell you the inside story on this. We've got an inter-departmental committee starting to work – in confidence at the moment, of course. And a proposal for doing something along the lines you suggest has just come back from a Cabinet sub-committee to be revised. So I can't tell you any details now, but let's keep in touch' – which amounts to the same thing.

All those who raised this criticism with us agreed that it is the Government's job to govern. They did not wish, as back-benchers, to usurp that function: merely to be allowed to peep into a few doors and to make sure, on the voters' behalf, that the job is being done properly. In the words of one of them: 'To come here and find oneself so utterly excluded from the real process of decision-making is a shock. After a few years here, many MPs choose to delude themselves into believing that they have a real say. They don't. They enjoy being in this splendid club, chatting to Ministers in the lobbies and tea room.' Meanwhile most decisions are made in Whitehall by Civil Servants, without a representative of the public having a full chance to examine them. Down the road in Westminster several hundred representatives of the public, who would be delighted to take on part of the job, are under-employed.

Part of the reason for this is the long standing tradition of Parliament as a fairly amateur shambles of Oxford Union debaters, country bumpkins, lawyers and self-satisfied burghers believing that laws can be written and the affairs of the nation supervised in spare moments from the serious business of earning money, hunting and living up to one's income. Such an assembly was, perhaps understandably, excluded from the expanding business of government in the first half of the twentieth century. But, we were repeatedly told, a growing number of MPs come into the House today ready to be full-timers, regarding Parliament not as a splendid club but as a place of work. However, they feel they are not encouraged. If, on the Standing Committee on a Bill, a Government back-bencher wishes to make a helpful contribution, he is liable to be rapidly told by his party whip to keep his mouth shut: he is there to help get the Government's business through quickly by voting when called upon to do so, not to slow things down by raising needless objections (see page 173 Crosland on Scott). When an MP seeks information about Government policy, he is liable to be brushed off by Ministers at Question Time with neat evasions and answers devised to reveal as little as possible, plainly indicating that Ministers and Civil Servants regard it as a triumph to keep information from MPs, where one might think it in the public interest that they should share it. Of course, there is a purpose behind the political game as played at Westminster. But the effect is to ensure that the majority of the 630 Members of Parliament are far less effective helpers in the government process than most of them want to be and are capable of being.

This view of what is wrong with the House of Commons was not reached quickly. It came only after conversations with many MPs, some of which led us down interesting side-alleys. One Shadow Cabinet member, for example, told us that the problem was the long hours the House sits: the most ludicrous of any legislature in the world; 'efficient work simply is not done after 8 pm except by owls and bats'.

Not only does this pattern of work make for inefficiency, it is also needlessly disruptive of MPs' private lives; if the hours were altered so that the House regularly rose by mid-evening, more women could become MPs; also many more able men in industry and the universities would be attracted to Parliament. It sounded like a good thesis for the programme.

Yet we did not pursue this theme in the end. Perhaps it would be a good thing if Parliament started work earlier in the morning and ended earlier in the evening. But many committees do start at 10.30 am already, and Ministers are said to need most mornings for their departmental work in Whitehall. In any case, morning sittings were tried in 1967 and were acknowledged to be a failure even by their sponsor, Mr Crossman; the Opposition sabotaged them and the House sat as late as ever into the night. Indeed, no matter how much they grumble or how mad it appears to outsiders, we gained the impression that MPs secretly enjoy their strange pattern of life. (This impression was supported by the results of an enquiry by the Procedure Committee in 1966 – a majority of MPs replying advocated no change in the times of sittings.) Furthermore, the argument about the quality of MPs being lower than that of some outsiders was not one we felt competent to raise. It would be almost impossible to compare the quality of MPs with that of, say, company managing directors, and the study by Anthony Barker and Michael Rush, *The Member of Parliament and his Information* (PEP/Study of Parliament Group, 1970) suggests that the level of education and the knowledge of public affairs of MPs are better than they used to be. If there is a fault, informed observers seem to agree, it lies not in the quality of the practitioners but in the present nature of the job.

One MP devoted a brilliant lunch hour with us to describing the iniquities of present procedure at Question Time. For example, putting down a question to the Prime Minister in such a form that it is in order and will not get transferred to the appropriate departmental Minister severely tests the ingenuity of the MP. Few forms can be relied upon to work: one, asking if 'the Prime Minister will pay an official visit to . . . (the MP's constituency or perhaps Brussels)', and receiving the answer 'I have at present no plans to do so, sir,' gives the MP a chance to ask a supplementary about unemployment or housing in his constituency, or the misdeeds of the EEC Commission; another, asking 'Will the Prime Minister place in the library a copy of his public speech at . . . on . . .?' and receiving the answer, which the questioner well knows, 'I have already done so, sir', allows the opportunity for a supplementary on the subject of the speech.

Even after he has surmounted such procedural hurdles, the MP will find Question Time of little use for sustained probing on policy or serious consideration of a constituency case. The cards are entirely in the Minister's hands; he is forewarned and his Civil Servants supply him with answers to all the supplementaries they can think of; and in the last resort the Minister can just refuse to answer. Each MP is allowed only one supplementary and the Speaker quickly moves on to the next tabled question, so a Minister can easily dodge difficult ones. The 'question rigging' scandal of 1971/72 (Ministers had lists of helpful questions prepared by their Civil Servants which they handed out to back-benchers to ask) showed how far Question Time had deteriorated into a party point-scoring game. So, our friend concluded, though widely regarded throughout the world as a superb institution for pressing the Executive, Question Time is now largely a matinee entertainment for tourists. Should this not be a major theme for our programme?

Again we made some enquiries, and eventually decided that, although what he said was true, this was not the right subject for us. The Select Committee on Parliamentary Questions had just reported and some improvements in procedure seemed likely to follow. Moreover, British MPs' outstanding talent is for raising a row. If a constituent has been wronged, if a civil liberty has been threatened, if the State is treading on somebody's toes, Parliament provides a grand sounding-board for the concern and sometimes the outrage of MPs. Whether by means of a Parliamentary question, an adjournment debate, or a Ten Minute Rule Bill, an MP who is deeply worried or scandalised about a matter can normally get a reasonable hearing in the House and a reasonable ministerial reply, and sometimes a surprisingly wide coverage in the newspapers the next morning. Parliamentary questions are not all they are cracked up to be, but they remain a useful weapon in the MP's modest armoury.

The Granada survey showed that the public's most persistent complaint against Parliament is the dominance – or the bickering – of the parties. The accusation that politicians put party before country is common, and large majorities, when asked by public opinion polls, have repeatedly favoured coalition above party government. The obvious fallacy in this complaint is well summed up in an essay Edmund Burke wrote in 1769, *Observations on a Late Publication intituled, 'The Present State of the Nation'*: 'Party divisions, whether on the whole operating for good or evil, are things inseparable from free government'. Of course parties can abuse their freedom. But nothing in the British party system suggests that the abuse is serious. To cry out against their excesses, to demand a government 'above parties' (as some have recently done), would have been anti-parliamentary and anti-democratic.

The aspect of the party system that is most criticised is the whips. Indeed, it would have been impossible to contemplate making a programme about Parliament without looking at this much criticised area: MPs as lobby-fodder, voting dutifully each night as the whips instruct them, a task as Christopher Hollis pointed out, that could equally well be performed by sheep. W S Gilbert put it even better in *HMS Pinafore*:

I always voted at my party's call
And I never thought of thinking for myself at all
(The Ruler of the Queen's Navee).

The picture some outsiders have of the whips as rigid disciplinarians, ordering MPs to do as they are told, is wrong. As one MP put it to us, the whips in the House of Commons have little power and are really less like whips than feather dusters. But the fact remains that most MPs regularly vote the party line, passing laws and rejecting motions as the whips tell them, without bothering to examine the content. Why? Because on most issues that come before the House, MPs have no strong view and are happy to be guided by like-minded colleagues. And even when they disagree with a particular policy, Government back-benchers are generally more concerned that the Government succeed than that the policy be changed; similarly Opposition back-benchers, though policy disagreements with their own front-benchers are more common, always share with them one overriding purpose: they want the Government out. Indeed this is the strength of the British system: that the Government chosen from the biggest party in the House of Commons can be sure of a voluntary majority for almost all its business. Thus the popular vote at a general election, however small a majority it gives to one party, enables that party effectively to govern, without the risk of daily defeat at the hands of changing back-bench alliances (such as weakened, for example, the fourth French Republic). That is why, in spite of the whips' lack of sanctions, MPs are so willing to obey. The whips are not simply the agent of the party bosses. Like the trainer of a football team, they help the players as much as the captain and the manager to achieve their common purpose. If what is needed is more strength or freedom for back-benchers, weakening the whips is not the way to get it: that would destroy more than it strengthened.

Our research led us down other promising side-alleys: Fixed term elections? Full-time MPs? The machinery to enable MPs to vote by proxy at the end of debates? Research staff for MPs or for the official Opposition? A system for better scrutiny of delegated legislation? Putting legislation in simpler language? Every one of them is, in the eyes of some Members or outside academics, the key reform that is now needed.

The process of sifting ideas about Parliamentary reform went on for some months, and not only did we reject many of the ideas put to us; we also found that most of our own original reasons for making a programme about Parliament at this time did not apply when we came to examine them in detail. For example, we began from the belief that Britain's entry into the European Economic Community would both rob Parliament of a substantial portion of its sovereignty and demand major changes. But a careful reading of the debates on the European Communities Bill suggested that, even though the most brilliant opponents of Britain's entry, Michael Foot and Enoch Powell, convincingly described the imminent demise of Parliamentary sovereignty, EEC entry involved for Parliament not a difference of kind in its relations with the Executive, but merely a difference in degree. Some of the powers attributed to Parliament during the debates on the European Communities Bill were exaggerated; most of them had long since passed to the Cabinet. John Mackintosh illustrated this point in a speech in the House on 16 February 1972 during the debate on the Bill. Critics of Britain's entry into the EEC had complained about the loss of control by Parliament over agriculture, with the introduction of the EEC's common agricultural policy and consequent control from Brussels. What, Mackintosh asked, was the situation now?

' . . . representing two agricultural counties, I recall going round before the annual price review collecting information from my farmers. I studied the statistics and prepared a memorandum on what I thought ought to be done in farming policy for the coming year. I wrote to my Rt Hon Friend the Member for Workington (Mr Peart), who was then Minister of Agriculture, Fisheries and Food, asking whether I could see him. I hope that he will not mind if I quote his reply, which I have always treasured: "Thank you for your letter and I am, of course, always glad to see back-benchers, particularly those with agricultural constituencies. However, as it is agricultural broad pricing and policy questions that you wish to discuss, I must point out that I am engaged with the NFU and the Treasury in the annual price review and it would be quite inappropriate for me to listen to, or be influenced by the views of a Member of Parliament on such a matter".'

This may be an extreme case but it reminds one that Parliament is not and never has been sovereign. Sovereign in Britain is the Queen in Parliament, which means the government with the consent of the legislature. This is made clear in the enacting formula which provides the opening words for all Acts of Parliament: 'Be it enacted by the Queen's Most Excellent Majesty, by and with the consent of the Lords Spiritual and Temporal, and Commons in this present Parliament assembled, and by the authority of the same as follows . . . ' In any case, there seemed little point in turning our programme about Parliament into a programme about Britain's entry into the Common Market.

Similar arguments applied to two other of our original arguments for making the programmes when we did. The report of the Royal Commission on the Constitution, which we had expected to seriously affect the position of Parliament, was long delayed, by the death of its chairman and dissent within the Commission leading to resignation; probably, therefore, its impact would be limited. In any event, the threat of Scottish and Welsh nationalism that had led to its creation had apparently diminished by 1972/73 and the Granada survey seemed to show, surprisingly, that the Scots and Welsh are no more dissatisfied with Parliament than are the English. Likewise, our expectation that television cameras would be, at least experimentally, admitted to the House of Commons with all the consequences that would have flowed from that, was proved wrong. In October 1972 the House of Commons voted against the proposal that it be televised for an experimental period, apparently closing the issue for the 1970–75 Parliament, although some Select Committees continued to try and get themselves on the air.

In sorting through all these ideas we had private conversations with about sixty MPs and about twenty academic experts in politics and government, from all parts of the political spectrum. Our full-time staff included Conservatives as well as Labour party people; close friends and advisors to the project ranged from a Monday Club member, Mr Edward Taylor MP, to a member of the Tribune group, Mr Norman Buchan MP.

During a trip to Washington, one of us talked to John Brademas, Democratic whip in the US House of Representatives. He showed us a Brookings Institution study of Congressmen, which employed a method that we adapted to provide a more systematic way of gathering the views of MPs. We arranged a succession of dinners with two small groups of MPs, chaired by Professor Anthony King, who edited the recorded transcripts into a book due to be published by Macmillan in spring 1974. An equally important purpose, of which the MPs at the dinners were fully aware, was to help to clarify our minds on some of the issues to be raised in the programme. The comments of almost all the MPs at the dinners on the mildness of the discipline of the whips are an example: they reinforced our previous belief that the whips should not be a major theme of the programme. The warm enthusiasm of all the MPs at the dinners for the development of Select Committees similarly reinforced our earlier view.

Our steps towards an orderly analysis of the subject were gradual; from conversation with MPs and others we went on to a careful working through a prepared agenda with groups of Labour and Conservative MPs over dinner. To help us take the next step forward we approached David Watt, the political editor of the *Financial Times*. He drew up for us the chart 'What's wrong with Parliament' on pages 24–26.

The chart represents, not one person's or one group's view of what is wrong with Parliament; it is an attempt to list the main functions, the most significant alleged malfunctions and some reform proposals. The chart helped to clarify our thinking, but even our unusually long television programme could not cover all of it.

The first two items in the chart, legislation and oversight of Government policy, seemed the most fundamental and had been subject to the heaviest array of telling criticisms. Further, as the chart shows, 'Poor scrutiny of legislation' and 'Failure to examine estimates or expenditure plans' share a single proposed remedy: specialist Select Committees.

When we came to plan our programme, we tried to construct a platform on which MPs, Civil Servants and Clerks could amplify the defects or virtues about which many of them had spoken to us. At the same time we wanted to convey to viewers the flavour of the House of Commons, to show MPs as far as possible conducting their normal business as they do every day.

To do this we set about showing – in the first part of our programme – the complex behind-the-scenes interactions that surround a Government decision. This involved our going into Parliament, into the Civil Service and into the private meetings of Ministers and back-benchers. We realised that it would almost certainly be impossible to get into Government meetings at which open discussion took place about public expenditure decisions. So we limited our hopes to following a small Government legislative decision and the parliamentary/ministerial talks it provoked. The negotiations to seek admission took some months and finally required approval at Cabinet level since we asked for a major constitutional innovation: Civil Servants do not publicly contradict their Ministers; by asking to be allowed to record their office conversations and their advice to a Minister before a decision was taken, we were in effect asking to see Civil Servants give advice which might turn out to be the opposite of the ministerial decision. Our request could be seen as a challenge to Mr Heath's commitment to 'open Government'.

The challenge was happily accepted and we were granted a degree of access that surprised some lobby correspondents and academics who had never been allowed anywhere near civil servant/ministerial conversations inside a department or even back-benchers' private meetings about tactics on the Standing Committee of a Bill. Indeed, even a Committee of the House had been turned down. In 1970, for its report on the process of legislation, the Select Committee on Procedure attempted to get permission to examine 'the initiative for amendment that was made in the course of proceedings on a particular Bill'. This permission was not granted.

Ministers, Civil Servants, and MPs were all extraordinarily helpful to us and enabled us to follow one episode: a part of the Fair Trading Bill during its passage through the Committee stage in the House of Commons. We proved luckier than we had expected. The part of the Bill we were allowed to follow dealt with the powers of the new Director-General of Fair Trading whose office the Bill created. This was not only an important matter, it was also politically extremely lively, with outside pressure groups and members of the Standing Committee seeking considerable changes which the Civil Servants felt bound to advise their Ministers to resist. Filming

WHAT'S WRONG WITH PARLIAMENT

FUNCTION	MALFUNCTION	POSSIBLE REMEDIES
1 **Legislation**	Poor scrunity of legislation by back-benchers	Specialist Committees dealing with legislation
		Two-stage scrunity
	Too much legislation	Voluntary time-tabling
		Abolition of 'sessions'
	Badly } drafted legislation Hastily	Pre-legislation committees
		Reform of draftsmen's department
	Total breakdown of oversight of delegated legislation	Worthwhile delegated legislation committee
	Lack of opportunity for controversial Private Members' Bills	Changes in Standing Orders Departmental Bills
2 **Oversight of Government Policy**	Inadequate information	Better pay } Research facilities } for MPs
	Complexity of government leading to loss of control	Ditto for the Opposition as such
	Breakdown of Question Time	Longer Question Time and positive will to make it work; more supplementaries

	Failure to examine estimates or expenditure plans	Development of specialist committee structure
3 Reflection and Education of Public Thinking	Remoteness Unrepresentativeness Arcane 'club' atmosphere Powerlessness } leading to lack of public confidence Failure to communicate with the public	More open selection procedures for Parliamentary candidates Improved physical facilities for lobbying at Westminster Reform of Lords to represent regional interests More free votes (less whipping) Better choice of debate subjects TV Simplification of procedure
4 Representation of the Subject	Breakdown of Question Time Failure of Ombudsman Breakdown of oversight of delegated legislation	Ombudsman with wider powers A Constituency Office, properly staffed Improved procedure for prayers against delegated legislation

FUNCTION	MALFUNCTION	POSSIBLE REMEDIES
4 *continued*	General weakness of the back-benches as against front-benches	Recognition that strong, independent Speaker is essential
5 **Pool of Executive Talent**	Lack of executive administrative } experience available Lack of quality in candidates General boredom leading to disillusionment, indolence, dispersal of effort among MPs	More/fewer part-time MPs New ways to harness outside expertise to the political process More conscious 'training' of junior Ministers Better use of Lords Involving government back-benchers in ministry work
6 **Cockpit of Party Struggle**	Not seen by public Cowboys and Indians despised by public	Televise chamber and committees More open procedure for selecting parliamentary candidates

any 'proceeding of the House of Commons' had been ruled out by the decision of the House against admitting television. So we filmed everything else we could: members of the Standing Committee on the Fair Trading Bill discussing their tactics for the Committee stage; Civil Servants discussing the meaning of amendments put down and how they should advise Ministers to respond to them; the Civil Servants briefing the Ministers (Sir Geoffrey Howe and Mr Peter Emery) on arguments to be raised in the Standing Committee; outside interest groups, like the Consumers' Association and the Confederation of British Industry, arguing among themselves and with both MPs and Civil Servants about how the clauses we were following should be amended; the Civil Servants attempting to re-draft the clauses, following discussion in the Standing Committee; and, finally, the Ministers privately presenting the amended clauses to their critics on the Standing Committee before the Report Stage of the Bill.

The careful historical record which we believe part one of our programme represents illustrated some problems that were then examined by the committee in part two. We invited MPs to do a large part of the work for us by conducting a hearing, in exactly the manner of a Select Committee of the House. Our committee included two 'reformers' on most of the themes to be examined (Mr John Mackintosh and Mr Nicholas Scott), and two of the leading anti-reformers (Mr Michael Foot and Mr Reginald Maudling) under the chairmanship of Mr Edward du Cann who, at the time we planned the programme, was chairman of the largest Commons Select Committee. As the transcript shows, they looked at, first, the size and complexity of Government leading to loss of parliamentary control; second, poor scrutiny of legislation; and third, failure to examine Government expenditure plans. Insofar as all five agreed with certain of the points made to them we may claim to have advanced the argument.

Sir William Armstrong, the Head of the Home Civil Service, told this committee that Parliamentary control over Ministers and the Civil Service had significantly loosened since he entered the service. All five MPs accepted this. When Mr Maudling put it to Sir William that some such loosening was necessary nowadays for the Government to get business through quickly, Sir William replied: 'I think there would be some spheres of activity where a slowing down would be sensible. Frequently Acts of Parliament are passed, then after a little while an amending Act is brought in, the thing is adapted and adjusted and it seems fairly clear, looking back on it, that perhaps the first one was brought in a little faster than it need have been. While it's quite true that speedy re-action is needed in some spheres, it doesn't follow that it's needed all over.' When Mr Foot said, 'Much of the evidence, including your own, Sir William, suggests that Parliament still has enormous powers against the Executive if they wish to use it. Is that correct? Is that your view too?' Sir William responded, 'Yes, that is so, but as also came out there is a big question – *if* they wish to use it.' The impression conveyed by Sir William Armstrong of Parliament slipping in its capacity (or will) to oversee both the growing volume and the growing complexity of Government business was strongly reinforced by the evidence of the Clerks of the House.

The evidence of poor scrutiny of legislation by back-benchers was not accepted by the members of the committee with such unanimity. Professor J A G Griffith's study of every Govern-ment Bill in three sessions, done for PEP and the Study of Parliament Group (a body of Clerks of the House of Commons and academics) formed the basis of the committee's examina-tion. His findings show that Parliament made very few *significant* changes to Government legislation[1]. In addition our committee looked at one Bill. Choosing the right one was not easy. The most common sort of Bill is short and non-contro-versial; 103 of the 183 Bills considered in the three sessions went through all their stages in less than ten hours (at an average of three hours a Bill) without even going upstairs to Standing Committee. These present no problem. Their simplicity and non-controversial character mean that the Civil Servants and draftsmen normally get them right. We therefore did not choose a Bill of this kind, but looked instead at the eleven Bills in the 1971–72 session which took over thirty hours each going through the Commons. These are either long and de-tailed, like the Housing Finance Bill, or short and highly controversial along party lines.

For our example we chose one of the latter sort, the Sound Broadcasting Bill. It was a Bill of some importance but short and easy to follow. And although it was a partisan Bill, it con-tained clauses which both sides of the Standing Committee be-lieved could profit from technical improvement. The Bill

[1]See page 184 for Professor Griffith's findings on 'significant changes' and pages 123-127 for his written evidence to the committee.

graphically demonstrated the limited effect of Commons scrutiny. In Committee, 167 amendments were moved by MPs outside the Government, of which only one was passed. A second defeat for the Government came when the Committee struck out Clause 7. At Report Stage, the two changes made in Committee were reversed and twenty-five further non-Government amendments were moved, of which none passed. The only lasting effect of four and a half months of Commons scrutiny was three Government amendments moved at Report implementing Government promises to re-draft back-bench Committee amendments (and one of these was a very trivial drafting point). The Civil Servant in charge of the Bill's drafting and parliamentary progress described the process to our committee of MPs. He was followed by one of the MPs on the Standing Committee on the Bill, who described its four and a half months' work as 'entirely wasted effort'.

The members of our committee did not accept that the Sound Broadcasting Bill is typical of all Bills that go through Parliament. What they did accept was that often, and particularly when the Bill is the subject of party battles, Parliament fails to carry out effective scrutiny. And while the members of the committee failed to agree on exactly how it was defined, they and the witnesses who appeared before them on this subject agreed that the problem is a serious one. Whether the concern is that Ministers may give binding undertakings to outside interests before a Bill comes to Parliament or (in Mr Maudling's words) that 'politicians go on bashing one another while the Civil Servants get the legislation right', or that the machinery is not suited to detailed scrutiny or liable to abuse by Ministers, a unanimous conclusion emerged that something is amiss with the process of legislation.

On inadequate scrutiny of public expenditure plans, the committee again reached some degree of consensus. All members agreed that scrutiny of past expenditure, as carried out by the Public Accounts Committee, aided by the Comptroller and Auditor-General and his staff of 600, is a great deal more efficient than examination of future expenditure plans. But there was no agreement on what to do about this. Sir William Armstrong and Mr William Rodgers, with the enthusiastic support of three members of the committee, argued for the further development of the House of Commons Select Committee system: investigatory committees hearing evidence, holding public enquiries, producing reports. By this method, they argued, debates in the House of Commons would become better informed, the scrutiny of government activity would become more vigorous. Mr Rodgers spoke about the work of the new Select Committee on Expenditure which, in the two years since its creation, had significantly improved the Commons' scrutiny. It caused the Treasury to reveal that the Government does not know enough to assess how the work done by departments matches up to the needs it is supposed to serve. Wynne Godley, an academic advisor to the committee, by producing examples, caused the Treasury to agree that such comparisons are feasible and to promise to provide relevant figures in future. The committee established the practice of close scrutiny of those Government activities in which actual annual expenditure suffered most from errors in the previous year's forecasts. The committee's first report on Defence contained 69 pages with sentences like this:

'The sub-committee was informed that increased costs were a matter of *** to ***%. The original contingency allowance was about *** and it has now been reduced to ***.'

The consequent public embarrassment led the Ministry of Defence to allow more information to be published in subsequent reports. The committee demonstrated that the Government had no consistent criteria for deciding: (a) why public money should go to one form of industry rather than another; (b) whether projects receiving public aid are meant to be profitable; and (c), most important, whether Government aid has its intended effect of speeding economic growth and raising living standards. While the impact on the Chamber and on the general public of all this work was so far slight, Mr Rodgers, Mr du Cann and Mr Mackintosh argued that these were real accomplishments, a more telling use of MPs' energies than many more publicised activities. Mr Foot and Mr Maudling however, while not putting forward any alternative proposals, made it plain that they do not think development of the Select Committee system is the answer.

The third part of our programme set about examining solutions. It took the form, in effect, of a debate about the Select Committee system. This was the central subject of Bernard Crick's book *The Reform of Parliament*. Thus our research began with Crick and ended with Crick. MPs and lobby correspondents kept telling us that Crick really didn't know much about Parliament, that they never saw him about the place, that he was wrong on all sorts of vital details, like so many theory-obsessed academics. But the more we looked into the matter the more we felt that, whether or not Crick's enthusiasm for the further development of Select Committees is justified, this is the issue which divides MPs more than any other when questions of parliamentary reform are discussed.

On one side are Crick's allies, the 'information first' men, who argue that Parliament is losing the power to influence major Government decisions because MPs don't know enough about the realities. The MPs on this side agree with the point put to us by one Civil Servant during our preliminary research: 'When I have had issues I am dealing with come before the House', he said, 'I know, of course, which are the really sensitive bits of the policy: the bits we may have got wrong, the bits where the balance of argument is very fine. I sit in the box [the Civil Servants' seats in the House] and mentally hold my breath. But Members nearly always miss these sensitive points. They parade over the wider issues – often issues they have been debating for decades – and the Government goes ahead with what it intended to do in the first place, not merely because it can muster a majority in the vote but because little if anything has been said that ought to cause it to think again about the policy.' This point was also made in the second part of our programme by the Civil Servant in charge of the Sound Broadcasting Bill. Asked by Mr du Cann how effective, how interesting, how important was the process of debate in Parliament in influencing the Bill, he replied that the debate, 'was, I think, a little bit disappointing. One thought all the time that there could have been a rather more informed debate'. In part three of our programme, John Selwyn Gummer gave a splendid example:

'I sat for months on the Agriculture (Miscellaneous Provisions) Bill – a matter of no argument at all between the parties. There was a long speech, when we were discussing slaughterhouses, on mink farms. Mink farms – we were discussing, at great length. None of us knew anything about mink farms. But the people who are concerned with mink farms would, I think, have been much helped if we had been able to call some evidence, instead of talking for a very long time about a point that turned out in the end not to be relevant to the Bill at all, which an expert, in two minutes, could have told us.'

The 'information first' men are seriously concerned that lack of knowledge prevents MPs from doing their jobs properly and believe that more Select Committees are needed to put this right.

On the other side are the 'Chamber first' men, who argue that the main purpose of the House of Commons is to raise the major political issues that divide the nation and not (in the words of one of them to us) 'to get buried in petty administrative issues like the line of the M4 motorway'. Michael Foot put it better during our programme when he said it is undesirable 'to turn Members of Parliament into auditors and accountants'. The greatest politicians, this argument runs, have not been the greatest masters of detail; they have been (as Brian Walden said in part three) the men most capable at the 'articulation of popular sentiment', most aware of fundamental changes in the direction of national feeling. The vital function of the House of Commons is to be responsive to these deeper currents, not to be distracted by the mere ebb and flow of daily tides – the detailed business of keeping an eye on the Civil Servants.

However Anthony Crosland argued in the debate in the third part of our programme that most of the 365 days each year are taken up, in the House of Commons, with 'housing policy, education policy, the social services', issues too detailed to provoke great debates. Indeed the great issues that fundamentally divide the Chamber – appeasement, Suez, EEC entry, nuclear disarmament, immigration – crop up rarely. Richard Crossman, a former Leader of the House of Commons, summing up the debate, referred to comments from the other side that the Chamber of the House of Commons is empty most days: 'I'll say why it's empty. Because it isn't worth listening to, because most of what is discussed on the floor is unsuitable for general debate between 625 people . . . The wrong things are debated there constantly.' So Mr Crosland, Mr Crossman and their allies asked for detailed matters to be removed from the Floor of the House to more effective scrutiny in Committee. Mr Crossman had already started this process with the removal of parts of the Finance Bill to Standing Committee (though not yet to an investigatory Select Committee). Enoch Powell opposed this development bitterly. He said in the debate, 'Surely all of us know by experience that quite suddenly in examining an apparently innocuous clause, first of all Members discover that it means something different from what they've imagined and is more important, and secondly they realise there is a political intention behind it: that lurking behind the apparent technicalities there was a political will.' For this reason he and Mr Foot and their allies opposed the removal of 'technical' matters from the Floor of the House into Committee.

The issue between the 'chamber' men and the 'information' men is not a narrow matter about how to run a debating society or a minor administrative machine. In recent years a kind of corporate state has operated, not merely in Britain but in all developed economies. The major interests in the community have to deal directly with the Government, and sometimes, inevitably, settle things before Parliament gets told. In such negotiations the public interest is usually represented by Civil Servants. This may have some advantages. Civil Servants may be better than MPs at mastering technical complexities. They usually seem to get things right. And some issues may be better settled privately between Civil Servants and interested parties rather than have politicians raise public concern or hopes that cannot be satisfied. But the public interest the Civil Servants represent is the Government one. Who – as John Mackintosh put it in our debate – is there to speak for the taxpayer, the consumer, the rank and file, the unorganised citizen? Only his MP.

Parliament already provides some checks: the risk of a political row is a significant restraint on Civil Servants; the public is not dependent merely on their being a splendid lot of public-minded chaps. But is the public interest adequately protected by a generally competent and public-spirited Civil Service, subject to occasional inspection by a busy Minister or the threat of a violent squall in Parliament? Or does the vast number and impact of Government decisions call for more regular exposure to public debate and questioning, more frequent testing of the political temperature, and, in effect, the development of systems by which MPs are enabled to keep watch on what Whitehall is brewing up?

Political historians are generally agreed that the dominant tradition of the House of Commons is one of subservience to the Executive. Normally, through the centuries, it has known its place. This tradition leads naturally to today's situation, where the Cabinet and Prime Minister have replaced the monarchy, with the Commons still subservient. It is no wonder that every ambitious MP wishes to be a Minister. But at odd moments in the past the House has asserted itself. In response to intolerable excesses, it connived at the overthrow of the Stuarts and legitimised the invitation to William III to become King, much as it had removed Charles I. For forty years in the mid-nineteenth century (during a period of weak government and political confusion) it gave orders to governments or voted them out. And in more normal times, the Speaker, as guardian of the traditional rights of the House of Commons, has often resisted the sway of the Monarch and Executive, has insisted that the Commons must not be by-passed. Through our programme MPs and others close to Parliament raised a similar question: does the simple arithmetic of growth in government business call for some such assertion today?

Part 1

A Law in the Making: four months inside a Ministry

Part 1

In the programme

Department of Trade and Industry (DTI)

Rt Hon Sir Geoffrey Howe	Cabinet Minister for Trade and Consumer Affairs. MP for Reigate
Peter Emery	Parliamentary Under-Secretary of State for Industry and Consumer Affairs. MP for Honiton
Patrick Shovelton	Deputy Secretary, in charge of information, competition policy and consumer protection
Cyril Coffin	Under-Secretary, in charge of Fair Trading Bill
Elizabeth Llewellyn-Smith	Assistant Secretary, in charge of co-ordination of Civil Servants on the Bill
Michael Casey	Assistant Secretary, in charge of consumer affairs in the Bill
Michael Ware	Assistant Solicitor in charge of drafting instructions to Parliamentary counsel for the Bill
Brian Armstrong	Principal, consumer affairs
John Meadway	Private Secretary to Sir Geoffrey Howe
Richard Luce	MP for Arundel & Shoreham, PPS (Parliamentary Private Secretary) to Sir Geoffrey Howe

Members of the Standing Committee – Conservative MPs

Janet Fookes	MP for Merton & Morden
Sally Oppenheim	MP for Gloucester
Trevor Skeet	MP for Bedford
Edward Taylor	MP for Glasgow, Cathcart

Members of the Standing Committee – Labour MPs

Alan Williams	Opposition spokesman on consumer affairs. MP for Swansea West
Bruce Millan	Opposition spokesman on monopolies and mergers. MP for Glasgow, Craigton
Rt Hon George Darling	Former Labour Minister of State at the Board of Trade. MP for Sheffield, Hillsborough
John Golding	Opposition Committee whip. MP for Newcastle-under-Lyme
Arthur Davidson	MP for Accrington
Richard Douglas	MP for Stirlingshire, East & Clackmannan
William Hamilton	MP for West Fife
Edward Lyons	MP for Bradford
Baroness Phillips	Opposition spokesman in the Lords on Fair Trading Bill

Outside interest groups:

Consumers' Association (CA)

Rosemary McRobert	Parliamentary adviser
John Pickering	Professor of Economics, Sussex University
David Tench	CA lawyer

Confederation of British Industry (CBI)

Harry Gray	Chairman of study group on Fair Trading Bill
Ivor Hussey	CBI lawyer and parliamentary liaison officer
James Carr	
Eric Felgate	

———

A Weights & Measures Inspector

Part 1

Transmitted at 10.30 pm on Monday 23 July 1973

Narrator

Traditionally the House of Commons is suspicious of the
Crown and its Ministers and Civil Servants. The Queen,
the formal head of the Government, may not even enter
the House. At the State Opening, the only Parliamentary
occasion ever seen on television, her messenger, Black Rod,
is ceremoniously resisted when he comes to summon MPs.

But as the power of Ministers and Civil Servants has grown,
some MPs say this tradition has become empty: that they
are now subservient to the Government machine – the
Cabinet, the Ministers and Civil Servants. Do MPs, our
representatives, still serve as the nation's watchdog? Do
they effectively review the laws that are passed? Do they
keep track of the money that is spent – our money?

These are the questions explored in the series of three
programmes that begin tonight, taking you deep into the
centre of Government, and the work of Members of
Parliament.

*   *   *

The Fair Trading Bill is just one of the sixty or so Bills passed by Parliament each year. Every Bill goes through something like the process we're going to see part of tonight.
First the Cabinet decides that its policy needs a law to be
passed. In this case the Fair Trading Bill followed a Government decision to pay more attention to consumer protection. A new Cabinet Minister was appointed to work in
the Department of Trade and Industry, Sir Geoffrey Howe,
the Minister for Trade and Consumer Affairs.

One of his first tasks was to guide the Fair Trading Bill
through Parliament. The Bill was given its First Reading
(which simply means it was published in the House of
Commons) on 30 November 1972, and two weeks later
had its Second Reading, a full day's debate on the general
principles, at the end of which the Commons sent it upstairs
to Standing Committee B for a line by line examination.

Our film this evening follows the impact of events in that Committee Room from their start on 25 January this year till their finish on 12 April. The impact, not the events themselves, because as with the main Chamber of the House, we're not allowed to film the actual debates.

The Standing Committee works like a miniature House of Commons. It has a built-in Government majority, in this case 11 Conservatives and nine Labour MPs. They debate the Bill clause by clause and vote on amendments.

We followed just two of the 123 clauses in the Bill, Clauses 2 and 3. These define the powers to protect consumers to be given to a new public official, the Director-General of Fair Trading. Those powers can be strengthened or weakened by a single phrase or even word in one clause, and outside pressure groups such as the Consumers' Association, lobby MPs on the Committee to put down amendments to the wording[1].

[1]The wording of the clauses as presented to the Standing Committee was as follows:
'General functions of Director.

Clause 2. (1) Without prejudice to any other functions assigned or transferred to him by or under this Act, it shall be the duty of the Director –

(a) to keep under review consumer trade practices which affect consumers in the United Kingdom and to collect information with respect to those practices, and the persons by whom they are carried on from time to time, with a view to his becoming aware of, and ascertaining the circumstances relating to, consumer trade practices which may adversely affect the economic interests of consumers in the United Kingdom, and

(b) to keep under review the carrying on of commercial activities in the United Kingdom, and to collect information with respect to those activities, and the persons by whom they are carried on from time to time, with a view to his becoming aware of, and ascertaining the circumstances relating to, monopoly situations or uncompetitive practices.

(2) It shall be the duty of the Director, where either he considers it expedient or he is requested by the Secretary of State to do so –

(a) to give information and assistance to the Secretary of State with respect to any of the matters mentioned in the preceding subsection, or

(b) subject to the provisions of Part II of this Act in relation to matters falling within paragraph (a) of the preceding subsection, to make recommendations to the Secretary of State as to any action which in the opinion of the Director it would be expedient for the Secretary of State or any other Minister to take in relation to any of the matters mentioned in that subsection.

(3) It shall also be the duty of the Director to have regard to evidence becoming available to him with respect to any course of conduct on the part of a person carrying on a business which appears to be conduct detrimental to the interests of consumers in the United Kingdom and (in

Much is at stake, for those words will shortly become the law of the land.

The film starts the night before the Committee's first session, with the nine Labour MPs, the opposition on the Standing Committee, planning their strategy for the debate on the first of the amendments. Their Chairman, Alan Williams, is Opposition spokesman on consumer affairs.

Labour MPs on Standing Committee – 24 January 1973
An interview room in the Palace of Westminster. Evening

ALAN J WILLIAMS

There will be a lot of amendments; some parts are more acceptable than others. We think that we'll spend more time obviously on the parts that we are opposed to but that

accordance with the provisions of Part III of this Act) to be regarded as unfair to them, with a view to considering what action (if any) he should take under Part III of this Act.

Clause 3. (1) In this Act "consumer trade practice" means any practice which is for the time being carried on in connection with the supply of goods (whether by way of sale or otherwise) to consumers or in connection with the supply of services to consumers and which relates –
(a) to the terms or conditions (whether as to price or otherwise) on or subject to which goods or services are or are sought to be supplied, or
(b) to the manner in which those terms or conditions are communicated to persons to whom goods are or are sought to be supplied or for whom services are or are sought to be supplied, or
(c) to promotion (by advertising, labelling or marking of goods, canvassing or otherwise) of the supply of goods or of the supply of services, or
(d) to methods of demanding or securing payment for goods or services supplied.

(2) Subject to the next following subsection, in this Act "consumer" means any person who is either –
(a) a person to whom goods are or are sought to be supplied (whether by way of sale or otherwise) in the course of a business carried on by the person supplying or seeking to supply them, or
(b) a person for whom services are or are sought to be supplied in the course of a business carried on by the person supplying or seeking to supply them, and who does not obtain or seek to obtain the goods or services in the course of a business carried on by him.

(3) For the purposes of any reference to consumers in subsection (1) of this section, or in any other provision of this Act, in its application to goods or services of any particular description or to goods or services to which a particular practice applies, "consumers" means persons who fulfil the conditions specified in subsection (2) of this section in relation to goods or services of that description or in relation to goods or services to which that practice applies.'

there's no reason why there should be any obstruction, no reason why there should be any delay. The Bill is so long and so complicated and so badly drafted that it's going to take us a long time anyway and there will be a lot of amendments to deal with.

WILLIAM HAMILTON

Are we going to have any long debates on the sittings' motion?

WILLIAMS

Well, it's thought we may have to. They [the Government] didn't give us a White Paper – on this they didn't even give us a Green Paper. The Bill was bounced on us, on the floor of the House and within ten days we had to have our Second Reading debate so I think we have to make the point that in part some of the number of amendments that will be down will be because the Government didn't give due time for consultation and didn't give enough information.

BRUCE MILLAN (Opposition spokesman on monopolies)

I think we have to make the general point that of course if they want to make progress with the Bill we're perfectly happy that they should, but they'll really have to give us decent answers. I mean a lot of the amendments, after all, are going to be asking for elucidation. We don't want to be palmed off with these inadequate answers. The more forthcoming they are, the quicker they'll get the Bill.

WILLIAMS

I think the first thing is to map out our approach to the Bill. It is a pretty lengthy Bill, 123 clauses and 13 schedules. It's going to take a pretty fair time with maximum co-operation. I assume that our approach to this Bill is that we'll get it through quickly but positively amended.

RICHARD (DICK) DOUGLAS

We broadly welcome it but we want to improve it.

MILLAN

We welcome the consumer side. The monopoly side is very poor. I don't think we can say that we broadly welcome it. There are one or two things we welcome. I think the consumer side, I think we did say, that we broadly welcomed that.

WILLIAMS

Well, we've got to be careful here because our approach

to the consumer side was that the general intention was good but that the structure they were building was in fact a very weak one and too much under the thumb of the Government.

MILLAN

It will need quite a lot of amendments to get the sort of objectives that we want on the consumer side.

JOHN GOLDING (Labour Committee Whip)

The one thing that we want to get home is the point made by the CBI [Confederation of British Industry] that this Bill is extremely complicated, badly laid out, difficult to unravel and exceedingly legalistically drafted. Now, I think we have got to get home in the first couple of sessions that this is true and we really have got to say to the Government that if they want it through very quickly, they themselves have got to go away and do their homework on the rest of the Bill and to produce for themselves an enormous number of drafting amendments to try to retrieve the situation.

WILLIAMS

Quite honestly if we don't make our stand on the first few clauses . . . Clause 1 sets up the Director, Clause 2 outlines his functions, Clause 3 defines what a consumer is and what a consumer trade practice is. [*Chat*]
The first six clauses or so really are fundamental. Once we've passed those if we let the argument go then we've lost it.

HAMILTON

Alan, have you any clues as to whether the Tories are going to be fed amendments by their front bench. I guess Howe has got something up his sleeve that he's going to feed out to his back-benchers.

WILLIAMS

Well, Peter Emery, in off-the-record discussion has indicated that they are willing to accept some amendments to the Bill and has said he's willing to have chats with us on the Bill outside the committee on things we regard as being important.

MILLAN

They've got one or two disaffected members on their side: Mrs Oppenheim, for example.

WILLIAMS

I think there are a couple of others who, if we place our arguments carefully, may well be persuaded occasionally to defect and either abstain or vote against. So we have got a chance of picking up a few amendments that the Government doesn't even intend us to pick up.

Consumers' Association – 25 January

A room in the CA offices.
Strategy Committee of three examines the Bill

DAVID TENCH (Consumers' Association lawyer)

This is a hell of a thing to digest, there's so much of it.

JOHN PICKERING (Professor of Economics, Sussex University)

I quite agree.

TENCH

This is a major Government Bill with a major Government policy behind it and we as lobbyists can't really hope to do more than tinker with it. It's no good our inventing a new policy and saying this is what we think the Government's policy should be – this *is* the Government's policy and we can only tinker with Government policy and improve it. We can't structurally alter it.

PICKERING

But also what you're saying is that you've really got to pick out perhaps three or four major issues on which it's *really* worth having a go: introducing a meaningful change; and not to go for peripheral stuff.

TENCH

Mind you, that raises a whole point if we've pursued that one sufficiently. This whole question of the limitations on the type of consumer trade practice that comes into the Bill at all . . .

ROSEMARY MCROBERT (CA Parliamentary Adviser)

This is Clause 14?

TENCH

First of all it raises its head in Clause 3 [1] where you're talking about the basic definition of consumer trade practice which in turn reflects upon the functions of the Director-General. So that he can't even *look* at a thing like shoddy

[1] See pages 40–41 for text of clauses.

goods which seems absolutely startling, or after-sales service.

McRobert

I think, David that the suggestion that we put down an amendment to Clause 3 and simply delete all these definitions, all these restrictions, is a sensible one. Because I don't see how you can possibly put in there the kinds of trade practices and abuses that you might want to cover at any given time in the future. I mean supposing this had been drafted ten years ago. Would one have thought of pyramid selling for example?

Tench

Yes, quite.

McRobert

I should have just thought, you know, put a full stop after consumers.

Tench

OK, let's go for that. I'll talk to the MPs about that particular question and see how they stand. I mean it could be that we are pushing on an open door and everybody will say 'No, no, no, no, if the Director-General is the right sort of chap everything will be OK'.

McRobert

Which brings us to another question. This question of whether an unfair trading practice has an influence on the consumers' *economic* position. It leaves out, so far as I can see, David, and this is mentioned all the way through the Bill, this question of health and safety.

Tench

Yes, if I understand it right, it's this: when you're looking at the Director's functions, which are defined in Clause 2, you find that, as Rosemary rightly says, its only consumer trade practices, as defined in Clause 3, which adversely affect the *economic* interests of consumers. Now, that means to say there's another amendment that we need to add.

McRobert

Yes.

Tench

Delete 'economic' in line 27 of page 2.

McRobert

That's right.

Tench

So let's make a note of that otherwise I shall forget it.
Add 'page 2', it's very easy to miss a thing like that, isn't it?
Page 2, line thingummy – here it is, 'economic' you see?

McRobert

Did you pick that up, John? 'May adversely affect the
economic interests of consumers in the United Kingdom.'
Do you think one can define it as 'economic interest'? It
seems to me a very narrow definition.

Tench

Mayn't it be this? This is a DTI [Department of Trade
and Industry] Bill and they only deal with the economic
aspects of trading; things like health and safety are either
for Health and Social Services or Home Office. That's the
argument.

McRobert

Oh yes – lovely interdepartmental problems, but that's for
them to sort out. I don't think at this stage we should miss
the opportunity to put down the amendment.

Tench

And you could hardly imagine a wetter notion than setting
up a grand Director-General of Fair Trading who's going
to be the great consumers' friend when he can't look at
health and safety at all. I mean, it would be absolutely
absurd, wouldn't it? Now, we must watch out for this
word 'economic'.

McRobert

I don't think it occurs again in Part I.

Tench

OK. Well that's fine.

Labour MPs – House of Commons – 29 January
An interview room in the Palace of Westminster. Evening

Alan Williams

Now Amendment 23. It's like reading out the hymns on
Sunday. This is one of the most important debates so far,
this is where you leave out 'economic'. Now, you know
that the criticism from the Consumers' Association, Public
Interest Centre, ourselves, literally everyone who's attacked

the Bill, has attacked it on the grounds that it is altogether too restrictive to confine its intentions purely to the *economic* interests of consumers. Obviously safety and health are the clearest other major interests. So I think we have to mount as strong and effective a campaign as possible here, and I think we must try and get them to concede. It would be a major widening of the scope of the Bill if we could get this accepted. I don't know if someone would like to move it particularly . . .

Rt Hon George Darling

If you think it's a major one Alan, and I'm inclined to agree with you, it ought to be done from the Front Bench.

John Golding

Could I say, if it's major there will be a vote won't there, so it'll be compulsory attendance really? You see suddenly the importance will be diminished. [*Chat and laughter*]

Narrator (in studio)

By now the Standing Committee has met twice and has almost finished with Clause 1.

As you saw, Labour MPs tabled amendments to Clause 2 which would widen the range of things the Director-General can look at. Amendment 23, to delete the word 'economic', raises the whole argument over the extent of his powers.

Opposition amendments are not usually put forward in the expectation they will succeed against the wishes of the Minister. The Government majority on each Committee ensures this rarely happens. The main purpose of amendments like 23 is to air an issue publicly, to put pressure on the Minister, to try to force him to commit himself to making changes to the Clause at a later stage in the Bill's progress through Parliament.

How to handle Amendment 23 in Standing Committee is the subject of the next discussion between senior Civil Servants of the Department of Trade and Industry and the Government team of MPs presenting the Bill – the Minister, Sir Geoffrey Howe, QC, his junior Minister, Peter Emery, together with Howe's Parliamentary Private Secretary, Richard Luce, who is their link with the Government's back-benchers.

Until tonight, no one outside the ministerial team and

Civil Servants has been present at these meetings – not even the other MPs on the Government side of the Committee. Such discussions have always until now been completely private.

Department of Trade and Industry Ministerial Briefing – 31 January
Sir Geoffrey Howe's office. Evening

CYRIL COFFIN (Under-Secretary)
I don't think we need spend a lot of time on the next group.

ELIZABETH LLEWELLYN-SMITH (Assistant Secretary)
This next group are purely drafting, I mean they're intended as purely drafting.

SIR GEOFFREY HOWE (Minister for Trade and Consumer Affairs)
They're either designed to abbreviate or make some point it's difficult to see. And then we come to 'economic'.

COFFIN
Economic?

HOWE
Yes, Amendment 23, essential to the basic concept of the role [of the Director-General].

Narrator
There is no set pattern for Civil Servants on a Bill. For Fair Trading, the team was led by Under-Secretary Cyril Coffin. Co-ordination was the job of Assistant Secretary Elizabeth Llewellyn-Smith. Consumer policy for the Bill was the task of Michael Casey, also an Assistant Secretary. They were supported by Assistant Solicitor Michael Ware and by Brian Armstrong who has the rank of Principal.

PETER EMERY (Parliamentary Under-Secretary Department of Trade and Industry)
It seems to me that the argument that they are going to mount is the factor of limitation. And they would wish, or it would seem they might wish to see the Director-General being able to look into the health and safety fields which 'economic' would exclude. And it seems to me we've got to very clearly be able to explain the reasons why we've had to limit it, the reasons of the existing bodies dealing with

this and, you know, make it quite clear how this is to operate in conjunction with those.

HOWE

One will have to explain that his power to propose new laws which comes in Part II operates only in non-health and safety, in the economic field. There's obviously a very good case for confining that, and not giving him the powers to propose new laws in relation to health and safety matters which are already covered by the Food and Drugs Acts and Medicines Act and are, in fact, under the surveillance of existing bodies on which consumers are represented.

COFFIN

Of course he has no expertise and will have no expertise in these specialised fields.

HOWE

No.

COFFIN

It would be duplication.

EMERY

That's the point. I mean he could obtain the expertise but as it exists already surely the one thing the Government doesn't want to do is duplicate the two or in fact run a competition between the two. This would be nonsensical.

HOWE

There may be an argument for saying that even if he shouldn't be placed under a duty to trawl around, if he discovers non-economic things, then he ought at least to know what to do about it.

EMERY

Yes, but it really would be foolish to have him resist or reject people giving him information because they send it to him because they understand him to be the consumers' watchdog; the right that he should be able to send it on to the appropriate bodies would seem to me commonsense; and I think people would have a right to expect that.

HOWE

Well, I think again it's a question of duty; because he's got enough power in any event on anything he receives information about; he wouldn't be disabled or disqualified from dealing with it.

COFFIN

No, he'll do just as we do now – pass it on to the appropriate bodies.

HOWE

He will become the repository for complaints and information and obviously handle that sensibly because that is what his function is meant to be. Again, that is something we can come back to look at in Part II.

Elizabeth Llewellyn-Smith's Office – 2 February

LLEWELLYN-SMITH [*dictating to secretary*]

Just do it as a draft and head it 'Amendment number 68: Resist' and then can you put in brackets after 'resist', but indicate willingness to look again at the structure of the Consumer Trade Practice provisions. [*Picture fades...*] This amendment is probably inspired by a suggestion circulated to certain members of the Standing Committee by the Consumers' Association, stop. [*Picture fades . . .*] And Ministers may like to take the line that they will listen sympathetically to constructive suggestions put forward in the Committee as to the powers the Director should have. Full stop.' That's the end. Put 'resist' again at the bottom and the date. I'll do a covering minute later on, but I'm not quite sure who I'll send it to.

Department of Trade and Industry – later on 2 February
The same office. Evening

BRIAN ARMSTRONG (Principal)

It never goes wider.

ELIZABETH LLEWELLYN-SMITH

Well, all this does is to bear out the case for taking a pretty cautious line on this and not defending it as it's drafted. And explaining the objective and also explaining the way it works, of course. I mean that's what Ministers have got to do.

ARMSTRONG

What does Cyril Coffin think about all this?

LLEWELLYN-SMITH

He seems quite prepared to consider changes to these clauses.

ARMSTRONG

I remember when we first had . . .

LLEWELLYN-SMITH

But what he wants and what everybody wants is to think about the actual practices. Sorry, what did you say?

ARMSTRONG

When we first had the first print of this thing we had about 24 hours to comment on it you know. I read it through first of all and my first reaction was 'Heavens, what do they want all this for? [the list of definitions of Consumer Trade Practice in Clause 3]. This will only run us the risk of excluding things.' But you know once these things get into print you can't get rid of them, it's terrible, and with the sort of time-table we had it just wasn't possible.

LLEWELLYN-SMITH

There is logic in excluding what's excluded but the line might not be drawn in absolutely the right place. Anyway we're not going to solve it between now and the next Committee day.

Department of Trade and Industry – next Ministerial Briefing 5 February
Sir Geoffrey Howe's office. Evening

CYRIL COFFIN

The principle on this, if there is any principle, is that he [the Director-General of Fair Trading] shouldn't be put under a duty to keep under review things which he then can't do anything about, one way or another. Either it should be relevant to his duty of giving information or assistance to Ministers or it should be relevant to his duty to publish information to help the consumers or to his duties under Parts II and III of the Bill.

SIR GEOFFREY HOWE

Yes, yes.

COFFIN

In other words there shouldn't be any sort of left-over bit which he's under a duty to keep under review but not do anything with.

HOWE

Is it going to be workable for the Director-General to have a duty to keep under review consumer trade practices across the board, for the purpose only of giving information and assistance to Ministers and of publishing information about it, but with other subsidiary purposes? Can one cast that role upon him?

ARMSTRONG

If you give him a general review function he's got to think creatively and originally and will need the sort of expertise that you have in these bodies such as the Food Standards Committee.

HOWE

Yes, yes.

ARMSTRONG

I think it is a big departure.

HOWE

It does make it very much wider.

MICHAEL WARE (Assistant Solicitor)

There's another possibility, that one can tailor the things he looks at by reference to the things he can do about them. For example, say, to make recommendations about the exercise of any powers under any enactment, or the need for new legislation. This would narrow the field in the sense that he would look at less things. The field would still be large but he would look at less things in it.

LLEWELLYN-SMITH

It would cut out the things he could do by private influence, like improving, say, trade arbitration schemes.

COFFIN

Which may be more desirable.

WARE

So far as the acquisition of information is concerned, I would have thought he would get the information anyway; because complainants are not going to stop to study whether it's a 'consumer trade practice' or not before they write to the Director-General. It will stream in. It's a question of whether to some of it he gives a stock answer 'that I cannot look at this' or whether he starts to investigate.

HOWE

I would have thought on the whole we ought to try and see if we can get him to live with, as it were, the wider remit, don't you?

COFFIN

Yes, it's a bit of an open ended thing. I mean you know, one doesn't . . . I would be hard put to it to say exactly how many staff he would need for this function.

RICHARD LUCE (Parliamentary Private Secretary to Sir Geoffrey Howe)

I think there's just one point here: I think Peter [Emery] was asking what the attitude of the Committee would be, and I would have thought that quite apart from the Opposition – you look at Amendment number 23 – certainly people on our side, people like Sally Oppenheim [Conservative back-bencher] who had this Hazardous Products Bill, is very concerned about health and safety; and although it can be explained you know that it's covered by various other parts of the Bill, it looks highly complicated and I think they will press very hard for the wider remit to be put into Clause 2.

HOWE

And in fact they achieve that in the simplest form by deleting the word 'economic' in line 27. That's what Amendment 23 is about.

LUCE

And the Consumers' Association would feel the same.

HOWE

And Janet Fookes [Conservative back-bencher]. My anxiety is whether one is not giving him [the Director-General] an impossibly wide remit and might be arousing expectations which would be very difficult to fulfil in the short term or difficult to fulfil without an adequate supporting expert staff.

LLEWELLYN-SMITH

I would have thought he would be more likely to be embarrassed if he had to deal with complainants by saying he'd got no power to act.

HOWE

I think what one might basically say is that if he was in the position that the Parliamentary Commissioner is in on a lot of things for example . . .

LLEWELLYN-SMITH

If he had to do everything, it would make his life very

difficult. But I think if he could establish his own priorities I should have thought all the advantages are in favour of giving him a very wide field.

COFFIN

How positive or mandatory is the duty 'where he considers it expedient' or 'where he is requested by the Secretary of State to do so'? To a layman it doesn't sound as though this is, you know, as if he can be sent to the Tower if he fails in the duty, because it is conditional – where he thinks he can play a useful role.

HOWE

You have to regulate it with common sense.

EMERY

Well, that's why we must resist the amendment that tries to take that out.

HOWE

And it may be that we ought to consider some kind of discretion conferring power, if we are going to broaden his remit to cover non-economic health and safety.

EMERY

Yes, that's what I think.

HOWE

There ought to be some degree of judgement invested in him so that he can frankly determine priorities. [Pause] I find great difficulty in drawing the logical line. In terms of his duty to keep under review, leaving everything else on one side, should he or should he not have a duty to keep under review shoddy goods, shoddy services, for example the frequent occurrence of under-inspected cars of a particular make?

COFFIN

But I think that it is important, while being open minded and offering to consider things, I think it is important to underline, you know, this chap – we can't have him as a one man Government.

HOWE

Yes.

COFFIN

And he's not going to be, he mustn't be given everything to do. The whole Bill – this part of the Bill – has been formulated in terms of things that are *unfair to consumers* . . .

HOWE
Yes.

COFFIN
That affect consumers directly, whether the manufacturer does it or it's the wholesaler or retailer that does it, it doesn't matter; if it affects the consumer and is *unfair* to him then, OK, this is within the Director's remit.

HOWE
OK well, yes, I think we shall have to hold that broad line. I find it very very difficult to believe we've got it accurately defined as it now stands, don't you?

COFFIN
Yes, I think this is so.

HOWE
In fact, the strategic line is, well, reasonable. We're not excluding everything that takes place on the part of the manufacturer or wholesaler, we're not excluding price altogether, but only in the general context of what is or is not fair to the consumer. Well, I think I'm clearer than I was. We shall very much have to defend the general framework of the distribution of functions and powers, explain it at least.

LLEWELLYN-SMITH
Explain it rather than defend it.

HOWE
And then react.

COFFIN
Express willingness to listen.

EMERY
But I think, defend the situation that we can't see the position of the Director-General being so expanded that his whole position is meaningless.

Narrator
In the Standing Committee on 6 February the amendment to delete 'economic' was withdrawn after the Government promised to re-draft Clause 2 and consider widening the Director-General's powers of review.

Department of Trade and Industry – 6 February
Cyril Coffin's office, just after the Standing Committee has adjourned

CYRIL COFFIN

They broke off on those drafting amendments of Mr Hamilton's about 'from time to time'?

ELIZABETH LLEWELLYN-SMITH

We did. I'm going to put up a rather tough little thing on this. I mean, again, Mr Emery was saying that 'I'll think about it and take further advice' and so on, but we really will wreck our relationship with the Parliamentary Counsel and also store up an awful lot of trouble if we start accepting . . .

COFFIN

Was he inclined to accept it?

LLEWELLYN-SMITH

Oh yes. Mr Lyons [Member for Bradford East] leapt to his feet and said that it wouldn't make any difference to a court if these words were in or out and . . .

COFFIN

So why didn't they accept them?

LLEWELLYN-SMITH

But I mean, once you start accepting them [Michael Casey enters] I say, I think I'm going to put up a tough little piece, if Michael Ware approves of it, on 'from time to time'. I think if we begin by crumbling on these things there's no end to the trouble.

Labour MPs – House of Commons – 6 February
An interview room in the Palace of Westminster. Evening

ALAN WILLIAMS

Now I think on Clause 3 we've got quite a lot of amendments down already. I think the Government's got itself into a mess; it's retreated quite a lot this morning. We haven't had a chance yet to fully establish the significance of the changes. I don't think we should withdraw any of our amendments (on Clause 3) in the light of what was said this morning. I think instead we should use them now to probe further how far he is willing to come to meet us. He made certain general concessions this morning. He'll have a chance on these amendments if we leave them on the paper to indicate just what he is willing to do.

ARTHUR DAVIDSON

Actually, it will be the same debates on Clause 3 as on
Clause 2. The issues are the same.

WILLIAMS

Well that's right, yes. Before I go onto the allocation, I
noticed that this morning – I expect you all had the same
note from the Consumers' Association – they have suddenly become very hostile to the Bill after Howe's interpretation of what it really meant. They suggested a further
amendment to Clause 3 suggesting that we should add to
the general provisions 'the manufacture, packing, marking,
labelling and distribution'. So I think it's worth putting
this down for them again as an exploratory [amendment].

Narrator (in studio)

At the end of the fifth session of the Committee the
Government had given ground on widening the area the
Director-General can look at – his review powers – though,
as we saw, they were quite open to doing that even before
the debate.

In the next part of the film, which deals with Clause 3, the
going gets tougher for those who hope to make changes
in the Bill.

After five two-and-a-half hour sessions of Standing Committee B, the pro-consumer group of MPs have won a
promise from the Government to consider widening the
area the Director-General can look at. Note the word
'consider'. The precise terms of the Government's changes
– if any – in Clause 2 will not be known for many weeks –
until the Report Stage, when the amended Bill is represented to the whole House of Commons. Then the
Government can, of course, use the full weight of its
majority to get clauses through in the form it prefers.

Clause 3 is more critical: it deals with the Director-General's
power to propose new orders that have to be obeyed by
traders – or else! The clause reads like this –

'In this Act Consumer Trade Practices means any Practice
which relates (a) to the terms or conditions of sale (b) to
the manner in which those terms or conditions are communicated (c) to promotion by advertising, labelling or
marking of goods (d) to methods of demanding or securing
payment.'

Sally Oppenheim, and other Conservative back-bench MPs

have tabled an amendment – number 99 – to add other practices to the list like '(e) quality, performance and reliability, standard of manufacture, or (f) availability of spare parts and servicing'. In other words, shoddy goods and spare parts.

Amendment 99 has the backing of the Consumers' Association, and to gather support for their amendment from the Labour side, the Association's David Tench visits George Darling, a Labour member of the Standing Committee and a former Minister of Trade.

George Darling's Office in the Palace of Westminster – 7 February
Morning

DAVID TENCH

I only speak for consumers whose interests I seek to promote. I'm not saying you should take the narrow view, all I'm saying, I only speak for individual consumers, you know, we don't purport to represent anybody else. There's a cutting down of the scope of the functions of the Director. This is serious because – assume we carry the day on the question of the wholesale as well as the retail side being within the scope of the Bill. One then finds, because of the definition of Consumer Trade Practice as propounded in 3.1 (a) to (d) inclusive that it is only *certain aspects* of the supply of goods which are in fact brought in. So that, for example, the question of the availability of spare parts, so that, in fact, the question of shoddy goods are not something that the Director-General can even *look at*. He can't even look at them! As you know, Sally Oppenheim has put down an amendment at our behest on that, and I suggest it's a good one.

GEORGE DARLING

I'm sorry I disagree with you on your amendment on shoddy goods. If people want to buy shoddy goods I think they should be allowed to buy shoddy goods.

TENCH

I'm not forbidding them.

DARLING

All that they need to know is that what they're buying is shoddy.

TENCH

Quite so. That's what the Director-General should be looking at. I'm not suggesting a law that makes selling shoddy goods illegal, I'm suggesting that they are something the Director should be allowed to look at.

DARLING

Look, I've got old allotments in my constituency where most of the land is now being tilled, if that's the word, by old age pensioners who rigged up their little huts beautifully. They don't want to buy carpets other than shoddy carpets, when what they've got on the floor of their hut wears out.

TENCH

Quite so. And they don't last probably very long, but they're entirely fit for the purpose. Now there are other people who think they're buying cheaply and are actually buying shoddy goods. If it be the case that the Director-General is not to have even power to consider questions in relation to shoddy goods, then the Bill is not taking us very much further is it?

Conservative MPs on Standing Committee – 7 February
An interview room in the Palace of Westminster. Afternoon

EDWARD TAYLOR

What about this question of Sally's amendment? Sally, what would it actually do?

MRS SALLY OPPENHEIM

It would be Clause 3, No. 1 (e) and (f) – after (d) in Clause 3. It is really that it has been felt that there is not a wide enough definition in the present Clause 3 (a) (b) (c) (d), and that it wouldn't deal with what we are now attempting to put in in (e) and (f) which is quality, performance, reliability, and standard of manufacture. This is a way of saying 'shoddy goods' in the context of the Bill – I think if we leave out shoddy goods, or shoddy workmanship for that matter, we are not carrying out the spirit of the Bill.

TAYLOR

And this would bring in garages . . .

OPPENHEIM

And then that brings in the further thing of servicing of goods and the availability of spare parts. This is your very serious problem of a monopoly situation operating once you are in the hands of one manufacturer and have to buy the spares, have to pay his price and have to put up with his service. That is why I think *extra* protection is needed.

TAYLOR

And we want to get clarification on these [from the Minister]. And I think quite honestly that from Sally's point if we don't get a very good assurance, I think we should press very hard on this one. Is that the general feeling? The feeling that we can get this clarified or we may have to go over the brink [i.e. vote against the Government] and if we do this they will certainly get something done in the Report Stage [i.e. change the Clause when the bill is re-presented to the whole House]. It's probably wrong to talk about a revolt in the presence of our friend the Whip but I really feel that this one is so crucial to the consumers of Britain. The Bill is doing so much for us and we just want to make sure it doesn't miss out something which they care about deeply.

JANET FOOKES

But I don't think it would come to that because I think Geoffrey [Howe] is genuinely interested; it is simply he sees the difficulty of widening it too much while we see the difficulties of having it too narrow.

TREVOR SKEET

But this is going to be a Consumers' Charter, and this can be simplified in quite a substantial way if we pursue what the Government are laying down here.

Department of Trade and Industry
Michael Casey and Brian Armstrong – 19 February
In Armstrong's office. Morning

CASEY

I'm just wondering about [Amendment] 99. Literally if we were to include anything on these lines we would be saying that the Director had a duty to review practices relating to quality and performance. [Armstrong nods assent]. Every manufacturing practice I can think of relates to the quality and performance of the product.

ARMSTRONG

Quite.

CASEY

And what about labour restrictive practices? [Armstrong sighs]. We've not had a Second Reading discussion on the implications of the work of the Director, and for the structure of the Bill the impact of some of the amendments which we've undertaken to reconsider.

ARMSTRONG

All we've had is discussions in one of the briefing meetings.

CASEY

Yes. They've asked for three things, I think. They asked first that we should widen Clause 2 by dropping 'economic' from the definition of trade practices to be looked at. They want non-economic factors such as safety to be considered. They've asked that Clause 3 should be widened in scope by including trade practices that are connected with this kind of thing, quality and performance. They've also asked that the definition should be deepened to cover transactions between manufacturers and retailers, trade practices there where the consumer is directly involved. So now there are these three things that you know would broaden and deepen it. And they want the limiting factor of economic performance to be removed.

ARMSTRONG

I would have thought that since this is the Government side they would shut up pretty easily on being given the undertaking [to consider the points in the amendment].

CASEY

But we've got a minute saying they want to press it pretty hard. I'll nip round and see Elizabeth. [Casey leaves the office]

ARMSTRONG

[throws down papers] Ugh!

Department of Trade and Industry – 14 February
Elizabeth Llewellyn-Smith on telephone in her office

LLEWELLYN-SMITH

Well I think that they will have to take a general look at the strategy and the speed at which this thing is moving at some point. Of course one keeps feeling, let's get through Clause 3 or if possible through Part I and then sit back and have a look at it . . . Yes. Anyway I don't think that Sir

Geoffrey will be at this meeting this evening. I think it's Mr Emery's meeting. So I think it'll only be a quick meeting just running over the programme for tomorrow. Right, thanks. [Hangs up]

Ministerial Briefing – 14 February
Peter Emery's office. Evening

PETER EMERY

'99' is spare parts, isn't it? The main argument I suppose which is new – they'll come back to the spare parts argument. That's what I would have thought that was mainly about.

MICHAEL CASEY

What I'm a bit worried about is that by always promising to reconsider we raise hopes that some kind of absurd function will be accepted for the Director. And while we are committed to looking at it again we'll obviously have to say that the Director-General can't be a valuer of the price of commodities in relation to their quality. Nor can he arbitrate between the parties.

EMERY

Nor should he.

CASEY

Nor should he.

EMERY

Nor should he. Exactly! You see what they are really trying to do is say that competition doesn't work and we must protect the fool from himself. And anybody who is ass enough to go and buy shoddy goods must in fact have some protection rather than *caveat emptor*. That is really what they're saying, isn't it? That we should set up a system whereby the ordinary person can believe that whatever they're buying is going to be better than they really think.

ELIZABETH LLEWELLYN-SMITH

They want a place where you can launch a complaint and have somebody else look after the complaint for them.

EMERY

Quite. Mark you I can see some difficulties on '99', I'm afraid.

LLEWELLYN-SMITH

Particularly these ones which are Government back-bencher amendments have: they're the dangerous ones.

CASEY

I think it's easy to see a number of things the Director-General can't do. I don't think he can say this product is too dear and I don't think he can say these are shoddy goods as such. I think then, there's a gradual shading into areas where in a sense you could see the argument for trying to bring them within the Director-General's ambit. For example, if a manufacturer decided that this year's range of products would have spare parts kept for them for only six months then that is something that consumers could legitimately complain about.

EMERY

But if it became quite apparent that a manufacturer was and had been for the last nine months always short of these gearbox spare parts, I would have thought that then the Director-General ought to be able to say to the manufacturer, 'Well now look, consumers are being taken in. This is something which you ought to correct. Can't you do it? I've had 130 complaints and I'm told that there are this number more. Now is this not something which you ought not to be looking at yourself'. I would have thought that's the type of contact which when we've been talking about contacts which we would have wanted him to be able to do.

CYRIL COFFIN

What we're talking about in relation to consumer trade practices in Part II of the Bill is the creation of new criminal offences. Now one can't really conceive that the Director could put up proposals which would stand up and be enforceable to create a *new criminal offence* on the part of a manufacturer for not having spare parts. You know, that's really not on.

EMERY

This is important that we get over, or that Geoffrey must get over, because I believe there is an immense amount of muddled thinking here. This is really the difficulty, people haven't really understood the Bill and don't see the differentiation between this part and Part II of the Bill.

LLEWELLYN-SMITH

I'm sure that's right. Part II they haven't really discussed at all, the Director's powers in Part II.

CASEY

Yes and its largely the fault of the Consumers' Association . . . in their literature sort of propagating this myth that the Director-General could operate in this way – but it wouldn't work. And there's this great bleat, that this is a 'puny bill'.

EMERY

We'll battle with that, anyway. All right, I don't think we'll have too much difficulty and if we get to Stand Part on Clause 3 it'll be a miracle.[1]

Labour MPs – 16 February

An interview room in the Palace of Westminster. Evening

ALAN WILLIAMS

On the next one, [Amendment] 99, the Tories have got this amendment down. It covers some of the points made by the Consumers' Association about quality, performance and servicing. Well, the amendment seems to cover most of the points. It's a matter of whether we want to risk them withdrawing them or not. We could tag a couple of our names on just to ensure that it stays on the Order Paper for discussion. What's your feeling on this?

BRUCE MILLAN

Mrs Oppenheim will not withdraw. I mean I think you should put our names on anyway because it's a bloody good amendment.

WILLIAM HAMILTON

That's right, it'll embarrass the Government.

WILLIAMS

I'll put all our names on. The whole lot. Unless any of our lawyers feel it could be strengthened by a separate amendment.

EDWARD LYONS

I don't think it matters for this purpose really.

WILLIAMS

OK. Fine. Then if we add all our names to that and let them launch the debate on it.

[1]'Stand Part' is the debate on the whole of the clause at the end of the debates on amendments. The House then votes on whether the Clause 'stand part' of the Bill.

Three Conservative MPs and a Weights and Measures Inspector – 20 February

An interview room in the Palace of Westminster. Afternoon of the start of the debate on Amendment 99 in Committee

EDWARD TAYLOR

And I think in particular, we should discuss the amendment that Sally put forward this morning. If I remember rightly, I saw you [the Inspector] sitting in the public gallery this morning in the Committee. Now we've got this particular amendment of course on Clause 3 which is the one Sally put down with the support of the members of both parties trying to clarify and probably explain, what is the description [of Consumer Trade Practices] in Clause 3. I wonder if you think this is something which would be helpful, something which is essential and generally what do you think about this and the other matters?

MRS SALLY OPPENHEIM

It's relating those matters to the function of the Director-General.

WEIGHTS AND MEASURES INSPECTOR

Well, firstly I think this Bill is excellent. I think in concept it's excellent. But, it's very important that you include the goods themselves, and the servicing of those goods. In fact if there's a loophole in the Trade Descriptions Act it is that in most transactions the shopper isn't sufficiently expert to ask the right questions. The seller doesn't give you the information that you require; the net result is that most commodities are sold without any description being applied to them at all.

OPPENHEIM

In other words, you are confirming that it is within the terms of reference, or should be, of the Director to refer to the quality, performance, reliability or standard of manufacture of the goods, and that this is in fact essential to any consumer protection exercise as we tend to feel it is.

INSPECTOR

Indeed!

RICHARD LUCE

Do you think this is the right place to do this? I mean the other argument is that competition should sort this out. You're saying that it doesn't sort it out.

INSPECTOR

I'm saying it doesn't sort it out because there isn't enough information. I think the answer is competition, but the point is competition must be *real* competition. It isn't real competition where there isn't the information whereby there can be prudent buying.

TAYLOR

The point is this question of Consumer Trade Practice is bound to Clause 2, where it states that the Director has a *duty* to keep under review consumer trade practices; so that if you extend it on the lines of the amendment, it's not just a question of where he says 'well, it might be a good thing to take a look into spare parts' – he's got an obligation.

OPPENHEIM

Yes, quite right.

INSPECTOR

In fact I would almost go further than you're doing: I would delete the whole of the sections (a) (b) (c) (d) in Clause 3 and I would finish where it says 'or in connection with the supply of services'. In other words, I'm just in effect saying no limits at all.

OPPENHEIM

I think that isn't quite on. We've intended to keep our amendments within the bounds of reality in that they may be more acceptable to the Government than the wider one, and certainly, in fact, that it may be more realistic to start off like that and possibly broaden it by amendment to an Act later.

Department of Trade and Industry, Michael Casey and Elizabeth Llewellyn-Smith – 16 February

In Casey's office. Morning

LLEWELLYN-SMITH

What she wants is for him to look at *actual quality,* not whether the quality is misrepresented or . . .

CASEY

I know what she wants, but it's rather difficult to cope with the amendment without discussing the philosophy behind the Bill; and saying that the only way to deal with quality is to deal with the rules of the game within which people make their bargain about quality.

LLEWELLYN-SMITH

Well, when Mr Luce says that Mrs Oppenheim is expected to press this amendment very hard, this could mean that like Mr Taylor this week she was prepared to actually *vote* for it; in which case obviously the Opposition will vote for it too . . . This is why I'm trying to think of how one can make absolutely clear the other ways. I mean this is not the right way, perhaps, to deal with improving standards of quality. But what are the ways that the Director will pursue?

CASEY

I think we can . . . Look, we've got two courses of action. One is to rehearse all these arguments which explain why we don't think this is a sensible amendment, that it pre-empts really what we hope to do at Report Stage when we've had a chance to deal with the thing as a whole, and therefore we think that it's undesirable. Or to get hold of Mrs Oppenheim behind the scenes and explain there, and say 'Now this is our view, we're going to be tough on this. Do you really want to press it?'

LLEWELLYN-SMITH

Yes. Well, if we're going to suggest that, the sooner we suggest it on Monday the better. I'd be in favour of doing that. I think probably on her part there's no misunderstanding. She knows what the Bill is intended to do and just thinks it should do something else.

CASEY

Well, if you think it's a silly amendment, you've got to say it's a silly amendment, or say that you'll consider the silly amendment, and consider it and deal with it at Report Stage.

Ministerial Briefing – 19 February
Peter Emery's office. Evening

PETER EMERY

Come on troops. [Everyone settles round the table]. Now then, all right. We then come to '99' which is Sally Oppenheim's amendment. Now Richard, have you got any views about how strongly Sally feels about it?

RICHARD LUCE

Yes, I think she feels very strongly and Teddy Taylor thought that she would want to push this one very hard unless she has some very firm reassurances on Number 99.

ELIZABETH LLEWELLYN-SMITH

I don't really know what reassurance we can give on that one. Even on the re-casting of Clause 2, it's unlikely to go that far; and certainly we couldn't consider these things going into Part II[1].

EMERY

Well now, let me just tactically look at this for a moment. Whilst you may be right, if Geoffrey's in Cabinet and Sally wishes to press this very hard, we will not carry this in committee, or we will not . . .

LUCE

If I may just say so, I think this is a growing and very serious problem. The West Sussex consumer protection chap who runs their show there said to me that one of the areas where it's really serious is imported consumer durables and cars. And the whole problem of servicing and spare parts there is a growing problem in Sussex.

EMERY

Yes, but that's what competition is about. If somebody is foolish enough to go and buy a [foreign] car then why should we protect him and ensure that the thing is right or proper, or if someone's Rolls has gone wrong, I'm not really too worried about protecting the consumer.

LUCE

Well I mean you'd be very worried if you bought the damn thing on an assurance, on an understanding that there was going to be normal servicing and there wasn't. And how the hell are you going to know yourself as an individual?

CYRIL COFFIN

Well, there might be a contract.

LUCE

I think this is a very serious problem, and you know, this will be pressed very hard, and I think we ought to take note of it.

[1]Part II has more teeth: it deals with powers to recommend that Parliament make orders against unfair consumer trade practices.

Brian Armstrong

What about this? If you wrote, if you ensured that all the contracts of sale included a provision and an undertaking that servicing would be available, then it would be a civil right to fall back upon and [Clause] 35 would operate[1].

Coffin

That's what I was saying just now. Create a contractual duty and you're home and dry. [*Chat*]

Emery

Why in fact whenever you sell anything you would have to have a contractual duty to maintain it – I mean, I'd get myself in very deep water with everybody, I think. You lawyers would be making money for evermore.

Michael Ware [to Brian Armstrong]

The flaw in your argument is that you assume the contract is with the manufacturer. But it's not, it's with some garage in the town which may well go out of business next week. You've got no contractual right with the manufacturers. And the problem is not restricted to imports; there's some complaint I believe with a manufacturer of pottery, dinner services, that people are deliberately making them for a very short run and you can never get any replacement bits when you've smashed a couple of dinner plates.

Armstrong

It seems to me that unless you write into the Bill some means of having orders which increase the information available to the consumer about these things or increase the term or improve the terms and conditions of sale you can't really do anything.

Emery

Well, my reaction is that if that is put in the Bill manufacturers would find a way of getting round it as quickly as humanly possible. Because they would try – and whether by an exclusion clause (which won't be any longer legal) or by some means they would attempt to get round that; because they are saying we cannot be responsible for everybody who sells an Austin car having the spare parts or being able to carry out service to the level which we our-

[1]Clause 35 (2) deals with action by the Director against breaches of civil obligations.

selves would require. And this would mean a centralisation structure which I think most of industry would not be willing to carry out. I think it would be a whole re-alteration of the retailing and selling structure within industry. And I really don't think that's what we want, or that in fact industry would accept it. I don't believe – I mean if we were going to do something like that, we'd have to go back to the Legislation Committee. I'm certain that is not what my colleagues think we're doing. Richard, I can see the point you're making. But, it's like you know, it's like the do-gooder. I want to get away from sin, I want to make all people be able to give the best service and provide that which they're saying they'll provide. That we should legislate to do this, or (I think because people would say we're not legislating to do it), but that we in fact should allow the Director-General to begin investigating it, when there is *not* a contract, would seem to me to begin implying that anything which affected the consumer which had not a contract would be open as fair game for the Director-General to investigate. Now I don't think that that argument is going to convince Sally. I think it's the right argument, but I think they see this as being something which has got a good popular appeal, an emotive factor, and what I'm wondering is as we – let's just think – we're going to have to re-do are we not, or it looks like we're going to re-do [Clause] 3 (a) (b) (c) and (d)?

LLEWELLYN-SMITH

This is going to be re-done on Report, anyway this definition – yes.

EMERY

Therefore, what I wonder is whether we accept these amendments – saying that I don't think they can be held in this manner and that we don't like them terribly in this area. We do see the point about maintenance. I would normally suggest that they were not essential and we should look at the assurances that have been given, but if she wishes to force it through well, I would not resist it. That sort of line. Then when it comes to Report we must have made up our mind absolutely and we wouldn't be down to a sort of single majority and we would be able to do what we want to with the whole of the clause. But, what I dislike about it is that it would give the impression to the outside world that we're widening it.

MICHAEL CASEY

And you're doing this in quite a number of issues aren't you? You're saying you're looking at this again.

LLEWELLYN-SMITH

I think one does want to keep clear about what the Director can't do. With the best will in the world, he can't be this sort of universal aunt who can do everything on quality and all the rest of it.

EMERY

All right. Well, we've been over this lot, and we believe that we do not think this is what the DG ought in fact to be spending his time doing. Is that right? Are we all agreed on that.

LLEWELLYN-SMITH

Yes.

EMERY

Richard?

LUCE

Also, if I may just re-enforce again, I'm a little bit worried about this from the Parliamentary angle of this earlier point of saying 'well, we'll look at this again'. Because I really do think we may be – though I'm in fact very sympathetic to their particular amendment – I think we might be storing up a lot of trouble for ourselves in Report Stage.

LLEWELLYN-SMITH

I'm sure we are.

COFFIN

There are already a number of points – quite serious ones.

LUCE

They're expecting radical changes.

EMERY

I have no doubt about that. But what then therefore are we suggesting? That we go down with flying colours, defeated, and defeated and defeated? And then we have to rectify it. It's not unusual, but it isn't the sort of thing that I'm very happy about doing.

LUCE

If it's any help I'll have a chat with them tonight just to see what – in what particular areas they're going to probe.

71

EMERY

Do you know, you see, its John [Gorst] and Ted [Taylor] and Sally, all three have their names on it and I have a feeling – hold on a minute, just to make it more difficult, is this not the one that all the Socialists have put their names down as well?

COFFIN

Yes it is. Well, three of them anyway.

LLEWELLYN-SMITH

Enough so it can't be withdrawn.

EMERY

So it's a major embarrassment, in actual fact. Well I don't like it I tell you. Does anybody have any other ideas because if not we must press on. And I think we may have to go down as saying that this is impossible.

LLEWELLYN-SMITH

I think for the record you ought to advise the Committee to vote against it even though knowing it's going to be carried.

EMERY

Well, that's fine for you, Elizabeth. I can see the headlines 'Emery can't conduct his committee very well' become constant as the weeks go on.

CASEY

I get the impression that a fair number of people on both sides have totally misunderstood the scope of this Bill. And that they are under the impression that the Director-General will have a kind of 'Which' function testing the quality of goods and being able to do something about it. They don't realise that the basic idea is that he lays down the rules of the game within which people make their own bargains.

EMERY

It isn't that I wish to disagree with you at all, but it is that they don't *want* the Bill to be that; they want the Bill to be very much wider, and they are setting out so to do.

CASEY

Since the Government will have to stamp its foot eventually and make perfectly clear the Director-General won't have this function, it would be, I think, very dangerous to give them anything from which they could say that they got the impression from the Committee. They're fooling themselves.

COFFIN

I think you want to say that of course we think that the consumers are entitled to good value for money, quality of goods appropriate to the price they pay, and so on; to proper servicing, availability of spare parts. Of course this is very desirable. But this Bill is not the most appropriate way of achieving this.

EMERY

All right. We certainly won't get further than that.

Three Labour MPs (Williams, Millan and Golding) walking to the Department of Trade and Industry – 20 February

Parliament Square. Afternoon

ALAN WILLIAMS

Well I think it doesn't matter how often we're meeting at the moment, or how infrequently, unless he can put something specific before us in place of Clauses 2 and 3, there's no point in meeting at all, you know. We're talking completely in a vacuum, and there'll have to be co-operation from him on the content of the Bill. But I'm not inclined to accept at this stage a revised timetable motion.

Narrator

The debates on Clauses 2 and 3 have taken longer than the Government expected, so the Minister has invited Labour leaders to discuss speeding up the Committee timetable. But Labour plans to use the occasion to press for news about the changes likely to be made to Clauses 2 and 3 at Report Stage when the Bill is re-presented to the whole House of Commons as amended or not by the Standing Committee.

WILLIAMS

It's so early in the proceedings, any delay there is, is hardly the result of filibustering. It's simply because we can't get clarification from them of what they're going to do.

Labour MPs in Sir Geoffrey Howe's Office at the Department of Trade and Industry – 20 February

A short time later

ALAN WILLIAMS

If we're not careful, what should be discussed at the Committee Stage in detail is going now to be put onto the floor of the House for the Report Stage. We've had no assurance on Report time. If we can have an assurance there that helps us to perhaps . . .

HOWE

Again that depends on when we reckon to get this back to the floor [of the House] and how long we can give it at that time.

WILLIAMS

But more important, before we go on to that, is whether you feel you're able at this stage to give clear indication of what you're going to do at Report on Clause 2 and Clause 3. If that can be done on Clause 3 Stand Part that may clear the way for Clause 4.

HOWE

I think to some extent I've indicated once or twice on Clause 2 the kind of areas we want to open up and the kind of limits to what we can open up.

WILLIAMS

But on the other hand we feel that what we've done so far has been worthwhile, in that it has produced a re-assessment of the Bill from you. What we now want is a firming up of that re-assessment if possible before we leave Clause 3.

HOWE

I'm under a difficulty because I don't think I can be there on Thursday either. Peter and I will have a word about it, twixt now and then.

EMERY

Well, I fully take the point of you saying this is a fundamental re-orientation of the whole of the Bill. Of course that isn't the case. But I do think that it's right that you should know where in fact we saw the additions and the alterations coming.

HOWE

We'll come back to this as soon as we can make some

specific suggestions, when we see what we're trying to make.

WILLIAMS

OK. Fine.

HOWE

Thanks very much indeed. And Bruce remains more or less mute.

BRUCE MILLAN

When you reach the monopoly section, I'll start.

WILLIAMS

Then it's my turn for a holiday when Bruce starts. [*Chat*]

EMERY

I say 'Amen' to that – would you like a permanent pair . . .? [*Laughter as they leave the office*]

Ministerial Briefing – 21 February
Peter Emery's office. Evening

PETER EMERY

Now, first things first. Will Geoffrey be able to be there for any part of tomorrow, because this is one of the factors?

PATRICK SHOVELTON (Deputy Secretary, Department of Trade and Industry)

All of it, I've been told.

EMERY

He's now going to be there for all of it. That I think will be useful.

SHOVELTON

He's been let off Cabinet.

EMERY

This shows some of the importance. Therefore what I would expect is then that he will deal with, or I would suggest that he would deal with Amendment 99 and probably the Third Reading. Not the Third Reading. [*Laughs*] We're getting way ahead of ourselves.

SHOVELTON

That'll be October, Minister.

EMERY

I'm still back in the Coal Bill of last night. [*Laughs*] Anyway the Stand Part [debate] on Clause 3. Because one of the things I think I would like to discuss with you quickly, because it did seem to me that the Opposition were trying to suggest that the Committee was in an immense muddle, because they weren't absolutely certain of what amendments we would put down on Report. Now I think this is being played rather to the political gallery, because the concept, as I tried to correct the other day, when they said there was going to be a fundamental change – well *none* of us have ever suggested that. What we have suggested was that we could see that there will probably need to be some changes, and these changes would not necessarily affect Part II of the Bill, or certain of the other operations. But nonetheless, what we did say was that we were willing to listen to all of their arguments so that we could take their advice in making certain that the Bill made sense. So that I therefore thought, that it would be very useful if we tried to define absolutely where we saw the areas of amendment that we were willing to bring forward on Report Stage. Now do you generally believe that that makes sense?

ELIZABETH LLEWELLYN-SMITH

I'm sure it's right, otherwise this thing, this myth will spread and it will be on record and they will come back on Report and say that they were promised enormous amendments to the whole of Parts II and III, which is not true.

EMERY

And the other thing is, you see, it's the Goebbels technique: you begin saying that there'll be radical revision or fundamental revision. They say it often enough and they'll begin to convince themselves that that's the case. And it isn't.

MICHAEL CASEY

Well, the point of the thing is you can't let the things they said yesterday go by default, and since they said it it's got to be rebutted.

EMERY (to Richard Luce)

Yes, well, you bring Geoffrey up to date on this discussion will you and I'll see him in the Division as well.

Interior Sir Geoffrey Howe's car – Parliament Square – 22 February

En route to the Standing Committee

HOWE

> Basically it's a question of explaining that there is scope for an amendment of substance on the scope of the Director's duties in Clause 2 – I think, going beyond that of merely removing 'economic' – but not much scope in enlarging the field generally on Clause 3.

JOHN MEADWAY (Howe's Private Secretary)

> How they're going to like this I'm not sure.

HOWE

> Well, I think it's merely a re-presentation of what we've said already.

MEADWAY

> I suspect they've got a rather more bullish impression.

HOWE

> Yes.

Narrator

> The Minister is missing a Cabinet meeting to attend the Committee in order to deal with both Amendment 99 and the demands for information about the changes in Clauses 2 and 3. After four weeks they're threatening to seriously hinder the Bill's progress – with 120 clauses still to go.

HOWE

> I'm going to have lunch here. I'll be staying 'til half-past one or twenty-to-two.

Narrator

> The Government came through the ordeal over Amendment 99 unscathed. Peter Emery had a private word with Sally Oppenheim in the division lobby of the House (where cameras are not allowed)[1].
>
> In Committee Sir Geoffrey Howe talked the members into not pressing the Amendment to a vote. He reassured the

[1]As the public are not admitted to the lobby with or without cameras, we have only indirect knowledge of this conversation, though that it took place we are sure. Mrs Oppenheim stated several months later she had no recollection of it, and that her views were not changed in this way.

MPs that something would be done but he made no clear and firm promises. He said, for example, 'if one looks at the definition of 'Consumer Trade Practice' as defining the scope of the Director's duties to keep matters under review that may be something we can unstitch and make wider'.

But people were not quite sure what Sir Geoffrey meant. This worried the Confederation of British Industry, whose members could be seriously affected if the Director-General's powers were widened. They have had a study group of executives meeting twice a week for three months making their own plans for amending the Bill.

CBI Study Group – 22 February

HARRY GRAY (Chairman)

Have there been any developments in the committee which ought to be reported?

IVOR HUSSEY (CBI Parliamentary adviser)

The point was made very firmly this morning that, in the opinion of the speakers, manufacturers are not doing their duty in ensuring that spare parts are available. And there can hardly be a consumer in this country who wouldn't agree with that, at any rate in a particular, even though perhaps not as a generalisation. It was clear first of all, that the Minister was concerned about this, as much concerned as the members advancing the amendments were. It was clear also that he was not prepared to accept the amendment because he didn't think it was the right place to put it. Now I can't recall the details of why he said this.

JAMES CARR

This is the same point we were discussing.

HUSSEY

But on the other hand we have to be, especially as the CBI, jolly careful about getting legislation to make sure that our members provide spare parts.

GRAY

But by all means let's raise this tomorrow [when they are to go to the Ministry].

CARR

What we ought to do tomorrow is ask them what they're up to because they're clearly up to something. And it is our duty as the CBI to seek out what's going on.

GRAY

This is exactly what I was going to say. I think we take the point. That we must be a little careful how we suggest they should add things which may prove to be a burden; but on the other hand we do want to know what they are talking about and what they have in mind to do.

Narrator

Like other outside interest groups, the CBI maintains regular contact with both MPs and Civil Servants including meetings at the Ministry.

CBI visit to the Department of Trade and Industry – 23 February

CYRIL COFFIN

Mike, you don't know Harry Gray from the CBI do you?

MICHAEL CASEY

How do you do. [*Chat. Then the formal meeting starts*]

PATRICK SHOVELTON

You don't mind about these cameras? Has that been fixed up? . . . We feel that on Second Reading speech and in the very important speeches which Sir Geoffrey Howe has made in the Committee, notably on the 6 February and yesterday, we would have hoped that our concept of the new arrangements for consumer assistance and how these will work in practice, as you put it, we would hope that this has helped a lot and has given a great deal of background information. But over to you –

HARRY GRAY

I see that there is to be revision certainly of Clause 3 and I think Clause 2 as well. Could you indicate what sort of revision is contemplated, because these are both rather fundamental to the Bill?

ELIZABETH LLEWELLYN-SMITH

Really, Clause 3 in itself is nothing but a definition clause. As he explained to the Committee, what is important is the places in the Bill where this concept of a Consumer Trade Practice is actually written into the Director's functions. Clause 2 gives the Director a general duty to keep under review Consumer Trade Practices, and in certain cases to make recommendations to Ministers. And what the Minister was saying on the 6 February was that he was open to argument that for that sort of general function, it was perhaps reasonable that the Director's terms of reference would be pretty widely drawn: in particular, that they needn't necessarily be limited as they are in Clause 2 as it stands to practices which adversely affect the economic interests of consumers. And it was in that context that he said that he would be having another look at the definition of a Consumer Trade Practice in Clause 3.

CBI REPRESENTATIVE

I think that what we were anxious to know was whether the re-drafting of Clause 3 would in fact widen considerably the definition of what you have in mind.

SHOVELTON

Our Minister is very conscious of the implications of widening the Bill. We've got the pressures on the other direction on us, of course, but we are endeavouring to stand fairly in the middle as usual.

CBI Study Group – 1 March

IVOR HUSSEY

Another little interpretation, if I may Chairman. Geoffrey Howe again in the course of his discussion said – 'I hope that without extending the Director's range of authority to keep under review under Clause 2, too widely' – God, how did he manage to say that? – 'we will be able to meet the servicing and availability points but not the quality points – and so far as it is practicable, that is the way in which I should like to unstitch the definition of his power under Clause 2 so as to enable him to bring that kind of matter under review.'

ERIC FELGATE

I'm not madly happy about this. One sees that there are strong arguments for not getting involved, but on the other hand the consumer interests have a real point here which they're unlikely to let lie doggo for very long if they're not satisfied on it.

HARRY GRAY

I think this is perfectly true. I wonder whether you can go on and widen the scope of this Bill and hope to bring in everything.

FELGATE

I view the widening of the Bill with as much apprehension as I think you do, Chairman. The point is that this is a not negligible point for those who wish to widen it, and unless they're satisfied, this is going to be a perpetual thorn in our flesh I think; and I'm not satisfactorily briefed from the people who are likely to be most concerned in this. I'm sure that a great many members would be horrified at the idea that they have to provide a spare parts service in perpetuity, more or less automatically.

JAMES CARR

Chairman, my point is, *I don't want* this Bill enlarged. What I want them to do is to clarify their own minds as to what they really are covering and what they're not. Then if there is something here that they want to cover let them go out and produce another Bill. There will be several other consumer bills. But what I think is particularly dangerous is a situation where the Director thinks and it is thought that he has wider powers, at least of headmaster's study intimidation, than the Bill actually gives him. Because then manufacturers will be leant on in a way that the law doesn't allow for and without having opportunity to discuss the thing properly.

CHAIRMAN

From what Howe has said, it seems to me likely that they will extend the function of the Director to keep this sort of thing under review, but he won't have any powers to do anything about it, except to make a report.

CARR

Well now, that's where we delude ourselves. He will have enormous powers. He will have headmaster's study powers. And if there's one thing we've learnt in the last ten years, of price control particularly, it is that headmaster's study powers are wider and more effective and more onerous on the manufacturers than if they'd been set out properly in the law. Well, that's what I want to avoid. [*Pause*]

GRAY

I don't think this is getting us very far.

CARR

Quite honestly, we're not going to know a damn thing about this Bill until we get to Report [Stage] and then it's too late to do anything about it.

Department of Trade and Industry – Michael Casey and Elizabeth Llewellyn-Smith – 14 March

In Casey's office

CASEY

> [*looking through Hansard*] But it could be read, you see, that he will propose under Clause 17. You see they've read into this far more . . .

LLEWELLYN-SMITH

> Well, this is why I think it's rather desirable to get on record exactly what he did promise and what he didn't promise. I thought I'd marked up this bit on here. Or was it 4a?

CASEY

> That's it there.

LLEWELLYN-SMITH

> Yes, well, we've quoted that several times. That's why it's in a box. Anyway, I've often given it to people to quote, I don't know whether they actually have. It's funny how difficult it is to track these down, because I spent about 45 minutes yesterday trying to track down something that Edward Taylor asked. In the end I got Mrs McDonald to mark up everything he'd said for three days and . . .

CASEY

> You found it?

LLEWELLYN-SMITH

> No, I didn't find it. In the end I gave up. It wasn't cost effective.

CASEY

> Anyway, Elizabeth, the comforting thing is that by the same token, it will be equally difficult to nail us the other way round and to quote it back that we undertook to do things we don't think we undertook!

LLEWELLYN-SMITH

> Yes, I quite agree.

Narrator, over exterior shot of Michael Casey and Elizabeth Llewellyn-Smith walking from the Department of Trade and Industry.

> One week later the Civil Servants meet to re-draft Clauses 2 and 3. It is their task to frame instructions for the Parlia-

mentary draftsman elsewhere in Whitehall who will actually write the words of the new clauses. If approved by the Minister and the other departments concerned, these will be presented to Parliament at the next phase – the Report Stage of the Bill. To meet the promise in Committee to broaden Clause 2, the Civil Servants proposed to let the Director-General review more than just Consumer Trade Practices. They suggest he should look at *all* commercial activities.

Department of Trade and Industry – Civil Servants' Meeting – 2 March
Michael Casey's office. Morning

MICHAEL WARE [*reading his notes on the discussion so far*]
    In essence, you want him to be able to look at the acts and omissions of manufacturers, wholesalers and retailers which adversely affect the interests of consumers.

ELIZABETH LLEWELLYN-SMITH
    In the UK.

MICHAEL CASEY
    I think that is exactly what Parliament wants. So how do we give him a discretion? It was the Minister who suggested we give him a discretion as to the scope of his duties. I'm not sure what this means or how it should be done.

WARE
    'It shall be the duty in any case in which the Director considers it appropriate . . .'

CYRIL COFFIN
    That sort of line.

LLEWELLYN-SMITH
    Totally subjective – so nobody can challenge his decision. I think that's what we want to achieve.

WARE
    A meaningless duty in a sense.

BRIAN ARMSTRONG
    Sorry, that is in regard to –

COFFIN
    Keeping under review, things which he thinks it is necessary to keep under review in relation to his . . .

LLEWELLYN-SMITH
    When he thinks it expedient.

CASEY
    So he has a duty, wherever he considers it appropriate to
    review 'commercial activities', with a view to identifying
    people who are carrying on those which may adversely
    affect the interests of consumers.

LLEWELLYN-SMITH
    Yes. Full stop.

CASEY
    Full stop. And we'll cover the UK point. I'm not sure . . .

COFFIN
    Sorry, what was the thing which may adversely affect . . . ?

CASEY
    Activities.

LLEWELLYN-SMITH
    Commercial activities.

COFFIN
    Commercial activities.

ARMSTRONG
    Isn't this in fact giving him more freedom to do nothing
    than he's got in the Bill already? So far as trade practices
    and economic effects of them are concerned, he's got to
    do it now.

LLEWELLYN-SMITH
    Well, fair enough.

CASEY
    I don't mind him being free to do nothing as long as he's
    free to do something that he feels he should do.

LLEWELLYN-SMITH
    These sort of general duty provisions are really pretty
    meaningless anyway. It's just an indication of what Parlia-
    ment expects the chap to spend money on. I mean the
    difference now is that we are deliberately bringing in these
    things where you have these advisory committees that
    you wrote your paper about – Food and Drugs and so on.
    I mean, what is the Director's relationship to be with them?
    Is he to go through them, and let them take the thing up

directly with their own Minister or is he to go straight to the Secretary of State, sort of bypassing them?

CASEY

In Committee, Geoffrey Howe's approach to this was to say that it would be sensible if the Director-General had power to react to information coming to him, for the purposes of informing or possibly advising other Ministers. It would be going too far, I think, that he should make *recommendations* to other Ministers because they have their own committees charged with recommending action.

COFFIN

Yes, yes.

CASEY

I mean, the Minister of Agriculture will not want the Director-General to make recommendations that Marks and Spencers shouldn't put cyclamates in orange juice, because he's already got a committee doing this. So we've got to cut out that.

LLEWELLYN-SMITH

He certainly won't want to recommend that to our Minister. [*Laughs*]

CASEY

No, it can be made perfectly clear can't it in debate, that we widen the fields of review to meet the point that Members made that where he gathers information on these matters, he should be able to react to them and pass information on? But we don't want him swamped, and we don't expect that he's going to duplicate the other bodies who are in this field. And that's it. It can be quite easily explained, can't it? That we envisage his role in this way. And no-one can then turn round and say that they expected him to do a lot of things that Parliament have been told he won't do.

LLEWELLYN-SMITH

That's the object we want to achieve, and I mean what it's going to look like, how it's worded, is nothing to do with us.

WARE

It looks politically about right, doesn't it?

CASEY

What procedures do we have to run through now to get this settled? There's interdepartmental clearance and the question of instructions. And then clearance with Ministers.

COFFIN

Well, I wonder whether Michael had better not have a shot at draft instructions, if he feels able to, on the basis of this rather desultory conversation. And then . . .

LLEWELLYN-SMITH

Yes, yes. And then at that stage it goes to the other departments before the instructions are actually delivered.

Civil Servants walking to Pub immediately after the previous scene – 2 March
Mid-day

ELIZABETH LLEWELLYN-SMITH

It does mean there will be some rather delicate ground, thin ice to cover while we plough through Part II. Either explaining the changes we make, or not, either of which is going to be a bit awkward.

MICHAEL CASEY

I'm glad Cyril came along. Now then we won't have to have a second reading of this. Shall we go down, there's a pub down there, let's try that one.

LLEWELLYN-SMITH

Yes. But apparently sometimes one isn't clear whether he has agreed something – like your thing about whether the majority of members were independent.

In Pub over lunch

ELIZABETH LLEWELLYN-SMITH

The absolutely low point was this time last year on the Europe Bill. We had two censure motions running, one on the chair and one on the Government, and we had loads of briefing. This all interrupted the Committee proceedings . . . it was the time I felt tiredest and most depressed in the whole of my life really. Why should one shorten one's life? You'd do it in a war or something like that for the sake of the country.

MICHAEL WARE

If you've got twenty Assistant Secretaries and twenty
Assistant Solicitors it doesn't mean you've got twenty good
quality ones. You'll still have ten good ones and ten useless
ones.

LLEWELLYN-SMITH

Yes, there's a dilution of currency.

Narrator

One month later the reactions have arrived from other
Government Departments concerned with consumer protection. The Ministry of Agriculture, Food and Fisheries,
known as MAFF, objects to the Director-General having
powers to review in its area of expertise – health and safety.
So after another long meeting, the Civil Servants at Trade
and Industry have worked out a more cautious wording.
It allows the Director-General to actively review economic
matters but only to 'take note of' complaints coming in
about health and safety. Now this formula must go again
through Ministerial channels to be approved.

Civil Servants report to Sir Geoffrey Howe on MAFF's
reaction – 19 April
Sir Geoffrey Howe's office. Mid-day

HOWE

Now widening the Director's role.

CYRIL COFFIN

I think the question turns in a sense on the construction of
the words 'keep under review'. MAFF regard these as conferring on him a duty, a mandatory duty. to go out and
explore their fields, what they regard as their fields . . .

ELIZABETH LLEWELLYN-SMITH

. . . and have an expert view.

COFFIN

And have an expert view.

LLEWELLYN-SMITH

Whereas they would say the Director's view is worth no
more than anybody's. You need staff, scientists, labora-
tories.

PETER EMERY

The prospect of drawing a distinction between Food and Drugs and the rest I think is just not on.

LLEWELLYN-SMITH

Quite. That's what we felt, and therefore it was probably better to have a slightly watered down duty for everything.

MICHAEL CASEY

Really, the most we could get Agriculture to accept was the sort of duty that was under Clause 2(3) 'Duty of the Director to have regard to evidence becoming available to him, in respect to, I suppose, commercial activities'.

EMERY

But I'm sure we're right in the view that to leave MAFF in an entirely different situation to everybody else just really isn't on, and therefore it seems to me we have to see just how far down the road we have to get in order to bring MAFF along with us. Do we have to fight about it or do we not?

HOWE

How far does 9(a) comply with our commitments, our undertakings?

CASEY

I think it's pretty good. I think it fulfilled what you said you would be likely to do on amendment. It doesn't satisfy some of the pressures that you were under. I think people went a lot further than 9(a) but *you* didn't go any further when you agreed to consider amending Clause 2.

HOWE

What the difference in practice is I entirely fail to see.

LLEWELLYN-SMITH

I think it's entirely presentation. I mean he will cut his coat according to his cloth. If he's got a limited number of staff he's obviously not going to spend a lot of time on dangerous drugs. He will in fact have a different role in the 'economic' and 'non-economic' problems, so that in one paragraph [in the new Clause 2] it will be different.

HOWE

I think let's try and go for that.

Narrator

Three weeks later the Bill was nearing Report Stage when it will be re-presented to the whole House of Commons as amended or not by the Committee. The Minister will tell his own party's back-benchers about the new clauses which are to be voted on as Government Amendments to the Bill. Meanwhile Labour meets to work out its strategy for the two-day debate.

Labour MPs two days before Report Stage – 14 May
An interview room in the Palace of Westminster. Afternoon

ALAN WILLIAMS

Now, I'm dissatisfied with the amendment the Government's put forward here. It goes part way to meeting us but I've put in provisionally an alteration. In the Government's amendment on Clause 2 you notice an (a) and a (b) there. (a) gives the power to review activities but purely economic activities; (b) gives power to 'receive and collate' but not to initiate as far as health and safety are concerned. This still doesn't go as far as we want it, so what I've done is to amend their amendment which makes sure we have a debate on our propositions. I've tabled it this afternoon. So that what it now means is that section (a) covers health and safety as well as economic interest and 'economic' is deleted. So this really now gives us everything we want and everything the Consumers' Association want, if the Government will accept our amendment.

Department of Trade and Industry – Ministerial Briefing for Report Stage – 15 May
Sir Geoffrey Howe's office. Morning

HOWE

So the effect of the division between us and them now is fairly limited, in fact, isn't it? We have broadened the Director's field of responsibility to cover the matters of health and safety but with a lower degree of duty. He doesn't actually have to go hunting around. And they want him to hunt around.

PATRICK SHOVELTON

Are the departments now happy about this?

CYRIL COFFIN

Well, I've just had the Ministry of Agriculture on and they are not terribly happy with some of the bits in the supplementary briefing notes. They recognise that there is this difference of view between the Home Office and themselves as to how far the Director ought to go on the health and safety line. But they were saying, for example, that to say that the responsible departments had developed considerable technical expertise considerably understates the case inasmuch as the Chief Medical Officer of Health, apart from being the Minister of Agriculture's brother [*laughter*] is also the expert, the top authority in the country on toxic substances. This is as far as they could possibly go and they're not at all sure they haven't gone perhaps too far.

HOWE

Well that's all right. And as long as they're content with where we are, we'll pay as much tribute as they like to their glowing expertise.

PETER EMERY

Family or otherwise.

COFFIN

The other thing was, you know, the Director's recommendations might be to the effect that the evidence before him appears to indicate that a particular danger exists. They suggest that all that he could really say is from the evidence he's had of complaints, you know, there *may* be a danger here. Well, they don't really like the concept of him as a ginger group for their great sort of committees.

EMERY

The whole of the debate and the questioning on this is actually how far can he go? What can he do and what can't he do? Those will be the real questions of the debate. And that's what I think, you know, we've got to be . . . we will be treading fairly carefully.

HOWE

Yes, but in fact basically, to the extent that he concludes that it's necessary and justifiable, he will be able to draw to the attention of the responsible bodies, things that seem to him to give rise for a case to answer. And that's . . .

SHOVELTON

Yes, and that's very significant in fact, isn't it?

HOWE

Yes it is.

SHOVELTON

And do we know what the Consumers' Association have –
I mean have we got any feel for the reaction of others
about this?

HOWE

Well, I think one must assume that the reaction of the
Opposition in wanting to have the total duty to keep
under review health and safety matters represents the line
of argument we've got to meet. And I think that it simply
isn't his function, it isn't within his capacity, in the light
of what you say about the expertise.

EMERY

If no action is taken on the advice, or the action that he
takes in drawing to the attention of MAFF or DHSS
[Department of Health and Social Services] his only line of
action is to publicise it in his annual report.

COFFIN

Yes, I continue to receive large volumes of complaints
about dangerous toys or . . .

HOWE

And then I daresay Alan Williams will ask a question about
it. [*Laughter*] And that is the sort of heartland of Part 1.

Narrator

The Fair Trading Bill passed the Report Stage in the
Commons with the latest Government version intact. The
Director-General was given wider powers to actively review
all commercial activities, while only passively receiving
complaints about health and safety. The list of things
he could act on still excluded spare parts and servicing and
shoddy goods[1]. The Bill now goes to the House of Lords,
where further changes can be made. So the Consumers'
Association met with Labour leaders including Baroness
Phillips, Consumer spokesman in the Lords.

[1]Though these are covered in his review powers in Clause 2.

St Stephen's Restaurant
A corner table facing the Palace of Westminster. Mid-day

ALAN WILLIAMS

I think the improvements on Clause 2 and 3 are useful, it's extended it quite substantially, but on the other hand I still don't think it's far enough. And in fact this is one of the things I thought we might discuss for the Lords.

BARONESS PHILLIPS

Yes, this is what I want to know. Which are the things that I can pick up as amendments, because sometimes in the Lords you can get things through by sheer default. In other words there's not enough people there to really vote against.

WILLIAMS

We widened the Bill and the old Clause 2, and we've got them to accept that health and safety are as much an interest to the consumers, but it is accepted in a very half-hearted way. And whereas there's full power to collect information to investigate as far as *economic* interests are concerned, under a new clause which will appear in the reprinted Bill and will appear at the start of Part II, all he can do as far as health and safety is concerned is to passively receive information and collate it. He can't go looking for problems and he can't go researching issues. Now this I think is a grave weakness still but you could still do a very valuable job of improving here.

DAVID TENCH

It's a very fundamental conceptual thing because this Bill, you see, was conceived basically as being a competition thing. Essentially economic. And we saw it as a consumer protection thing, which is really potentially quite different. That's where the crunch comes on that, don't you agree? Because they still see it as Fair Trading. They say it's got nothing to do with health and safety, that's something else.

BARONESS PHILLIPS

They're more concerned really with the other angle, the monopoly angle, I think.

TENCH

It really stems also from the fact that health and safety as a consumer protection thing is a Home Office responsibility. And the Home Office is very unconsumer-minded . . .

[Lunch is served. Film credits appear]

Narrator (in studio)

Standing Committee B of the House of Commons took nearly as long to deal with Clauses 2 and 3 of the Fair Trading Bill as they did to deal with the other 121 clauses put together.

The arduous Parliamentary process of passing the Bill is now coming to an end with the Royal Assent, the Queen's signature of approval turning the Bill into an Act and making it law.

Tomorrow night in THE STATE OF THE NATION a committee of inquiry will examine the effectiveness of that process and other Parliamentary activities – and the arguments for reform.

Part 2

Law-making and Public Money:
has Parliament lost control?

The transcript of Part 2 of the programme is not
exactly as transmitted.
The written evidence received by the committee
from all witnesses is given at some length.
In the programme as transmitted, only a few small
extracts from the written evidence were read out
by the narrator.

Further, some parts of the hearing, which on
transmission were summarised by the narrator, are
here given at length. Sections included in this
version but not transmitted are indicated by
vertical rules.

Part 2

The form of Part 2 was a committee hearing: five MPs, behaving roughly as though they were a House of Commons Select Committee, heard a succession of witnesses and discussed among themselves the evidence they had heard. The hearing was recorded in County Hall, London – across the river from the Palace of Westminster – on 9 March 1973.

In the Programme

THE COMMITTEE

Chairman The Rt Hon Edward du Cann MP
(Conservative, Taunton)
Mr Michael Foot MP (Labour, Ebbw Vale)
Mr John Mackintosh MP
(Labour, Berwick and East Lothian)
The Rt Hon Reginald Maudling MP
(Conservative, Barnet)
Mr Nicholas Scott MP
(Conservative, Paddington South)

THE WITNESSES *In order of appearance*
Sir William Armstrong
(Head of the Home Civil Service)
Mr Michael Ryle (Clerk, Public Bills Office
– House of Commons)
Mr Frank Allen (Clerk to the Public
Expenditure Committee – House of
Commons)
Mr D G C Lawrence (Under-Secretary –
Ministry of Posts and Telecommunications)
Mr Phillip Whitehead MP
(Labour, Derby North)
Professor John Griffith (Professor of
English Law, London University)
Mr George Cunningham MP
(Labour, Islington South-West)
Sir David Pitblado
(Comptroller and Auditor-General)
Mr William Rodgers MP
(Labour, Stockton-on-Tees)

EDWARD DU CANN

Gentlemen, if you are ready we will start immediately on
our examination of this crucial question which is in front
of us, whether or not the control by Parliament of the
Government of the day is adequate. As Members of Parliament we represent the people of this country who elect us.
We are really discussing whether or not in this democracy
there is adequate control of the Executive. We have a
number of witnesses to examine. I'm sure you'll all agree
that the written evidence that's been put in front of us is
extremely interesting. Our first witness is Sir William
Armstrong, the Head of the Home Civil Service. Call Sir
William Armstrong please. [*Enter Sir William Armstrong*]

[Sir William had submitted evidence that in his three
decades in the Civil Service the work of government
had expanded enormously and increased in technical
complexity (see below). This expansion had created
problems for the Government, increasing work loads
and increasing the difficulty of effective ministerial control within the department. Parliamentary account-
ability, 'to protect the individual and ensure a watch by
the legislature over the activities of government' had
also become more difficult. He concluded: 'Because
Ministers need to be advised on this parliamentary business, Parliamentary control in itself creates more work
for the Civil Service. So far we have always been able
to meet Parliament's wishes, but there is a relationship
between the size of the task of government, the extent
of its answerability, and the resources available to do
the work.']

DU CANN

Sir William, we are most grateful to you for coming before
the committee as Head of the Home Civil Service to give
us your evidence. Do you think the attitude of Ministers
to Members of Parliament, to Parliament as a whole, has
changed during the span of your career in the Civil
Service – is it more deferential than it used to be?

SIR WILLIAM ARMSTRONG

Are Ministers more deferential? No, I don't think so.
What does seem to me to have changed is the actual be-
haviour. When I first came in it would be normal for a
Civil Servant in a department to say to his Minister: 'I'm

sorry, you can't do that, you haven't got the authority to spend that particular money.' And that wouldn't necessarily be the end of it, but it would mean a big break. There would then have to be a legislative process and the getting of the authority might cause a delay of perhaps a year. But increasingly Ministers have been unwilling to wait. I've seen the practice grow up where there can be a statement in the House, to the effect that it is the Government's intention to do this; in due time we will get the powers to do it; if it's a question of money we can do it in the Appropriation Act. So the brakes are off, and that has been quite a change since I first came into the Service.

du CANN

Government activity, as your written evidence makes clear, has grown enormously. What would you say the most striking evidence of that has been?

ARMSTRONG

Perhaps I could give you three sets of figures. If you take expenditure, in 1938 when I came into the Service, the total was £739 million. Last year it was £16,000 million. More than sixteen times growth. Then if you take legislation, when I came into the Service in 1938 there were 935 pages put on the statute book by Parliament that year. In 1971 it was 2100.

MICHAEL FOOT

In view of the absolutely vast increase in Government powers and Government business which you described, don't you think it's rather remarkable that such a ramshackle institution as the House of Commons keeps any control at all – if you do think it does keep any control?

ARMSTRONG

Oh it certainly exercises some control, certainly a very great influence. Things are quite different when Parliament's not sitting. In a recess, especially the long summer recess, the feel in Whitehall is quite different – a certain slackness sets in.

FOOT

You mean you've got a feeling that somebody's got an eye on you after all?

ARMSTRONG

That's right.

FOOT

And wouldn't you say that one of the main reasons the Civil Service has to keep a watch out during such periods is because of what may suddenly blow up in the House of Commons quite unexpectedly.

ARMSTRONG

Absolutely.

FOOT

And isn't it the case that it's on the Floor of the House of Commons that that is most likely to happen?

ARMSTRONG

Oh yes. If I may give an illustration. I happened to be visiting the Welsh Office in Cardiff on the day when there had been an oil slick in the Bristol Channel. So naturally there was a great deal of activity going on and when I arrived at the office the man in charge there was beginning to get people in to start assessing the situation. The first question dealt with was – what was to be said in the House? It was not – how much mess there was on the beaches and what damage had been done, and how progress could be made in clearing it up: that came next. The first question was – 'the Minister's been on the line, there's almost certain to be a Private Notice Question, the line I suggest should be taken is such and such'.

FOOT

I've no doubt Members of Parliament would be very gratified to hear this belated assurance.

DU CANN

Which of the Parliamentary methods of control with which we are familiar do you regard as being the most effective?

ARMSTRONG

I think the most effective, in the sense of a Parliamentary activity that the Government simply has to pay attention to, are the views of its own supporters – what its own back-benchers feel about its activities and what it is doing. That may be expressed in debates on the Floor of the House or more likely in private talk about what will happen in a debate; or it may come out in committees, in Select Committees or Standing Committees.

99

FOOT

Why do you think Ministers are much more ready to think they can get things through the House of Commons without much trouble?

ARMSTRONG

This is a process which has gone on a long time. I think that one result of the expansion of Government activity, into fields in which before World War II Government was not very active, has been that the pace of reaction of the Government has had to be quicker. They were into business where more or less instant reaction has to take place. And that is not simply reaction in a political sense, but action involving spending money, and that has meant Ministers have been less and less willing to wait, and of course Parliament has accepted it. If Parliament had insisted on their waiting, then it would have been different.

FOOT

Could you say there's a Civil Service attitude towards this comparative decline? Has the Civil Service welcomed it or has the Civil Service done anything to try and guard against it? There have been suggestions in some quarters that the top Civil Servants form a kind of Mafia since they stay while Parliaments and Ministers come and go and that therefore the Civil Service really runs the thing. Would you repudiate that utterly or would you accept any part of it?

ARMSTRONG

Well, obviously the Civil Service must have a great influence. I repudiate any suggestion that we run the country or that decisions are taken by anybody other than Ministers. In the *big* issues.

FOOT

But if Ministers can find it easier to get away with it, surely the Civil Service find the same thing and apparently both, according to part of your evidence, both Ministers and the Civil Service have accepted this situation.

ARMSTRONG

Yes. Coming back to the first part of your question, I think the Civil Service is divided on this. Obviously for some purposes this is very convenient. Business can, as it were, move more smoothly. You don't have to wait – you can get Parliamentary authority in this way more quickly, and that suits quite a large part of the Service. But in the Treasury, where I spent a great deal of my time, we regretted this very much, because the Parliamentary system put a brake on expenditure; we felt that the Treasury, Parliament, and the Public Accounts Committee formed a kind of alliance. That is not as strong as it used to be.

FOOT

I'm rather disturbed by what you say about the cosiness of the relationship between the Treasury and the Public Accounts Committee which is supposed to keep an eye on it. Does your answer mean that the relationship is so close that the Treasury really retains its control over this body which is making some of the investigations?

ARMSTRONG

It never seemed cosy to me. It was close in the sense that we in the Treasury felt that in maintaining control over the spending departments, we had the same objective as the Public Accounts Committee. So we were allies in that sense. But that didn't mean that we always saw eye to eye or that the Treasury itself could escape criticism. The Treasury came in for a great deal of criticism over the years.

REGINALD MAUDLING

I want to be clear on one point, Sir William: the question of rather looser Parliamentary control and what Michael Foot elegantly described as 'getting away with it'. I thought your evidence largely arose from the need to act quickly nowadays, and if it is necessary nowadays for Government to act more rapidly, and react more rapidly, doesn't it mean that some loosening of control is inevitable?

ARMSTRONG

Yes, but how you behave to quite a large extent turns on how detailed the scrutiny of your behaviour is going to be afterwards. And it is partly the speed of reaction, also the sheer complication. You know that in the great mass of activity reflected in enormous numbers of reports, estimates and so on, the mass is so great that an awful lot of it is going to get overlooked through the sheer size of it.

MAUDLING

The strengthening really would be *ex post facto* – examination of the Government's actions, possibly leading them back to more caution, not strengthening the control over the Government before it's able to act at all in a situation calling for action?

ARMSTRONG

I think there would be some spheres of activity where a slowing down would be sensible. Frequently Acts of Parliament are passed, then after a little while an amending Act is brought in, the thing is adapted and adjusted and it seems fairly clear, looking back on it, that perhaps the first one was brought in a little faster than it need have been. While it's quite true that speedy reaction is needed in some spheres, it doesn't follow that it's needed all over.

DU CANN

Sir William, we're grateful to you. As you know, we're going to see a succession of other witnesses; then we might like to ask you to come back and see us again, for a further discussion, if that could be convenient for you.

ARMSTRONG

Well I'll certainly try and make it so. [*Exit Sir William Armstrong*]

DU CANN

John, were there any points that you think that we ought to have in mind?

JOHN MACKINTOSH

No, but it seems to me that Sir William has given us the real problem, and that is that in his experience as the Head of the Civil Service, Parliamentary control has declined over the last twenty years, and that we have to see how it has declined and in what ways we could possibly recommend filling this gap, whether it needs to be bridged. I think he's therefore set the context of our inquiry.

DU CANN

Reggie, what did you think?

MAUDLING

Well, I'm sort of biased. I spent several years in the Treasury with Sir William as you did yourself. I thought his evidence was extremely sound and I think what he says is true. My problem is: isn't it inevitable that Parliamentary control will get looser, is it necessarily a bad thing that it should, in the purposes of the efficient management of the country, particularly the economy?

du CANN

What did you think Nick?

NICHOLAS SCOTT

I thought that there was a distinction between detailed control and a general influence on the machinery of government and I think we perhaps might be able to bring this out more as other witnesses come in. Perhaps a need to strengthen detailed control, but certainly not to dilute in any way this general influence that we have.

du CANN

Our next witnesses then are two of the Clerks in the House of Commons. We want to talk to them chiefly about the resources of Parliament, to establish exactly what resources Parliament has to enable MPs to do their work. Nick, you're going to be responsible for questioning them in the main, are you not? Perhaps you could call our next witnesses please, Mr Allen and Mr Ryle. [*Enter Mr Allen and Mr Ryle*]

[Mr Allen's written evidence asserted that, while 'the House of Commons' control of expenditure and taxation is the source of its power . . . little or no detailed examination of either is now done on the Floor.' To remedy this the new Expenditure Committee which replaced the Estimates Committee in 1971, is enabled to examine the Government's five-year economic forecasts in the Public Expenditure White Paper, to hear witnesses (including Ministers), and report on policy questions. At present the Committee is staffed by a few 'generalist' Clerks who advise on procedure, organise programmes of evidence, draft reports and collaborate with temporary part-time expert advisers. The extension of the specialist staff presents problems but 'if the Public Accounts Committee (PAC) can have the Comptroller and Auditor General and his staff, why not the equivalent service for the Expenditure Committee?' Possible improvements to the Commons scrutiny of finance include the merger of the PAC and the Expenditure Committee and the establishment of a permanent Taxation Committee.

Mr Ryle's written evidence described Parliament as the forum in which the policies of the Government 'have to be publicly explained, justified, attacked and defended'. The growth of government meant that if Parliament was to continue to speak 'to and for the people' it must ensure that there are *opportunities* for criticising the whole range of Government activity, and appropriate *techniques* for making that criticism effective. Effective criticism required information. He suggested that the further use of Select Committees for legislation as well as expenditure scrutiny, so as to inform and enrich the public debate in the Chamber, might be considered.]

DU CANN

Mr Ryle, Mr Allen – and firstly can I, on behalf of the committee, welcome you and thank you for coming before us. That pile of books, Mr Ryle, looks very intimidating but I suppose they mainly derive from your responsibility as Clerk in the Public Bills Office?

MICHAEL RYLE

They're only designed, sir, to illustrate in another way a point that Sir William Armstrong made. The new statutes for 1910 in this one thin volume; the statutes and laws of the land for 1951 in one thicker volume; and 1971 in these three thick volumes.

DU CANN

Now Mr Scott, would you like to begin the questioning for us please.

SCOTT

Mr Ryle you've demonstrated fairly graphically this increase in the size of legislation and amount of legislation, and Sir William mentioned that Government expenditure had increased something like twenty-fold during his time in the Civil Service. I wonder whether perhaps you'd like to start by telling us, as one who's served in the House of Commons for a number of years, how you see the role of Parliament in relation to the Government and to the Executive.

RYLE

It seems to me, Mr Scott, increasingly apparent that, putting it over-simply, the role of Government is to govern, the role of Parliament is to be the critic of Government. Gladstone I believe once said, addressing the House, 'You have been summoned here, not to legislate or to govern, but to be the constant critic of Government.' I think this is the starting point for any appraisal of the functioning of Parliament. If you start with a different assumption, that

Parliament's job is actually to govern, to take decisions, then you will reach different conclusions about how it should be done and about the efficacy of our present procedures.

SCOTT

To what extent has the expansion of resources of Parliament matched the expansion of the work that they've had to do over the past twenty years?

FRANK ALLEN

If you're thinking about the number of staff, people like ourselves, and other sorts of specialist advice, the numbers of permanent staff, I don't think at our level they have changed so very much. This may be, of course, a point of credit to us, that without increasing our numbers we've been able to do more.

SCOTT

Information doubles now every eight or nine years; to what extent are we using modern methods of retrieving information for Members of Parliament and for the staff of the House of Commons?

ALLEN

To my knowledge, not probably as much as you would think necessary. Certainly within the staff of the Clerk of the House Department, I don't think that our methods have changed very much, simply because I don't think that it's our function to do this.

SCOTT

Mr Ryle, this must be a problem that faces legislatures all over the world. I wonder what studies the House of Commons has done of the way that other parliaments manage this problem – whether you think we're doing rather better or rather worse than other parliaments?

RYLE

I think one must confess that, officially as it were, the House itself has made very little study of this. When I was over in Canada about a year ago I was particularly struck with some very recent developments in the Canadian parliament in their technique for examining Bills. They for years had used the same methods as we use in our several Standing Committees (or debating committees), debating amendments and debating clauses in the Bill. But in the last two years they've begun to use a little more of what we would call the Select Committee technique – the taking of evidence on Bills before they proceed to the political debates. I think myself (and this is a matter which was recommended by the Procedure Committee) that we could perhaps make greater use of the fact-finding technique. You referred, I think quite rightly if I may say so, to the need to get information. If you are to be an effective critic you must have information on which to base your criticism.

DU CANN

I think this is a point which we will want to follow up with other witnesses. Can I just turn to Mr Foot and then Mr Mackintosh shortly please?

FOOT

One question I'd like to put to Mr Ryle. Surely, whatever Mr Gladstone may have said, it is a very cramped view of the function of the House of Commons to say that it should only be the critic – the House of Commons, Parliament, is a legislative body and therefore Parliament makes legislation, and if it chucks away that power surely it is surrendering its main power – isn't that the case?

RYLE

I wouldn't deny, of course, that Parliament in the end passes legislation but the initiative lies mainly with the Government. They lay before Parliament in considerable detail what they wish to achieve, and the Government through their control of the party whips on the whole can ensure that what they wish to achieve is achieved.

MACKINTOSH

Two points if I may, Mr Ryle. Isn't it true that one of the contrasts between your 1910 and 1950s and then the 1971 block of legislation is that legislation now tends to be much more extensively prepared and pre-negotiated between the Government and outside bodies before the Bill is printed and presented to Parliament? The real information one wants is to know what deals have been done between the Executive and the pressure groups. What were the real arguments which conditioned the form of the legislation?

RYLE

I would have thought that that was a further point in favour of the hearing of evidence by committees when looking at Bills. Not only could they get direct evidence from the Civil Servants on the technical details, but they could hear the interested parties, they could hear the people who are affected.

DU CANN

Mr Maudling?

MAUDLING

I don't quite understand why you need a committee for a Member of Parliament to know what his constituents are thinking about Government measures. I used to get a certain number of letters saying some very forthright things about Government measures. Why is a committee necessary for that?

ALLEN

I would have thought that, after all, Members of Parliament have to have many, as it were, irons in the fire. Of course they'll get a great deal of information from their constituents no doubt; but much of that is probably slightly adjusted to the particular frame of mind of the constituent who is making the representation.

DU CANN

You mean they may be political rather than factual?

ALLEN

Yes, or indeed personal.

DU CANN

Absolutely, yes.

ALLEN

I think the Members, as far as they have time – and this is a point that I would love to talk on at some length – certainly need to have access to as much *official* information as they can possibly get hold of.

RYLE

Could I just elaborate on one point very briefly.

DU CANN

Yes, Mr Ryle.

RYLE

In response perhaps to Mr Maudling's question, and to the point that I think was in Mr Foot's mind – I don't think I envisage, and I don't think the Procedure Committee envisaged when they made this recommendation, that this process of taking evidence and so on would replace debate. It would be designed as I said, to enrich debate, to make the debate better informed so as to make the debates on the Floor of the House themselves more valuable.

DU CANN

But perhaps I could just follow that if I may – Mr Allen is Clerk to the new Select Committee on Public Expenditure. If one argues that Parliamentary control rests on the ability to control expenditure, does Mr Allen think or does Mr Ryle think that we do have effective control at the present time? [*A long pause during which both Clerks remain silent*] Are we improving our techniques, let me make the question easier?

ALLEN

Yes, I think so, but I think that improvement of technique will follow the establishment of a real need and a demonstration of the ability to use improved techniques.

DU CANN

There must be a scandal first you mean?

ALLEN

Not a scandal, but I think Members have got to be able to put up a really solid case to show that they need the additional facilities and staff that – with all respect – they say they do. I don't want to be disrespectful to Members, I wouldn't have been in my job for so long if I had been otherwise I hope.

DU CANN

We are very anxious to establish the truth, Mr Allen, you may say what you wish in this privileged forum.

ALLEN

I think it is very easy to say, for example, in the case of the Expenditure Committee – here is a Committee of a number of important people doing a very important job, they ought to have a very large staff to assist them. But I think you've got to go beyond that and say – this, this, and this are precisely the things they need to know.

DU CANN

These are the jobs to do, define the jobs first?

ALLEN

Yes, I think they should be defined first.

DU CANN

Mr Foot, the final question?

FOOT

Don't you think there's also a danger in these committees, whatever may be their virtues, that Members of Parliament get divided up into different compartments so that the only experts on expenditure are those who have had the good fortune to have been instructed by yourself and others, whereas those who haven't had that are a sort of second class lot, and that that is going to injure the House of Commons itself where, after all, judgements have to be made upon a whole range of matters.

ALLEN

I haven't so far noticed that the activities of any Select Committee have injured the interests of Members as they perform on the Floor of the House.

FOOT

As you're so free in giving your views about Members of Parliament, wouldn't you agree that many members of Select Committees do talk as if they're the only people who know about it, and surely that's a danger?

ALLEN

I think if you're involved in any particular current activity you're bound to talk as if you knew all about it – this is what you're in business for. But I don't believe that it has been shown that the expertise of members of Select Committees in any way militates against the effectiveness of Members in debates on the Floor of the House.

DU CANN

Mr Mackintosh has, I believe, just a final question.

MACKINTOSH

Just one point. Surely it's better when you get a debate, that you have a few Members on the Floor of the House who are really well informed as otherwise the only people who are really well equipped are the Ministers. It's better to have a few first-class informed people than everybody knowing very little but all equal.

DU CANN

The Committee is deeply grateful to you, Mr Allen and to

you Mr Ryle, for your kindness in coming here and for giving us such frank and clear evidence.

BOTH

Thank you. [*Exeunt Clerks*]

DU CANN

Well I would very much have liked that session to have been able to continue for a good deal longer. I think that we were learning a great deal about ourselves as Members of Parliament. Nick, you started the questioning, what did you think?

SCOTT

I think that one of the things we ought to be pursuing now is how effective our Standing Committee procedures are, for improving and examining legislation in detail. My experience has been that too often Standing Committees instead of talking about the particular clause or a particular amendment rehash the whole debate which took place on Second Reading on the Floor of the House, probably a dozen times in Standing Committee.

DU CANN

Are you really saying, Nick, that when we have the opportunity to look in detail at a Bill, we tend rather to rehearse the political arguments than to put the Bill itself under a microscope?

SCOTT

That's right – and that's why the Select Committees system could be adapted.

DU CANN

John, what do you think?

MACKINTOSH

Well I think now we've really got to look at the point Michael Foot made when he said that if Parliament isn't a legislature it's nothing. I think we want to look in what sense we're a legislature and what difference we make to Bills. What influence we have on the Government's proposals as they go through the House.

DU CANN

Take a case – take a Bill, take draft legislation and take it through some of its processes. Michael what do you think?

I think that's the right way to proceed.

Legislation

[*Enter Mr Lawrence*]

DU CANN

Mr Lawrence thank you for coming to see us today. You know our responsibilities as a committee. We're looking into the relationship between the Executive and Members of Parliament, seeing how well or how badly the democratic process works. Now we thought, if it's agreeable to you, we'd follow through one Bill in all its processes and we've chosen the Sound Broadcasting Bill. We were much obliged to you for your written evidence.

[Two pieces of written evidence were received on the Sound Broadcasting Bill. Mr Lawrence's described its genesis. 'The Conservative Party's manifesto had stated that it would permit local private enterprise radio under the general supervision of an independent broadcasting authority and that local newspapers would be allowed a stake.' This being a statement of firm intention, the question for Civil Servants was: how could it best be turned into reality? They had two main areas to study: technical, how could the new service be brought to as many people as possible; and administrative, should the ITA have a role, and how should local newspapers qualify for their stake? Before decisions were reached on the administrative questions there were extensive consultations with broadcasting and newspaper interests, trade associations concerned with advertising, representatives of local authorities, trades unions, and with many other groups of people interested in radio from a technical, commercial or social point of view. A White Paper: *An Alternative Source of Radio Broadcasting*, was debated in the Commons in May 1971. A number of organisations already consulted submitted comments on the White Paper.

The decision to make the Independent Television Authority responsible for local radio meant that the legislation would take the form of an amendment to the Television Act 1964. Officials examined the Act, put proposals to the Treasury Solicitor, who instructed

Parliamentary Counsel, who drafted the Bill. It had its
Second Reading in November and became law in June
1972. The one major change made during the passage
of the Bill was the insertion of an additional section
(now Section 9) providing safeguards against the possibility of an excessive concentration of newspaper
ownership in local radio.]

DU CANN

You are, as I understand, the Under-Secretary in charge of
the Broadcasting Department, at the Ministry of Posts and
Telecommunications. Now could you tell me please, what
sort of consultation did you have with outside interests on
this Bill?

DENNIS LAWRENCE

There was a great deal of consultation with broadcasting
organisations, with the BBC and the IBA – the ITA as it
then was – with trade unions, with representatives of the
local press who are particularly affected. These were the
main bodies.

DU CANN

Now what about the consultation with Members of Parliament? How was that arranged, before the Bill in fact
appeared?

LAWRENCE

To the best of my recollection there was no consultation
with Members of Parliament on this particular Bill before
it reached the House.

DU CANN

How was the Government's intention announced? Was
there a White Paper?

LAWRENCE

Yes there was. It was – if I remember rightly – in May 1971;
a White Paper was published and debated and this laid
out the broad scheme for the development of the new
service as the Government envisaged it.

DU CANN

Now what about the process of debate in Parliament? How
effective was it? How interesting was it? How important
was it?

LAWRENCE

The general debate?

DU CANN

Yes.

LAWRENCE

It was, I think, a little disappointing. One felt all the time that there could have been a rather more informed debate. I should think from both sides. This was the impression one had. There were some Members, obviously, who'd made broadcasting their special interest who had quite a bit to say and had some very valuable things to say. But by and large I think one felt a slight sense of disappointment.

DU CANN

But let me come on to the Committee stage, the detailed examination of the Bill. How long did that take?

LAWRENCE

Oh it started in November and went on until February next year – about three months with at least two sittings a week, some of them pretty late sittings.

DU CANN

Yes, a long process.

LAWRENCE

A long process.

DU CANN

Now how effective was it?

LAWRENCE

I think one has to ask what one means by effective – you're conscious if you're working on a Bill, of course, that this procedure is going to take place; it's there before you start. I think the mere fact of having to go through a Committee Stage is a pretty severe discipline on the people who are preparing legislation.

DU CANN

Yes, now who else would like to join – John Mackintosh?

MACKINTOSH

Could I just ask one point? You say you drew up the Bill after this elaborate set of consultations and before speaking to a single Member of the House of Commons, except Ministers?

LAWRENCE

This is so, yes.

MACKINTOSH

Now when you'd drawn up the Bill and published it, what difference was there in the content of the Bill – significant difference between the end result after all the procedures in the House of Commons compared with the Bill which you placed before them? Were there any changes?

LAWRENCE

Yes there were some changes. As a result of the Committee Stage of the House, an additional clause was written into the Bill which was directed to limiting the total amount that a single press interest could hold in the new service as a whole. This reflected a great deal of anxiety on both sides.

MACKINTOSH

How significant was this change in the form of the Bill?

LAWRENCE

I wouldn't have said that it was in the end likely to make a vast difference to the way in which the legislation would be administered by the authority.

DU CANN

Mr Foot you had a question I think.

FOOT

I appreciate your answer saying that the threat of the discussion influenced the Bill itself, but if people were to take the view that you had the whole thing cut and dried in advance and that that was really what got onto the statute book, would you not agree that that may have been due to the Government Ministers, the particular Ministers in this particular Bill, not listening to the House of Commons? They could have listened more couldn't they? Much more.

LAWRENCE

They could have listened more. You assume, of course, in putting the question that the things which the House and particular Members will have to say will always be of specific value or relevance. I mean sometimes they're not – one is not complaining about this – Parliament in many ways represents the man on the Clapham omnibus and all sorts of other things, and – you know, they're not always frightfully relevant.

FOOT

Going back to the pre-process before it ever came to the House of Commons to which John Mackintosh referred, did any Minister say to you: 'Now you must be extremely careful in any discussions with outside interests that no commitment is made in any sense whatsoever which will prevent the House of Commons from having an absolutely free play in making its decision about the details of the Bill'?

LAWRENCE

No, no Minister said anything of that sort to me. I should not feel that I was doing my job properly if a Minister said to me something of the sort you've just suggested. But I might have to say to him, 'I'm not sure, Minister, that you can really go that far – there's Parliament to be considered – you've got to go through Committee Stage. How will you explain this or that attitude?' Of course if the Minister gives you an instruction, then you're there to do what he says.

DU CANN

Mr Lawrence thank you very much indeed. [*Exit Mr Lawrence*]

FOOT

Well I think it is an interesting matter to discover whether there has been a change in the general practice about commitments to outside bodies. Certainly years ago the House of Commons was extremely jealous about any kind of arrangement being made with an outside body before a Bill was brought before the House, and the Minister who came to the House of Commons without having absolutely free hands would be pilloried on that account. I don't know whether that's the same today or not.

MAUDLING

That's exactly the point: that any Minister who made a commitment outside Parliament which Parliament then refused to honour would himself be in the most terrible trouble. I think that is the reason why this does not happen.

DU CANN

Of course there's no reason why outside interests should not be consulted about draft legislation. Indeed in these highly complex technical days, it's very important, particularly in a Bill of this sort, that there should be some consultation on the technical details.

FOOT

But it's a difficult line to draw, isn't it? I understand a commitment with an outside body which a Minister feels he's got to honour in order to maintain his relationships with them. All the same I think the answers we've had are extremely interesting on this point because they do show that there is a very strong element of parliamentary control available. But I think we should see whether it has been weakened or not.

DU CANN

We must follow this point through. We've obviously got our teeth into an important one. John?

MACKINTOSH

There are two conventions on this and I think we're getting close to the heart of the matter now. One convention is that the bodies consulted in the preliminary process may not reveal to the public or to Members of Parliament what happened at the consultation, so you can never dig out whether a commitment was entered into or not, and no Minister's going to say this. The other convention is that the Civil Service doesn't show the outside body the actual clause or draft clause, but it can tell them what's in the clause, so it's a very fine adjustment.

MAUDLING

It's not a question of whether any undertaking given by a Minister becomes public knowledge. If he's given his undertaking, he's given it, whether it's private or public. I think any Minister would recognise that if he gives an undertaking which he can't subsequently honour he's in very serious trouble. Therefore if he's a wise Minister in any sense at all, he doesn't give that sort of undertaking.

MACKINTOSH

But what was going on when Heath was discussing with the TUC the other day about a package deal on inflation? He was offering commitments – you do this and I'll do that, on the assumption that this could be plugged through the House. Now Heath wasn't saying to the TUC – look I will be overturned by the House. He was doing a direct negotiation.

MAUDLING

Because he was going to put to Parliament what he believed to be right. But if he is in danger of being overthrown by Parliament, then he's in a very difficult situation.

MACKINTOSH

Well he knows he isn't because he's got a majority.

MAUDLING

. . . the sanction on the Minister is not to give an undertaking of a kind he's not prepared to stake his entire career
on.

FOOT

Now what we were asking about legislation is whether
that has grown up as well in legislative matters and I must
say my first impression on reading Mr Lawrence's memorandum was that we were getting very near to that
situation. I'm not making any accusations but it was very
near to the situation where the Bill went through unchanged because they wanted to keep to the arrangements
that they'd made in the first place.

DU CANN

I think what we'd better do now, if you agree, is have a
look and see exactly what did happen to this Bill when it
was going through what we called earlier, the Standing
Committee Stage, that is to say its detailed examination by
MPs in Parliament. Now we're going to call Mr Whitehead,
who is a Member of Parliament, one of our colleagues in
the House, who actually was a member of the Committee
that examined this Bill; I think we might well ask him about
this. [*Enter Mr Whitehead*]

[Mr Whitehead's written evidence described the four
and a half months Commons Standing Committee. 'Because of a working alliance between the Labour Opposition and two Conservatives with a close interest in
commercial broadcasting, debates on most amendments
were substantial, and the Bill was much mauled in the
Committee.' Clause 7, which gave newspapers the right
to acquire a shareholding in local commercial radio
from the successful contractors and at the instance of the
IBA, was struck out by 10 votes to 9 after 92 columns
debate. In addition two major additions were made to
Clause 2. The first, introduced from the Conservative
back-benches, stipulated that the first sixty stations
should all provide an all-round service and struck at the
Government's proposal to have two stations in London,
one all-news, one general. The second, a Labour amendment, required each local station to have a news service

staffed by qualified journalists. On each, the Government was defeated by a combination of the votes of the Opposition and two Government back-benchers. No other major amendments were carried. The Minister did introduce a new clause on publication of applications for local radio station franchises along the lines of an undertaking he gave the Committee. On the Government side over half the Members spoke either once or not at all; one went so far as to wear ear-plugs throughout the proceedings, and an Opposition Member complained that 'there is scarcely any reason for making speeches in this Committee other than to try to delay its proceedings'.

'So far as the substantive alterations made to the Bill in Committee are concerned, the Government simply used the brute force of its majority in the full House at Report Stage to expunge them. The additions to Clause 2 of the Bill were deleted by a majority of 157 to 138, the Government finding only one MP to speak against them. The old Clause 7 which had been deleted from the Bill returned, substantially unaltered. It was added to the Bill, in an apathetic House, by 179 votes to 154, with the two Conservative back-benchers who had rebelled in Committee, voting with the Opposition.'

The Sound Broadcasting Bill therefore passed through the Commons substantially unaltered by its four months in Committee. The ITA, to which so much additional responsibility was being given, was at that very moment under scrutiny by the Select Committee on Nationalised Industries, which reported five months later. The report was highly critical of the then ITA's handling of commercial television, but no attempt was made to use the Committee's findings in improving the Bill. 'I cannot say that my own four months on Standing Committee F persuaded me that this sort of close scrutiny of Bills can possibly be effective.']

DU CANN

Mr Whitehead, thank you very much for coming to see us. You were one of twenty Members of Parliament who in Committee had the responsibility of giving a detailed and thorough examination to the Sound Broadcasting Bill which we've just been discussing with Mr Lawrence. The Sound Broadcasting Bill wasn't very long, about ten clauses, I think, and you spent four months examining it. Would you say that your work was effective?

PHILLIP WHITEHEAD

No, quite the contrary. We spent four and a half months on the Bill and I would imagine that most of us felt, when we brought the Bill out of Committee, having very substantially altered it, that some at least of those alterations would go into legislation. That was not the case. They were struck out, all the main ones. And the clause which we had taken out of the Bill in Committee was put back, very substantially the same clause, by the Government at the Report Stage.

DU CANN

Mr Foot.

FOOT

Are you saying then that the failure on this Committee was due to the machinery itself or rather to the way the Ministers used the machinery?

WHITEHEAD

I think it was due largely to the fact that the machinery was not employed as it might have been.

FOOT

So it could have been employed in a quite different way and it could have given the opportunity for really fundamental changes to be made by the process of discussion?

WHITEHEAD

If the Minister had been prepared to accept the voice of the Committee as the voice of the House.

FOOT

And on the question of these other interests that you describe, which we've been discussing with some of the other witnesses, was it your impression that in effect the Ministers, the Government, or the Civil Service, had made such binding arrangements with outside interests that they couldn't escape from them and therefore whatever the Committee said they had to reassert what they'd previously agreed?

WHITEHEAD

Partly so, yes. I think they felt a strong commitment, firstly to the party manifesto, secondly to the discussions which they had had before the Bill came into Committee. So they didn't significantly alter the Bill as a result of the Second Reading debate, nor indeed as a result of what went on in the Committee.

FOOT

I'm not concerned about the almost unique instance of an attachment to the party manifesto. I'm concerned about the question of whether in fact they had entered into private consultations which took a superior place to the public discussions in the House of Commons.

WHITEHEAD

I think they had but I would be the last person to ask because Members of Parliament were not consulted. We didn't know.

DU CANN

Mr Maudling.

MAUDLING

I thought the phrase 'commitment to a manifesto' was rather an unusual one. Is not a commitment to a manifesto a commitment to the electorate who voted for it?

WHITEHEAD

Possibly so, but in this case parts of the commitment as printed were shown to be pretty unworkable in the Committee. Nevertheless they were adhered to.

MAUDLING

I gather the Committee introduced changes but those changes were reversed by the will of the whole House on Report. Isn't that what happened?

WHITEHEAD

Well, if by the 'will of the whole House' you mean a given majority voting on a given day, yes that's correct.

MAUDLING

The only way to determine the will of the House is by voting, isn't it?

WHITEHEAD

Well, it's not a very well-informed way. It's people voting according to the party whip.

DU CANN

Mr Mackintosh.

MACKINTOSH

Your point, Mr Whitehead, is that during the debates in the full House on the Report Stage no new evidence was adduced to change the view of the Committee Members, and many Members voted who had no idea what the Bill was about. They voted to put back clauses you had struck out?

WHITEHEAD

Absolutely so.

MACKINTOSH

And what then is the end difference between the Bill as it went into law and the original proposals of the Government in their White Paper before it came near the House of Commons?

WHITEHEAD

Very little. There were two small amendments accepted at the Committee Stage. I would find it very hard now, looking at the Act, to see any difference from the Bill as it came before the Committee, before all that four and a half months of discussion.

DU CANN

So you felt your four and a half months were wasted time?

WHITEHEAD

Totally.

SCOTT

And much of the discussion that went on in the Standing Committee was on purely party lines and many of the people who were voting up there were voting on straight party lines? Not because they were particularly involved in the discussions, or interested in the discussions? Are we right?

WHITEHEAD

I think that's so on both sides, yes. On the Opposition side there is a feeling that you must frustrate legislation. There were three major Bills before the House at that stage. There were late night sittings going on on the committee corridor. It was a point of principle and prestige to the Opposition to see how long these Bills could be kept there. On the Government side the Bills had to be taken through. They had to be taken through with as little amendment as possible. On the Government side too there were people on the Committee who were drafted to be part of a majority and who made it quite clear by personal minor protests that they were unwilling to be there in the Committee at all. They didn't want to be there.

SCOTT

So you've got a fundamental conflict between the theory of a Standing Committee, which is to go over the Bill line by line and improve it, and what happened in practice which was a continuation of the political argument and a political confrontation that ought to have been settled by the vote on principle at Second Reading?

WHITEHEAD

I think that is so, yes. And when you say we examined this Bill line by line and clause by clause, that is so only in the sense that if you have only a ten-clause Bill and you have months for discussion of it, you are bound to look at every line. But it wasn't, I think, a detailed and informed argument, and it was not an argument which was taken seriously by the Government or the Civil Servants.

SCOTT

Now would you say that within those twenty Members on the Committee, there were a group across the parties who would have been able to sit down with the Minister and on an informed basis do the theoretical job, that is to say go over the Bill without too many preconceived political conceptions and actually improve the legislation?

WHITEHEAD

Yes I think among the twenty Members of the Committee were almost all of the Members of Parliament who have a special interest in broadcasting and some special knowledge of it. And they tended to share certain views about the Bill and their views were expressed in the votes which the Committee eventually took. But of course, that was ignored when the thing came back, at Report.

DU CANN

Mr Whitehead, that document that you have on your right-hand side, is that the printed record of the proceedings of the Committee?

WHITEHEAD

That is the printed record – two volumes, two very fat paperbacks – of the proceedings of Standing Committee F for four and a half months. And I would suggest that almost all of it is wasted effort.

DU CANN

Well, thank you very much indeed.

WHITEHEAD

Thank you. [*Exit Mr Whitehead*]

DU CANN

It seems now that we should look more widely. We've looked at the process of one Bill. There could be arguments on both sides. It may be that a lot of the matters proposed in that Committee were not wise matters. We can't tell without looking at the detail of the record; we were not there. What we ought to do presumably is to look at Bills in general and see how wide-ranging the discussion is, how many occasions there are changes when Bills come before Parliament.

Shall we call our next witness? He's Professor Griffith, who is Professor of English Law at London University. [*Enter Professor Griffith*]

Professor Griffith, thank you very much for coming to see us today. The committee is obliged to you for your substantial and most useful written memorandum.

[Professor Griffith's memorandum stated:

Whether the role of Parliament in the legislative process is considered to be adequately or inadequately performed under present conditions depends in large part on how this role is envisaged. If the two Houses of Parliament are regarded as being the bodies which should be primarily responsible for the making of laws, then the actuality – which is the control exercised by the Government over the legislative process both in and out of Parliament – will seem a travesty of the constitution. For the range and quality of amendments made on the initiative of those who are not Ministers are small when set against the volume of Government proposals which are passed through the two Houses without alteration. But if the making of laws is looked on as a function primarily of Governments who submit their proposals to scrutiny by, amongst others, non-ministerial Members of Parliament, then the impact made by such Members will be seen sometimes to be of some significance and on occasion to be of genuine importance.

'If we look at three sessions we can see that Members not being Ministers moved 3510 amendments in Committee of which only 171 were agreed to. Whereas out of 907 amendments moved by Ministers 906 were agreed to.'

Government Bills 1967–68, 1968–69 and 1970–71

COMMITTEE STAGE

	Moved by Ministers	Moved by Government back-benchers	Moved by Opposition
Number of amendments moved	907	436 _____ 3510	3074
Number of amendments withdrawn	None	294 _____ 1797	1503
Number of amendments negatived	1	102 _____ 1542	1440
Number of amendments agreed to	906	40 _____ 171	131

'These figures are somewhat misleading. First, because a large number of amendments moved by Ministers are technical or drafting amendments. Secondly, because some of the amendments moved by Ministers are in response to pressure brought on Ministers by other Members of Parliament. Most importantly, note the large number of amendments moved by those not Ministers and withdrawn. Of these, about 40 per cent in these sessions are withdrawn because the Minister in charge of the Bill promises to look again at the point raised by the amendment. This leads us to the next stage – the consideration by the House of Bills as reported from the Committee.'

Government Bills 1967–68, 1968–69 and 1970–71

	Moved by Ministers	Moved by Government back-benchers	Moved by Opposition
Number of amendments moved	865	89	599
		688	
Number of amendments withdrawn	1	41	167
		208	
Number of amendments negatived	None	38	403
		441	
Number of amendments agreed to	864	10	29
		39	
Number of amendments moved and agreed to as a result of undertakings given in Committee	365	—	—

'Here the pattern is the same: out of 865 amendments moved by Ministers, 864 were agreed to; out of 688 amendments moved by those not being Ministers, only 39 amendments were agreed to. But note the figure of 365 amendments below the double line being the number moved by Ministers in response to points made by other Members in Committee. These figures can be used to support the view that Members who are not Ministers make very little impact. Or they can be used to support the view that this impact is not inconsiderable. It depends on the position of the observer.

'Occasionally, the impact on Ministers is much greater. The biggest defeat suffered by Ministers in recent years was when back-benchers on both sides in 1969 combined to force the Government to withdraw the Bill which was to have reformed the House of Lords. In 1970 an Education Bill was defeated in Committee because of the failure of the Government to ensure that its supporters were present in sufficient strength. And in 1971, the Immigration Bill was defeated on one very important question by a combination of some Government back-benchers and the Opposition and this change was not restored on Report.

'During the debates on a Bill, Parliament performs two separate functions, sometimes both at the same time. The first function is to examine the Bill critically to see whether it achieves what it sets out to achieve, to improve it technically, to consider whether it should be extended or limited in its purpose or its scope. The second function, generally for the Opposition alone, is to examine the political policy that lies behind the Bill.

'The problem which faces all those who seek to improve the procedure of Parliament as it applies to the legislative process is how to cater for those two separate functions of technical improvement and political argument.'[1]]

du CANN

We've just been examining the process of one Bill, one single piece of legislation, through all its Parliamentary stages. Now you, sir, we understand, have made an analysis of some three years' legislation and what we should greatly like to do, if we may, is to work through with you exactly what your conclusions are as a result of that detailed examination and see if they're the same as ours or how they differ. Mr Maudling.

MAUDLING

I think the work you've been doing, Professor Griffith, is extremely interesting and very thorough. I was a bit doubtful about your statistical method. You seem to be trying to prove by statistics, by the number of amendments moved by Government and Opposition respectively, and their fate, the extent to which in practice the Committee Stage is

[1]Professor Griffith's evidence is based on a study of the legislative process carried out for Political and Economic Planning and the Study of Parliament Group, financed by a Social Science Research Council grant, to be published by Allen & Unwin.

126

effective. Do you really think this is an effective, a useful test, of the influence a Committee Stage has upon the Government?

GRIFFITH

I don't think that one can simply add up amendments and answer questions of that kind if for no other reason than that one amendment may be of extreme importance, and a hundred amendments may be trifling. No, it was simply that it seemed to be a useful exercise to see in figures what were the answers to certain questions. When one uses those statistics to come to conclusions, one has to be extremely careful of them, I entirely agree. Parliament, a living organism, is not a subject that can be reduced to statistics which will produce valuable results. Nevertheless, these things had never been done. Many statements are made by many people – parliamentarians and others – of a general kind about the nature of amendments, about how often amendments are carried, about the effect of the Report Stage on Committee and so on. And in one particular respect I think these statistics do show something, that is about withdrawn amendments.

[Professor Griffith was referring here to figures in his evidence about Government amendments moved at Report as a result of undertakings given to the Opposition or to Government back-benchers in exchange for the withdrawal of amendments in Committee. It is often said by MPs that their influence on legislation is greater than would appear from the statistics, because the Government often accepts the substance of withdrawn amendments and introduces its own amendments to meet the points on Report. But Professor Griffith's figures show that in the three sessions studied, only 365, less than a fifth, of the withdrawn amendments resulted in Government amendments on Report. Further, the Government is not often defeated in Standing Committee. In the three years studied it happened only twenty-five times. Usually (in seventeen of the twenty-five cases) the Government used its majority in the whole House to reverse such defeats. The figures above, coupled with the 5 per cent of back-bench and official Opposition amendments agreed to in Committee and the 7 per cent agreed on Report, are measurable effects of the Commons' scrutiny of Government legislation.]

MACKINTOSH

Professor Griffith, you have had a chance to look at the evidence that we've just had from Mr Whitehead about the Sound Broadcasting Bill. Could I ask you, given your study of three sessions, how typical do you think his conclusion was that after four and a half months' work only a very trivial change was made in the Bill by members other than the Government?

GRIFFITH

There are no types, as far as I know, of Bills. Every Bill is an original Bill. Every dilemma and problem that comes before a Standing Committee tends to be special. There are groups of Bills, like the one which he spoke of, where a great deal of discussion takes place and at the end of the day the effect on the Statute Book, on the Bill itself, is negligible or nil. Naturally these tend to be the ones where political controversy is most deeply involved. Governments, if they are committed to a line of policy, are not going to be deflected from that. On the other hand there are other sorts of Bills, which are not controversial at all, where the whole atmosphere in Committee is quite different. You can move from one committee room in the corridor to another and you move from a scene of hot conflict and ill-temper to a group of people sitting down trying to improve a measure. There is no type. All I know is that both sorts of things happen.

FOOT

Does not your answer about the variation of Bills, the unique character of every Bill, go to the root of the whole question, because if that is true is it not the case that the House of Commons still retains enormous legislative power?

GRIFFITH

No, I think you overstate the case by putting it in that way. When we talk about the House of Commons doing something, what we mean, 99 times out of 100, is the Government majority. That is perfectly proper. That's the way government is carried on. It is the will of the Government that is likely to prevail but I don't think one should identify the will of the Government with the will of the House except simply as a form of words. The political reality is, as we know, that the Government will get its way very frequently, but then there will be exceptions, as always.

FOOT

All I mean is that in the main the machinery whereby the House of Commons, Members of Parliament, can act as legislators, still remains, however much Governments of different complexions have tried to invade it, or the Civil Service wishes to invade it.

GRIFFITH

One point about machinery, coming out of what I said earlier about the different types: it is unlikely, it seems to me, that the same machinery, the same structure, the same sort of committee, is appropriate both for the highly controversial Bill and for the uncontroversial Bill. The two exercises, as I have said, are different exercises and it seems to me improbable that one procedure, the Standing Committee procedure, is likely to be sufficiently flexible to serve both purposes. Nor do I believe that it is sufficiently flexible.

DU CANN

This is a point that has come out in other evidence that we have received.

GRIFFITH

The great importance of the Standing Committee it seems to me is not how much amendment Opposition or backbenchers may be able to make to the Bill, it is that here you have a situation where the Minister is required to stand up in a relatively small room with a relatively small number of people, facing particularly the Opposition who, as somebody else said, sit there on the front bench smiling like razors. And the Minister has to stand up there for day after day, perhaps month after month, being cross-examined by people who know their business. A common criticism, with which I agree, is that they do not have enough information on which to base their cross-examination.

DU CANN

I think we've found your evidence most useful, very helpful and illuminating. Thank you very much. [*Exit Professor Griffith*]

MAUDLING

I think what's emerged is that it would be a good thing if the old idea, that the Second Reading settled the principle and then within that framework your Standing Committee tried to improve the Bill for the purpose approved in

principle, that might make more effective work in Standing
Committee than the present system where – quite honestly
– it is a bit mixed.

DU CANN
  Yes it is.

MACKINTOSH
  What Professor Griffith did say was that wherever you get
  a hotly controversial Bill, then for practical purposes there
  are no changes at Committee Stage. You get a repetition
  of the major political arguments and this is I think the case.

Financial scrutiny and how to re-assert control

  [The next witness was George Cunningham MP. In his
  written evidence he stated: 'Whatever is the ideal way,
  the way we do it now can't be it. Government always
  gets every penny it wants. Members would not pretend
  to understand the Estimates they have approved. The
  only occasions when expenditure is approved (Consoli-
  dated Fund Debates) are taken by Members as days off.
  Yet these occasions are not a formal approval of what
  has already been examined: they are the only time when
  expenditure proposals are looked at.'
  The House does look carefully at expenditure that has
  already taken place through the Public Accounts Committee; it is scrutiny of proposals for new expenditure
  that is at fault. It now looks at expenditure proposals in
  two forms: the Public Expenditure White Paper and
  the Estimates. The White Paper is in too general terms
  to allow policy decisions to be based on it and the debate
  on it has not turned out to be the great rival to the
  Budget debate which people expected. 'It never will,
  because the White Paper does not tell the House what
  the marginal options are – i.e. what things would be
  done with an extra bit of money in housing, or what
  things would have to be dropped if there were a bit less
  on roads. This is the information which Ministers have
  when *they* take their decisions and you cannot take
  decisions without it. The Estimates are not the purely
  consequential nuts and bolts that Members (and
  Ministers) think. Big items of expenditure which get no
  mention in the White Paper find a place in the Estimates. The application of funds to *this* specific purpose

rather than *that* within a given field is a proper subject of Parliamentary scrutiny. At the moment it is not done.' The Estimates can be properly examined only by the subject committee for a given area of policy looking at them *and* the long-term forecasts for its area. This function is complementary to the work now done by the Expenditure sub-committees and would give the sub-committees a closer insight into their policy areas.]

[*Enter Mr Cunningham*]

DU CANN

I'm going to ask Mr Maudling, former Chancellor of the Exchequer, to ask you some questions on our behalf first.

MAUDLING

I think there's only one main question. You attach great importance to the control of expenditure, but I'm not quite sure which purpose you have in mind. Is it to save money in the sense of making sure that money is not inefficiently spent? Or is it to enable Parliament to establish priorities between different objectives on which to spend the money? In other words is it still an efficiency operation or is it a policy choice operation?

GEORGE CUNNINGHAM

I think it must be both. When a Government decides how much money to spend and upon what purposes to spend it, it takes account, of course, of both those considerations. In respect of both the Government is, in theory, subject to the approval of Parliament. In practice it has no scrutiny from Parliament at all. The Government always gets every penny of what it wants and gets it for exactly the purposes which it first thought of without ever any change at all. That seems to me to be not only contrary to constitutional doctrine but totally contrary to the demands for scrutiny over what the Executive is doing.

MAUDLING

Wouldn't you say that in practice the scrutiny of how the money has been spent is pretty detailed and the control pretty firm?

CUNNINGHAM

Yes, but the significance of that is that you say the way in which the money *has been spent*. The Public Accounts Committee of the House is an excellent organ for making sure that it has been spent upon the purposes which Parliament envisaged, or rather the Government envisaged, but there is absolutely no equivalent for looking at the proposals for expenditure and modifying them or for subjecting them to any kind of examination at all. The House receives the proposals of the Government to spend money in an enormous book of thousands of pages. And it simply lets the thing pass on a vote without examining it.

DU CANN

Are those the Estimates in fact that you have there, Mr Cunningham?

CUNNINGHAM

These volumes are the once-a-year request for funds by the Government. They are supplemented by three or four other requests for funds which amount to about half as much again, both in bulk and in terms of cash. And on each occasion that the Government asks Parliament to vote this money for the specific purposes in these books, Parliament gives it the money without ever looking at the detailed purposes set out therein.

SCOTT

Mr Cunningham, you would want then to dilute the ability of Government to make policy decisions and obtain the money to carry those policies into practice?

CUNNINGHAM

I wouldn't put it like that. I want to subject the activities of Government in the field of expenditure to something approximating to the scrutiny by the Legislature which theory says the Legislature has got. The Legislature may be relatively uninfluential on the matter of the legislation that the Government wants, but when it comes to expenditure the Legislature is not only totally uninfluential but doesn't even *try* to influence the specific purposes for which the money is voted.

SCOTT

But surely the increasing complexity of Government means that Governments have to be able to react much more quickly and to take policy decisions much more quickly. Do you think it's possible so to reform Parliamentary procedures that before those policy decisions could be taken they would come and get approval for expenditure from Parliament in the way that you suggest?

CUNNINGHAM

No, in any sensible system it would be possible for the Government to put its hand into the kitty and take money out for an emergency purpose, subject to subsequent Parliamentary approval. This it can do now. But this must constitute perhaps 1 per cent at most of the total money that the Government gets its hands on. What I'm saying is that in respect of the other proposals for expenditure the sensible thing to do is to refer those proposals to subject committees of the House so that they can have a preliminary look and submit their views to the whole House.

MACKINTOSH

Your point, Mr Cunningham, is that the decision by Government to spend money on roads as opposed to schools, or universities as opposed to nursery schools, is a prime matter of political choice, and that this kind of choice isn't put in that form before the House.

CUNNINGHAM

I would say that. But the House has organised itself better for scrutinising that kind of choice than it used to do. I'm rather making the point that in addition to looking at the broad policy options the House, since it imposes upon itself the duty of voting the detail of these expenditure proposals, must equip itself to look at the detail too.

MACKINTOSH

What do we lack in the way of this equipment now?

CUNNINGHAM

Subject committees of the House. If it is proposed that £6,000 million should be spent this year, for example, in the field of the Department of the Environment, and if you have a committee of the House, as we do have, which is supposed to be concerned with the affairs of the Department of the Environment, then it seems to me to be barmy not to refer the proposals for expenditure in that field to that committee. At the moment we don't, and anyone who suggests that should be done is regarded as a crank.

FOOT

Well, wouldn't your proposals, if you were able to find the means of carrying them through, be inclined to turn Members of Parliament into auditors and accountants? You may say there are enough of them already. Surely that's a different job from the major job of political choice.

CUNNINGHAM

Yes, I think that is right, but I am not suggesting that Members should go into the very finest detail. I would just point out to Mr Foot that at the moment Members do have to vote this detail. Now if someone wants to say that in modern conditions we ought not to have to vote it and that the Government should be allowed to put its hand into the kitty any time it wants, and we'll only look at that afterwards, then that is at least a consistent position. But for us to have to approve it and not to take an interest in what we are doing, which is the case at the moment, I think is totally unacceptable. [*Exit Mr Cunningham*]

[The next witness was Sir David Pitblado – the Comptroller and Auditor General – whose written evidence described his job and that of the Select Committee he serves. The Comptroller and Auditor General is independent both of Government and Parliament: he has statutory duties of auditing and certifying Government accounts and reporting on them to Parliament, and is assisted by a specially trained staff of Government auditors in the Exchequer and Audit Department. 'The effectiveness of his work depends on the action taken by Parliament and in the Executive in response to the points he raises. The Public Accounts Committee has examined his Reports for Parliament since his office was created in 1866. The primary purpose of the Comptroller's audit and of the Public Accounts Committee's examination of government departments on matters arising from it is to ensure that money has been spent, with proper authority, for purposes for which it has been granted by Parliament. But, arising naturally from this, the Committee has been concerned with sound financial practices, the prevention of waste and extravagance, and obtaining value for money, and has encouraged the Comptroller to develop these aspects of the work of his department.']
[*Enter Sir David Pitblado*]

DU CANN

Sir David, what are your statutory duties?

SIR DAVID PITBLADO

In brief, to audit all the Government accounts and a number of others, and report to Parliament that the money has been spent in accordance with legislation, in accordance with Estimates, in accordance with the policies which have been put forward by the Government to Parliament.

du Cann

You have a large staff to help you in this work?

Pitblado

I have a staff of just under six hundred scattered round the country.

du Cann

Can you just mention for us the subjects of a number of your recent reports?

Pitblado

Well, I report on all the accounts and select items out of them which will be of interest to Parliament, I mean matters such as the Rolls Royce RB211, the hospital service and the control of expenditure in Government-owned companies. From the whole sweep of Government expenditures, we pull out items which it is worth while for the Public Accounts Committee to discuss with a view to getting things done better in the future.

Foot

Sir David, in view of the fact that your position and that of the Public Accounts Committee is absolutely pivotal in the control of expenditure, could you say something about your independence which you note in your report to us. How independent really are you? What are the relations with the Treasury, for example? Sir William Armstrong told us how close were these relations. Don't you think there's something peculiar in the watch-dog being on such good terms with the burglar, if I can put it that way? The burglar representing the Treasury, of course.

Pitblado

Well I think the relations with the Treasury are really based on the fact that for over 90 per cent of the work the Treasury is not the burglar but the watch-dog. The Treasury is within the Government the watch-dog that expenditures are not incurred unnecessarily and are incurred properly.

Foot

And where is the initiative taken? How much initiative

comes from the Treasury in suggesting these are the places where you ought to look, or where does the initiative primarily come from?

PITBLADO

It doesn't come to a very great extent even from myself. It comes from the auditors who are going about their work and finding out things which need to be explored. And then a selection of those things, which have previously been discussed with the departments, are brought up. But I'm under no instructions or pressure, either from the Treasury (or for that matter from Parliament) in the selection of items to be brought up.

FOOT

Would you tell us exactly what was the origin of the investigation into the North Sea oil, the recent report which is obviously one of paramount importance for the whole country, millions upon millions of pounds involved? How did it start and why was it that the matter was not taken up before? Could you give us an account of how it actually happened?

PITBLADO

Well the account under which the receipts from licensing and so forth in the North Sea are recorded comes before the Public Accounts Committee. Although the round of licensing in which auctioning had taken place was not within the year on which I'd just reported, there was considerable concern. So the chairman of the Public Accounts Committee asked me if I would produce a memorandum for them and also get evidence from the department. So this was an initiative by the chairman and committee, in which they asked me to give them assistance, which I did.

DU CANN

In other words by a committee of the House of Commons.

PITBLADO

By a committee of the House of Commons.

MACKINTOSH

Sir David, you are running a sort of anti-Civil-Service Civil Service in that you have a big staff specialising in watching over the Civil Service and you work through a Select Committee of the House which can take evidence and examine officials. Now to my mind you're associated with such famous discoveries as profits on Ferranti, Hawker-Siddeley contracting, now North Sea oil. Without your anti-Civil-Service Civil Service and without your Select Committee these would have gone by default?

PITBLADO

Not necessarily, but it is the function of an audit in all countries to bring out matters of this sort for discussion by Parliament.

MACKINTOSH

Would you consider that there was room for an extension of this kind of well-staffed Select Committee looking into administration and detailed conduct of policy in other areas than simply financial accounting?[1]

PITBLADO

I think there is room for further examination of particular issues; though I myself feel, if Parliament has discussed policy in deciding upon legislation and if it has considered policy in other debates, the people who are entrusted with particular jobs need to get on with arranging to do the jobs, to carry out the policy, and that a scrutiny after they've established the way they're doing it is in some ways more valuable than breathing down their necks while they're trying to decide how best to do it.

MACKINTOSH

But policy on North Sea oil, for example, could not really sensibly be discussed without your very valuable report on this matter: on the taxation and the profits and the whole procedure. We could discuss policy till we're black in the face but it would be meaningless if we didn't know what you'd told us.

PITBLADO

Oh, in this case the committee operated on the account, which was published to Parliament and the world, and on answers by the department to the questions which they put to them. [*Exit Sir David Pitblado*]

DU CANN

I think it's quite plain that Sir David's evidence brings out that we certainly do have the machinery for inquiry after the event and that it is working effectively. I don't think there's any doubt about that. Do you agree Michael?

[1]Since the making of the programme the Exchequer and Audit Department has loaned two auditors to the Expenditure Committee.

FOOT

Well, with some qualifications; I'm not prepared to give quite such a holus bolus agreement as that. For instance, North Sea gas was on the initiative of the chairman and that in turn was due to political pressures of a one-man committee if you like – very often the best committee – Lord Balogh, who's been pursuing this matter for a long time, and eventually he breaks through. Now as far as I understand it, that wasn't hit upon by the Public Accounts Committee itself originally and it wasn't the Treasury that came along and said 'Here boys, why don't you inquire into North Sea oil, that's the place where you really should be looking', so I think that qualifies what you say.

MACKINTOSH

And I think what matters is not where the idea comes from but that we have the machinery to do it. Lord Balogh may have had the idea, but without the Public Accounts Committee the detailed work couldn't have been done.

MAUDLING

Certainly my experience both as a Civil Servant and as a Minister is that the Permanent Secretary who's told he's got to appear before the Public Accounts Committee really gets cracking. It is a very effective discipline indeed on the departments and I think by and large the way it operates – everything always can be improved – came out of his evidence as completely good.

DU CANN

Well we've been looking at the examination after the event. The next witness we were proposing to call, if you remember, is Mr Rodgers, one of our colleagues in the House of Commons who's been one of the original members of the newly-formed Select Committee on Public Expenditure, and indeed a very effective chairman on one of its sub-committees. [*Enter Mr Rodgers*]

[Mr Rodgers' written evidence assessed the role of the Expenditure Committee in improving Parliament's financial scrutiny: 'Public expenditure', he explained, 'must be determined by the Government of the day on a political basis. Its overall level will be influenced by commitments entered into and the necessities of economic management; its distribution by political priorities.' The Opposition's proper role is to scrutinise and challenge this expenditure in the broadest way through debate in the Chamber. Even Select Committees of the House work within a political framework; MPs are (and should be) political animals, alert and well-informed, but not much taken by financial drudgery. However, to be effective in a Select Committee, they must be coaxed into discarding their party labels for some of the time and grow to feel a loyalty to their colleagues and their task.

The Public Accounts Committee has the help of the Comptroller and Auditor-General. There is no reason why the Expenditure Committee should not have similar staff. The Expenditure Committee is inevitably feeling its way, but nonetheless has considerable achievements to its credit: the General sub-committee, with the help of its specialist advisor, has produced pioneering reports and the Trade and Industry sub-committee has successfully investigated the controversial question of public money invested in the private sector of industry. Evidence has been taken in public adding to the long-term educational value of such enquiries. Perhaps most important, it is arguable that the Expenditure Committee is better placed than any other body to help push the Executive towards more open government. It cannot usurp the traditional function of the Chamber and it takes time to learn how best to break into the bastions of departmental secrecy, but at a time when the power of the Executive has increased and is increasing, any means by which it may be diminished deserves support. Without Select Committees there can be none of the intensive probing that scrutiny properly involves.]

DU CANN

Mr Rodgers, I'm going to ask Mr Mackintosh if he'd begin the questioning.

MACKINTOSH

Mr Rodgers, could I ask you a practical question on the matter of expenditure. Over a number of years now there's been a great argument as to whether Concorde as a project should go on or not. Do you think that – apart from Ministers – the rank and file Members of Parliament know enough about this to take any reasonable informed view of the matter?

WILLIAM RODGERS

No, I think they know very little about it.

MACKINTOSH

Is it not possible that if one got out the facts on this matter that they would be so overwhelming that they would influence the form of the political conflict?

RODGERS

They would. I think they would certainly influence the debate and perhaps influence the decision, whichever way it went. That is what I think Select Committees ought to be doing, finding more of the facts and laying them before the House. I think scrutiny through Select Committees of the House is the way we have discovered more about Concorde than we would have known otherwise.

MACKINTOSH

Have we got sufficient equipment to do this job over the whole front of public policy at the moment?

RODGERS

No we haven't. I think it's fair to say the House finds its own way forward and the Expenditure Committee has existed for two years and we're finding our way, but I think that if the House wants it, and if members of the Select Committee believe it's important, certainly we can move forward and extend the sphere of activity of Select Committees and their effectiveness without in any way detracting from the important debate in the Chamber.

DU CANN

Thank you. Mr Scott.

SCOTT

The Select Committee on Expenditure is looking at existing policies of expenditure as it develops. The Public Accounts Committee is looking at expenditure that's taken place, and auditing it. We've heard that the Public Accounts Committee has a staff of about 600 people. What's the staff of the Expenditure Committee and its sub-committees?

RODGERS

I think I could count it on the fingers of two hands, but with respect I think the distinction you make is not absolutely the way it is. Inevitably as the Expenditure Committee is concerned with objectives and policy, it doesn't lend itself in the same way to the very detailed examination which the PAC must have. But my guess is that nevertheless to be effective the Expenditure Committee must develop an expertise which will mean more people; I think, yes, this is the direction we are moving.

FOOT

Do you not think that in fact future expenditure covers such a wide range of the whole of our politics that in the selection of particular subjects you're bound to be making political choices of one sort or another. Party political choices too.

RODGERS

I think the choices we're making are about the things which matter to the country and to Parliament and to both parties. Both parties have spent a great deal of money in the private sector of industry. This is a highly political subject and yet it lent itself to scrutiny by an all-party Select Committee.

FOOT

Do you think there's any danger of blunting the battle between the parties by their approach to these highly tender political questions in this way? In other words, that it might encourage a form of coalition-mindedness in approaching these great subjects?

RODGERS

No, on the contrary, I don't like shadow-boxing. I don't think politicians are at their best when they speak out of ignorance or when they contrive their confrontations. I think Parliament will have a higher reputation the more honest it is. And it will be more honest if it has the facts at its fingertips about which it can argue.

FOOT

Yes, but don't you think there's a sharp line to be drawn between investigating facts which can really be regarded as objective and making up your mind say about regional policy which involves clashes between say socialism and capitalism, and that, therefore, you cannot try and pretend that certain facts are objective when in fact they're bound to be coloured by politics.

RODGERS

Well, members of a Select Committee can't become political eunuchs. If that's what you're saying, that is true. And we have two lives. And yet I think it is possible for a Select Committee made up of people who have very different political views, to look at the question of objectives and at the same time retain their ability to debate in the party political sense.

DU CANN

Mr Rodgers, the Expenditure Committee has been in existence now for just about two years. What would you say its successes have been?

RODGERS

I think its success has been already in certain areas to have influenced Government policy. The taking of evidence itself, which, of course, is taken in public, widely reported, has influenced Government policy in a very substantial way. But it's much too early to say what we shall finally put on the record. I think we shall influence Governments, but more important we shall inform Parliament and Members of Parliament.

DU CANN

Mr Rodgers, we're very much obliged to you. [*Exit Mr Rodgers*] Well, gentlemen, there we are, we have, in fact, come to the end of our witnesses. We did say at the beginning that we might wish to examine Sir William Armstrong, the Head of the Home Civil Service, again. It does seem to me that a number of points have come up during our questioning of these witnesses about which we might wish to have Sir William's opinion rather shortly. Can we ask Sir William to come back and see us again for a moment please. [*Enter Sir William Armstrong*] Sir William, I'm afraid you're having a double ordeal. I think we're now at the end of our inquiry. We've seen a number of witnesses and I take it that you've had the opportunity of watching our examination of them?

SIR WILLIAM ARMSTRONG

Yes, I have.

DU CANN

Mr Maudling.

MAUDLING

One point does occur to me, raised several times: that if the Parliamentary system, given the limitation on the amount of time in relation to the amount of business we do, is to be more effective, some people say Members of Parliament should have more information at their disposal. I suspect really the procedure should change so that the subsequent stages of a Bill and the detailed examination is carried on on the basis that the principle is settled and that you can then get down to the details of making the Bill work as well as it possibly can in the light of Parliamentary approval in principle. Do you think there's something in that line of approach or not?

ARMSTRONG

I think there might be, but again I don't see how Parliament and Members of Parliament can be expected to restrict themselves, as came out on a number of occasions in the evidence. The political conflict is there, is a fact of life, and great ingenuity is adopted in keeping that conflict going, and that often means that detailed examination takes second place or maybe even hardly happens at all. But the reality is the political conflict. And I think that one could make all the pious hopes in the world but parliamentarians would go on behaving in this way.

MAUDLING

So the politicians go on bashing one another while the Civil Servants get the legislation right.

DU CANN

Mr Scott.

SCOTT

Two points really, which are sort of slightly linked on this subject. The first of them is we've heard I think from other witnesses that the Select Committee process seemed, at least while the subject is being discussed, to reduce the element of party conflict. And wouldn't it therefore be better, taking up Mr Maudling's point, that when you had a Bill which was the subject of acute controversy on the Floor of the House that a small Select Committee should go over it in detail, once that fundamental debate on political principle had taken place on Second Reading?

ARMSTRONG

If the real object of the exercise was to say, 'Yes, we've had that debate, we all accept it, that principle is accepted, what we now turn to is getting it right in detail', yes. But often that isn't the case. The debate, the political conflict, in fact, still goes on, and the detail has got to be done as best one can.

DU CANN

I think this is exactly the point Mr Maudling brought out a little bit earlier, that too often the agreement in principle is not accepted. The argument continues during the whole passage of the Bill and that may well prevent the detailed examination being effective. This is really what you're getting at.

ARMSTRONG

Yes, it is, yes.

DU CANN

Mr Mackintosh.

MACKINTOSH

Sir William, I take it that the burden of your evidence is that Parliamentary control is not as effective now as it was when you joined the Service. Would you be saying that?

ARMSTRONG

It certainly has loosened, yes.

MACKINTOSH

Now, this loosening, how would you think it would be best to remedy this? Parliament is naturally slow in its reactions; would you think one could do this simply by, as it were, more activity by MPs on the Floor of the House, or would you think one wants more other institutions like the Public Accounts Committee doing detailed supervisory work?

ARMSTRONG

I think it probably does require more activity, more institutions, more expert scrutiny. If one compares the present situation with the last century when the whole thing was supposed to be much simpler, the Select Committees of the last century were not only much more influential, some of the big reforms came out of Select Committees. I think it's true that they were quite accustomed for the Committees to be formed partly of Members of Parliament and partly of people from other walks of life. The notion that a Select Committee could only consist of Members of Parliament seems to have grown up later, and I think one might experiment with scrutiny committees – which not only included Members of Parliament, but brought in people from outside.

MACKINTOSH

For example, this report we've had this year from the Public Accounts Committee on the profits, or failure to tax profits of North Sea oil companies; this kind of valuable investigatory work which the Government accepted couldn't be done by the Floor or the mass of Members of Parliament operating in the House as a whole?

ARMSTRONG

No, I think that's right.

MACKINTOSH

So, you could see a room for extension of this, over other aspects than finance?

ARMSTRONG

Yes, I think I would.

MACKINTOSH

Is the burden of your reflection then that Parliament is well organised for the political blow-up but relatively poorly organised for the rest, and it's difficult to tell when the one seeps into the other?

ARMSTRONG

I think, yes, there are certain areas where that does seem to us to be so. Many times a Finance Bill gets on the Statute Book and the experts know that it's not perfect or that there are areas of it that have not been fully discussed. And in this year we'll be amending the legislation of last year or the year before, given the fact that it wasn't fully examined. Of course, with a lot of legislation that's not possible because the opportunities for legislation are much less frequent than they are in finance.

DU CANN

Mr Foot.

FOOT

Much of the evidence, including your own, Sir William, suggests that Parliament still has enormous powers against the Executive if they wish to use it. Is that correct? Is that your view too?

ARMSTRONG

Yes, that is so, but as also came out there is a big question: if they want to use it. Who are *they*? Parliament in the sense of a decision-taker is ultimately the will of the Government. The Government has the majority so long as its supporters will vote for it. So, one element in Parliament, which remains important, are the back-bench supporters of the Government, because they are the people who hold the majority in their hands.

du CANN

Sir William, we're most grateful to you. Thank you very much indeed. [*Exit Sir William Armstrong*] Well, gentlemen, I think if it's agreeable to you we should adjourn at this point. As I said earlier, we've got a great deal to think about and to discuss with our colleagues. I will try and arrange for that to be done as promptly as possible. Thank you all for your help and co-operation.

> [The subsequent meeting Mr du Cann referred to was the third part of the programme in which a dozen MPs, including the five Members of the Committee, debated reform proposals arising from the evidence presented in the first two parts. On one side in this debate were the 'Chamber-first' men, who consider the main function of Parliament to be the voicing of fundamental political issues, which is best done – or perhaps can only be done – on the Floor of the House. To the protagonists of this view, extension of Select Committee investigations threatens to turn MPs into administrators and accountants, too busy with detail to notice the big causes that need to be watched for.
>
> On the other side were the 'Information-first' men, who consider that Parliament can in no way be effective unless it is well informed, that the ignorance of MPs on many issues that come before them is a disgrace, and that the development of Select Committee investigations is the way to restore effectiveness to Parliament – both informing debates on the Floor and strengthening the authority of all Members.
>
> Like the film of work on the Fair Trading Bill and the committee hearing, the debate was designed to air the issue, not to settle it.]

Part 3

A Debate: Are MPs too ignorant to do their job?

The three motions debated:

That Members of Parliament are too ignorant to do their job properly

That the strengthening of investigatory Select Committees is Parliament's most urgent need

That legislative Select Committees are the only way to restore Parliament's proper role in law making

Part 3

In the Programme

Chairman: John Jennings MP (Conservative, Burton)

Supporters of the Motions

Rt Hon Anthony Crosland MP (Labour, Grimsby)

Rt Hon Richard Crossman MP (Labour, Coventry East)

Rt Hon Edward du Cann MP (Conservative, Taunton)

John Selwyn Gummer MP (Conservative, Lewisham West)

John P Mackintosh MP (Labour, Berwick and East Lothian)

Nicholas Scott MP (Conservative, Paddington South)

Opposers of the Motions

Michael Foot MP (Labour, Ebbw Vale)

Angus Maude MP (Conservative, Stratford-upon-Avon)

Rt Hon Reginald Maudling MP (Conservative, Barnet)

Rt Hon Charles Pannell MP (Labour, Leeds West)

Rt Hon Enoch Powell MP (Conservative, Wolverhampton
South-West)

Brian Walden MP (Labour, Birmingham, All Saints)

Narrator: Debates are the basic method of the House of Commons for conducting its business. But tonight that basic method is under question. Speeches and debates: are these the most efficient, the most informed way for MPs, our representatives, to keep a check on the growing activities of Government?

For the last part of THE STATE OF THE NATION on Parliament we have tonight a debate. Not inside Parliament, of course, but as near as we can get to the real thing. Again MPs have crossed the river to the Greater London Council to debate for you, as they regularly do, hidden from all cameras, in the Palace of Westminster. The form of this debate is closely patterned on a Standing Committee of the House of Commons, with just one difference: *there* Conservative and Labour sit on opposite benches; *here* supporters of the motions for debate sit on one side, opponents on the other. So Labour and Conservative are mixed together. The divide tonight is on attitudes to the way the House of Commons should work. I'm not going to introduce the MPs in the debate to you, as it is the convention in Standing Committees that the Chairman invites Members to speak or interrupt by clearly naming them. The Chairman is John Jennings, Conservative MP, a senior member of the Speaker's panel of chairmen of Standing Committees and, in recent years, regularly Chairman of the Standing Committee on the Finance Bill.

I

JOHN JENNINGS: Order, order. Nowhere else in the world is it likely that a group of Members of Parliament could or would gather together to discuss and debate their own ignorance. But that's what we're going to do here. We will all realise, as the debate goes on, that this word ignorance in its context doesn't mean exactly what many people think it means. There will be three debates: One a general debate, and the two following deriving completely from the first one. This Committee is assembled not on party lines, but on opinions held as to how the functions of Parliament can best be carried out, and we will find this is what the debate is all about.

The first motion to be debated is *'That Members of Parliament are too ignorant to do their job properly'*. This will be proposed by Mr John Mackintosh, and opposed by the Rt Hon Enoch Powell. I now call Mr John Mackintosh to propose this motion.

JOHN MACKINTOSH: Mr Jennings, I am glad you made the point in your opening remarks that the word ignorant is to be taken in the Oxford Dictionary meaning of 'lacking information'. There is no suggestion that Members of Parliament are lazy, that they do not work or that they are not well informed, as much as the limits of the present situation allow. The suggestion is that they are not equipped with sufficient information to be as effective as a modern member of a legislature ought to be.

Now I know that in replying to this there will be many Members opposite who want to make the case that the chief function of Parliament is a political function, to have political rows, to see what the Government's doing, to get a sense of how the public are reacting, to build this up and to make the maximum political impact. And that the task of the House of Commons is to continue between elections the struggle for power. And that therefore no more information is needed than the average well-informed person can get from the press and from their full-time work in and around the House, meeting people, meeting pressure groups and so on.

I want to start by saying I accept that this is the primary function of Parliament, to make political rows and to struggle for power. But what I am wanting to argue in supporting this motion, in moving it, is that we could be far more effective if we knew a great deal more about what was going on inside the Executive, if we could elucidate and discover information. I know this is disputed. I remember once listening to Michael Foot making an attack on the Labour Government's policy of keeping troops East of Suez, a brilliant attack I thought, without being disrespectful a little insubstantial in places. And I remember saying to him, wouldn't it have been a good idea if we'd had a Defence Committee which could have discovered the cost of the bases East of Suez. We could have heard the generals and the admirals on how effective they thought our forces were there, and heard about our treaty commitments, and discovered a little bit of the thinking behind it. And Michael said to me, 'No, it wouldn't have helped me at all.' He said 'I only find facts confuse my arguments'. Well I know some people do take this view, but I think sometimes more information clarifies the air, it makes the political blow-up more effective.

Let's take a recent case in the news just now. Take Concorde. No-one would object politically to building Concorde if it cost a hundred million pounds. It's when the cost goes up and up that the question of cancelling it has arisen. If one had had a Select Committee that could have found out not only the existing costs, but the projected costs, and indeed some costs that might have been hidden elsewhere in other items of the accounts, then we could have done a much more effective job on the overall question of go on or not.

Let's take another question that recently occurred where facts help. Take the political blow-up which really threatened the Conservative Government, in a small way, over the Maplin airport. Now here we have suddenly a piece of information that you didn't need a new airport because the existing airports could provide all the facilities this country would need in the foreseeable future. Is this true or false? Members didn't know. If we'd had a Select Committee and we could have moved in the House 'Let us wait until we have a report as to whether this is accurate or not', then the discovery of the facts would have loaded the political situation and made the arguments so much clearer and more decisive. Indeed the Government might have given up before the facts came out, rather than have continued.

There are other situations where we do not already have an intense political argument but where one might exist if we knew what was going on. We've seen something of the work of the Public Accounts Committee with its big staff. The traditionalists who like the House of Commons as it is, they accept the Public Accounts Committee for the simple reason that it has existed since 1860: it is not objectionable though it has a staff, it's effective, because it is there. Well let's look at what it has done. It took on a question MPs really knew nothing about, and that is public contracting, the taxpayers' money going out on defence. They discovered, over the Hawker Siddeley case, that money was being spent and contracts were being made which were going all to pieces, where forward forecasting was unsatisfactory. This became a big political row. So did the Ferranti profits case. Neither of these would have come to the light of day but for the Public Accounts Committee. I think there was another good example only a month or so ago, when the Public Accounts Committee discovered over an existing political row about North Sea oil companies that this was much more important because the companies were dodging paying income tax. They rearranged it so that they avoided paying any tax at all. Now this could never have been discovered by Members of Parliament operating on their own. They might have, but how would they have had a clue? It was the Comptroller and Auditor-General and his staff of five hundred that discovered it and contributed something to this political storm about the whole Government handling of North Sea oil.

So my argument is that this investigatory work, this finding out what's going on inside the Executive, helps Parliament to do its traditional function, to struggle for power and policy, to criticise the Government.

I remember a case not long ago where the Nationalised Industries Committee, which the Labour Party originally resisted on the grounds that it would weaken Parliament – nobody takes that view now it's been working for ten or fifteen years, but they opposed it originally – I remember when the Committee said, 'We want to find out relations between the Bank of England and the Treasury.' Members of Parliament didn't know; they were conducted, these relations, in secrecy. We passed a Bill setting up the present situation in the Bank of England, we weren't allowed to look at it. Now who got together to demand information, the right to investigate? A Tory Member, Colonel Lancaster, and a Tribune Group Left-winger, Ian Mikardo, the Chairman and Deputy Chairman of the Committee. No-one suggested that Colonel Lancaster had become a member of the Tribune Group, and no-one suggested that Ian Mikardo had suddenly become a Right-wing Conservative. Nor did anyone suggest that they were in the pocket of the Treasury. They said 'We are entitled to know' and I think Michael Foot backed them up. Now that is the kind of work which stimulates Parliament as an agency where political rows can take place.

One further point. Michael Foot has said, I think, earlier, that if Parliament isn't a legislature it's nothing. Now what we have discovered and what I think we all know is that the process of legislation, a great deal of it, is prior secret discussion between the Government and the pressure groups, the lobbies, the private organisations. But you know the one group of people that's not represented there is the public: the citizen, the taxpayer, the consumer. They are represented in Parliament and Parliament doesn't hear about these deals and arrangements until the whole thing is nearly finished and concluded and a Bill is presented to the House.

I am moving this motion because I believe that as a Parliament we would be far more effective if we could elucidate the facts, we could investigate the Executive, we could find out the prior deals and get in on the formative stage of legislation. I want to make Parliament much more effective so that we are once again looked upon as we should be, as the forum of the nation. I beg to move. *(Hear, hear)*

JOHN JENNINGS: The question is '*That Members of Parliament are too ignorant to do their job properly*'. I call the Rt Hon Enoch Powell.

THE RT HON ENOCH POWELL: Mr Jennings, if I were a Prime Minister whose object was to turn himself into a dictator, if I hated the House of Commons as much as I love it, and if I wanted to deprive it of all real political effectiveness, then I would seize with both hands and with gratitude the arguments, the line of thought, and the developments foreshadowed by the Hon. Member opposite. I should encourage the House of Commons to set up as many committees as possible. My object would be, especially in the afternoons and evenings, to have Hon. Members busily and I am sure happily employed upstairs. As long as they didn't come into the Chamber I wouldn't mind what they were doing upstairs in the committee rooms. Of course I would bring them into consultation on all the legislation beforehand, naturally in the form of a Select Committee: balanced, of course, in party terms, but hand-picked by the Whips. And therefore by the time my legislation came before, as a perfunctory last stage, the House of Commons itself, I would not only have allies on both sides of the House, who had been through it all, who were committed to it, but my Ministers would be able to confront the House with the undeniable fact that really all the work had been done. There's no point in the ignoramuses on the floor of the Chamber – of course they might be allowed to ask a question occasionally, satisfy a little ignorant curiosity. But the main work of course had, as would be quite logical, been fed into the preparation of the legislation itself. And as for information, of course I wouldn't be satisfied with the present excessive services provided by the House of Commons library. I would take Hon. Members and I would stuff them with information as one stuffs a goose to produce pâté de fois gras. They should have information until it was coming out of their ears. Because they would be quite unable, with absorbing the information and working the computers and keeping their staff of researchers and secretaries well occupied, they would be quite unable to get together in the lobbies, to meet, to talk to one another. And above all, they wouldn't come into the Chamber very often. *(Interruption:* MR JOHN MACKINTOSH: They don't anyway!) Aha! But it's the people that do come into the Chamber – and the occasions when what's happening in the Chamber draws hundreds of other Members there – that I should be really afraid of. I say, Mr Jennings, above all they wouldn't come into the Chamber.

Now I went along partly with the analysis of the Hon. Member, of the function of Parliament, of the House of Commons. That it is a political forum which protracts the essential debate in the electorate, that it is a representation of the people which is constantly watching Government, constantly asking it questions, striking the finger upon the weak places. But it does this in a particular way. It is the power to force a Minister in the Chamber to make a case and to sustain that case, whether he is arguing the question that Clause 33 of a Bill Stand Part or whether he is arguing a major matter of Government policy.

Now I would like to take very briefly some of the cases, because they are very instructive, which the Hon. Member raised. He mentioned Concorde. I'd like to throw in another couple for good measure. He mentioned the ignorant approach of Michael Foot in a defence debate. Well I was for a period spokesman for the Opposition on Defence, and two of the proposals of the then Government were in the range of advanced weapons, the purchase of an American aircraft called the F-111, and the construction of an Anglo-French variable geometry aircraft. And I said they were nonsense. I said they wouldn't happen, and I said that the policy based upon them would collapse in ruins. Not only did I not need the advice of Air Vice-Marshals, Air Marshals, or experts from the aviation industry in order to do this; they would have been a positive nuisance. Indeed I had to restrain my colleagues from going and getting that sort of misleading advice. I said, 'No, just read the White Paper. And you will see that when a politician, when a government has to write paragraphs like that, then there is nothing behind it and they know there is nothing behind it.' And sure enough, there was nothing behind it, because the simple questions, the simple questions which any intelligent member of the public could have asked, but wasn't in the House of Commons to ask, could not be answered. What the devil are you going to do with fifty of those aircraft? Whatever they were like, however good they were. The Government could never answer that question, and in due course, in incredible humiliation, the policy collapsed.

Now debate. I come back to this central point. Mr Jennings, everything which diminishes true debate on the Floor of the House of Commons strengthens the Executive and weakens Parliament. We must in order to do our business, be un-involved. We are not participating in government, we are not experts, we are even less the puppets of the experts. We have our own expertise, and our expertise is as politicians and would-be Ministers facing other politicians and actual Ministers, to strike our finger upon the places where it hurts, or upon the places where the great clash of politics is going to take place, and fight it out. We can only do that through debate, we can only do that on the Floor of the Chamber. And those who wish Parliament and the House of Commons ill, will support this motion. (*Hear, hear*)

JOHN JENNINGS: The debate is now open. Mr Nicholas Scott.

NICHOLAS SCOTT: Mr Jennings, I think if one compares the sort of political ping-pong that goes on at Question Time in the House of Commons with all too often political slogans being used as an alternative for political argument, with the way in which members of the Executive in the United States are cross-questioned on matters of detail before Congressional Committees, you see how really a legislature ought to be able to subject members of an Executive to pressure.

When I first came into the House seven years ago I began attending an annual conference on Africa – a joint conference, of members of the American legislature and our own Parliament. And I suppose at the outset part of the object of the exercise was avowedly to educate Americans, using the benefit that many British Members of Parliament had of African affairs over a number of years. And certainly when this process started the American participants were significantly less well informed about African affairs than were the British Members of Parliament. And it took I think three years for the extra resources in terms of personal staffing and in terms of the facilities of the House and Senate Committees on Foreign Affairs, to swing that balance.

And so really the point I am seeking to make at this stage of the argument is that we are less well informed than we ought to be. Other legislatures in the world do it better than we do. We ought not to be ashamed, simply because of our dogmatic adherence to the status quo, to be ashamed to change and to learn from their experience. (*Hear, hear*)

JOHN JENNINGS: Mr Angus Maude.

ANGUS MAUDE: I thought that at some stage in this argument we should hear about the Congressional Committees in the United States. And in case anybody should be impressed by this argument, let us get it quite clear at the outset, that it is wholly irrelevant and based on an entirely false understanding of the differences in the constitution of the United States and the United Kingdom. The fact of the matter is that in America, unlike Britain, the legislature and the executive are completely separated. Neither the President nor any member of his Cabinet is a member of either House of Congress, and the only way in which ministers can in fact be interrogated in depth is through the Senate and Congressional Committees. Members of the Senate, members of Congress, do not normally aspire to become ministers or members of the President's Cabinet. What they aspire to become is Chairman and Vice-Chairman of Senate or Congressional Committees. This is almost the ultimate ambition of a Congressman in the United States, to become Chairman of one of the important committees: Foreign Affairs, Finance, where the television cameras are always there and there is always a juicy scandal like Watergate to deal with. Yes indeed. (*Interruption*)

JOHN MACKINTOSH: Why does the Hon. Gentleman think it would be such a disaster if Members of Parliament were not all desperate to become Ministers? It is one of the greatest weaknesses of the House of Commons that every back-bencher with ambition and ability wants either to become a Minister or a Shadow Minister. Surely to become a permanent critic of the Government is also an honourable and worthwhile objective?

ANGUS MAUDE: It can be argued whether all Members of

Parliament want to become Ministers. It has been said that they either want to become Ministers quickly or knights slowly. *(Laughter)* Either of those is no doubt a harmless enough ambition. And it isn't the expert, as often as not, who really embarrasses the Government. *(Hear, hear)* It isn't the expert always who improves Bills, discovers scandals. It is very often the rather thick uninvolved chap who perhaps has been half asleep through most of the Minister's speech in a Standing Committee or on the Floor . . . *(Laughter)* And who suddenly wakes up and says 'What does that mean?' Or who wakes up and says 'Prove that!' Or 'Could I have the figures?' And very often it is almost by accident, as it were, by the ordinary commonsense bloke asking the ordinary common-sense question that the experts have never thought of, that we get the improvements, the changes of policy and so forth, that really affect legislation. The Chamber is getting thin already with the number of Members that it has there. More Select Committees, more Legislative Committees, will make this infinitely worse. What we need is more informed debate in the House. And on the question of information, it isn't Select Committees that give you information, it is every Member's outside sources to which he can already get access. What a Member wants is not official information or officially inspired and provided information. It's the information which he has the nous and the commonsense and the acumen to go and find for himself.

JOHN JENNINGS: The Rt Hon Edward du Cann

RT HON EDWARD DU CANN: Mr Jennings, of course Mr Maude is right in what he says. I quote a phrase from one of his last few sentences. What we need is a better informed debate. In other words, he admits we are not as well informed as we ought to be at the present time. I thought, Sir, if I may say so, that his speech largely consisted of tilting at a series of Aunt Sallies, which he set up for his own intellectual pleasure. But, Sir, if I may, I would like particularly to refer to what Mr Powell was saying. It seemed to me we could divide his speech into two parts. There was first the serious part. He said it is the job of Parliament to control the Executive. How very right indeed that is. He said, or inferred, second, that there is a danger that we can become too absorbed with minutiae and we might not spend an adequate time talking about the great issues in Parliament. *(Interruption)* I said 'inferred that' and I believe that he did. I believe that to be correct also.

JOHN JENNINGS: Mr Powell.

ENOCH POWELL: Isn't this a case of tilting at Aunt Sallies; I wondered what that could mean. *(Laughter)*

EDWARD DU CANN: If Mr Powell thinks so, then now he knows, and I am glad at any rate that this debate is better informed in that sense.

But I come now to the more entertaining part of his speech, that is to say, the less serious part, where I believe he was entirely wrong. He suggested, Sir, that we might have in future Members of Parliament stuffed with information like Strasbourg geese, tripping over themselves. *(Mr Powell explodes into laughter at mention of Strasbourg geese)* I thought he might pick that up *(Laughter)*, I thought he might pick up that point in particular. Sir, that would be absurd. Of course. And he knows – he knows it would be absurd. I think the view that some of us take, however, more rationally and much more seriously, is that if anything Members of Parliament at the present time are more like skeletons than stuffed geese. We are not as well informed as we ought to be. It is perfectly true, Sir, as you began by pointing out, that Members of Parliament are not ignorant people. Indeed they are extremely well-informed on a vast variety of subjects. The question is, whether or not we have all the information in the ways that we need to enable us to do our job effectively. I don't believe that we are doing our job as effectively as we might.

JOHN JENNINGS: At this point I am forced to adjourn the debate for a few moments, but let me first explain what will happen for the rest of the time. We will debate two other motions, then we will return to this first motion. The debate will then be open for Hon. and Rt Hon Gentlemen to participate again. And then the winding up will take place by Mr Michael Foot for the Opposers, and the Rt Hon Richard Crossman for the Proposers. Debate now adjourned.

2

JOHN JENNINGS: Order, order. The second motion to be debated is *'That the strengthening of investigatory Select Committees is Parliament's most urgent need'*. This will be moved by the

Right Honourable Edward du Cann and opposed by Mr Brian Walden. I call the Right Hon Edward du Cann.

RT HON EDWARD DU CANN: Mr Jennings, I beg to move the motion on the paper. My point, basically, is a simple one. A Member of Parliament is a trustee for his constituents, the people of our country. It's his job to see, irrespective of party, that we get value from the Government of the day, that the Government of the day is as efficient as it can be and that Parliament, by and large, comes to the right decisions in the national interest. In a word, it's his job to be effective.

Now, sir, let us look at the business of government. In another committee[1] we heard some time ago of the way in which the business of Parliament, the legislative process, has grown from I think some 900 pages of legislation back in the year before the War to well over 2000 today. The scale of the work we do is vast. And then if you measure it in money terms we heard also in that same committee that Government expenditure has risen from some £700 millions before the War to £16,000 millions today and in this document, Mr Jennings, the public expenditure for the years ahead, we see the figures as high as £30,000 millions. Indeed, we heard a little time ago from Sir William Armstrong, the Head of the Home Civil Service, that Parliament's control of the Executive has effectively loosened – those were the words he used. Then we heard, sir, from Clerks of our own House of Commons and they said that Parliament's resources have not matched the growth of its work. These are the facts and it is a fact too that the power of the Executive has increased and is increasing. I believe, sir, that Members of Parliament have an historic duty to contain it and indeed some may think – I hope I carry Mr Foot and Mr Powell with me – some may think that before we preach to Europe about how it should organise its affairs, we have a special duty to put our own house in order.

So the question then is how? Our procedure over the last hundred years or more has been very largely unchanged. My constituents would think me eccentric if I went off down to Somerset to my constituency in a 1938 car. Still less an earlier model, an 1838 model. I wouldn't attempt to run a business with the same tools, with the same methods, that were employed twenty, forty or a hundred years ago. And I suggest to this committee that a serious examination of huge pro-

[1]See pages 97-100.

grammes, of which I've spoken in sum, cannot be achieved alone by general debate, nor can we compare alternatives effectively, road against rail, let us say, more money on preventive medicine or on treatment. We cannot compare alternatives alone by general debate.

We are all familiar with the work of the Public Accounts Committee and with some of the more sensational discoveries that that has made. North Sea oil is one which my colleague, Mr Mackintosh, is fond of reminding us about. But last night, Mr Jennings, I went into the library of the House of Commons, I took down the first volume that I could find of the annual record of the work of that Committee and I picked from it at random just two examples of the sort of details of the day-to-day work that that Committee is doing. I take overseas aid – bilateral, budgetary assistance to Malawi. Does anybody seriously think you can examine whether or not overseas aid to Malawi is effective by means of speeches in the House of Commons? No, sir, this requires serious examination. And there is a catalogue of detailed work which that Committee does, exposing difficulties, exposing problems, getting the information for Members of Parliament. *(Interruption)*

JOHN JENNINGS: Mr Powell.

ENOCH POWELL: Could I ask what use the House of Commons has made of that information?

EDWARD DU CANN: If I may say so I think that's a very different point. If Mr Powell is going on to say ought we to allow more time in the Chamber for debates on reports of Select Committees, I will be the first to agree with him.

So there is one Committee which is generally known to be doing effective work. Then sir, we have the Select Committee on Expenditure. The tools are there. Why do I put such great emphasis on matters of expenditure? I don't suggest that committees looking at expenditure or committees looking at anything are a panacea. I do say however that the control of expenditure is the foundation on which the power of Parliament rests, that Government expenditure is not under full control. Discussions of money resolutions or debates about supply in the sense of voting the money, are the exception rather than the rule. I say, finally, Mr Jennings, it is shocking is it not, that our Parliament will vote millions of pounds, tens of millions of pounds, on occasion thousands of millions of pounds, 'on the nod' as we say? We are perfunctory whereas we should be scrupulous.

No-one surely can deny the need for modern methods. Nobody can deny that we should do our work effectively. No-one can deny either that these Committees have been effective. We need to be better informed, we need to do our work with greater competence, sir. I suggest this is one way by which it could be done. I beg to move. *(Hear, hear)*

JOHN JENNINGS: The question is *'That the strengthening of investigatory Select Committees is Parliament's most urgent need'*. Mr Brian Walden.

BRIAN WALDEN: Mr Jennings, if the motion we were debating merely affirmed the value of some investigatory Select Committees, I wouldn't oppose it. But that isn't the motion. It isn't a simple assertion that such committees have a value. That wouldn't suit the purpose of the proposition at all. We have to assent to the improbable assertion that it's Parliament's most urgent need. And the real reason for that is – it came out clearly in something that Mr Scott said in an earlier discussion – that what is really sought is a transformation of the House of Commons as we know it into a radically different institution, patterned on the Congress of the United States of America. However inappropriate that might be to our institutions and traditions, that is what is sought, and for very good reasons, as the proposition see them, as I shall go into in a moment. *(Interruption)*

JOHN JENNINGS: Mr Scott.

NICHOLAS SCOTT: Another explanation is that we on this side are not so arrogant as to maintain that we can't learn anything from these other legislatures (WALDEN: No) and that simply we ought to incorporate at least some of their good ideas into our own methods of work. *(Hear, hear)*

JOHN JENNINGS: Mr Walden.

BRIAN WALDEN: And there would be no objection to that, of course, and I don't object. Who would object to a certain number of investigatory sub-committees? That isn't the motion that's being put forward. But what is being said is that these investigatory Select Committees represent – their strengthening represents – our most urgent need. I don't think it does at all.

In fact the role of the House of Commons is as a mediator between governors and governed and that is best done by an articulation of popular sentiment, and frankly, that's what rankles. A lot of people in the House of Commons now don't particularly like the raw meat of democracy, they find it uncongenial. The articulation of popular sentiment has become a role that they do not feel at ease in carrying out and what they want is a different type of structure to allow a different type of activity. That's what fuels these demands for fancy devices. Now I quite admit that a bad motivation doesn't spoil a good case, but this isn't a good case. It's a mechanistic case. It came out very clearly in the way the proposer proposed it. In all this stuff about the main function of the Government of the day to be as efficient as possible. He even had an 1838 car worked in there somewhere! The truth of it is that many members opposite see politics as a science and prefer it that way. They don't want it as an art. To them that's the boring bit. Many of us think otherwise. And of course you must have information, it would be foolish to say otherwise, and of course some people must carry out detailed investigations. But the main function of a Member of Parliament as a Member of Parliament is in the Chamber and his main duty is to have some imagination and some flair and some understanding of popular sentiment. Not be a walking compendium of what various experts may or may not have asserted to him.

Now, that seems to me to be, in fact, the crucial issue that's involved in these investigatory Select Committees. And I assert that their proliferation would have in my opinion two quite inevitable consequences; the first is it would distract press and public and parliamentary attention away from that already ailing institution, the Chamber of the House of Commons. That's the first thing it would do. And the second thing that it would quite inevitably do is turn even more debates into cosy little confrontations, or, more likely, collaborations between the apparatchiks of the Select Committees. Of course, other members would be allowed to speak, naturally, but they would speak from below the salt. We're already told that they're very largely uninformed. They'd be allowed their day in court and they would speak in an atmosphere heavy with the kindly patronage of their supposedly better-informed colleagues from the Select Committees.

And what about the members of the Select Committee themselves? Is it supposed that if we allow them to proliferate they will choose the least publicly appealing topics to investigate? Of course they won't. They don't now with the Select Committees we currently have and they won't in the future. They will take the appealing, if you like, the sexy issues, and is it really the case that a chap who is holding forth in front of a gratifyingly large press audience, doubtless with the television cameras in the course of time there to record it for prime viewing, and he's investigating Lonrho or he's investigating vice in Soho or corruption in the bureaucracy; are we really going to be told that that fellow is going to rush down to the Chamber of the House of Commons for another debate, to sit for three hours waiting for his turn to be called and then sitting another three hours to hear his colleagues' opinions on what he said? Plenty of Members already find that tedious, they already find it beneath their dignity. That is the thing they want to avoid. Often because they don't like the Chamber. There are plenty of Members of Parliament who don't, who find its discussions uncongenial. They prefer a different way of going about things. In the name, in fact, of a better system they intend to impose their valuations on us and I can see no logical reason why we should assent that they should.

JOHN JENNINGS: The Right Hon Richard Crossman.

RT HON RICHARD CROSSMAN: Mr Chairman, I don't want to make a personal reply except to say that I think the honourable Member knows that I quite enjoy the Chamber and I'm not likely to want somewhere else where things aren't quite as rough. I'd like to explain to you, Mr Chairman, the two examples which made me change my mind on this. They're some years ago. They are still relevant. The first example was the production of the British atomic bomb which, we now know, was made successfully by the Labour Government without any awareness of Parliament. All the finances were suppressed successfully. People have talked as though we are only concerned with getting experts to give us nice little bits of information. Mr Walden you live in the most secretive country in the world. You live in the country where the Government, by profession, is the biggest coverer-up that's ever been. One of the functions of Parliament is to stop cover, to expose scandal. Does he really tell me he thinks it's a good thing that governments are able to suppress the fact that they're spending hundreds of millions a year on a secret weapon, and get away with it? That was the first example.

The second, of course, was Suez. Does he think that it was a good thing that Government was allowed to drag this country into war and suppress the fact that it was doing so, just like President Johnson? Is that a good thing?

Now after Suez – because this is another kind of investigation – I thought it was a good thing to have a post mortem. So did Mr Michael Foot, that great anti-committee man. You can't have an investigation without a committee of enquiry. Yes, it'll be party biased, there'll be violent feelings in it, somebody will be defending, somebody opposed, it'll be balanced. Let me assure you that when you sit on a committee of this kind and you investigate for months, the bias gets a bit blurred and mixed and, in fact, something is got out. Wouldn't we have been a better democracy if we'd set up a committee of enquiry after Suez to investigate Suez and get the truth which we still don't know? Well, those are the two points I want to make Mr Chairman.

JOHN JENNINGS: The Rt Hon Michael Foot – Mr Michael Foot.

MICHAEL FOOT: Mr Chairman I've had to wait a long time for this promotion! And in this unorthodox assembly! I would like to reply directly if I can to what Dick Crossman has just said. Of course, as Brian Walden said at the beginning, we on this side of the House, certainly speaking for myself, we are not denying that there is a requirement for investigatory committees at certain stages. They can be extremely important, and that is why, of course, if I had got in earlier I would have anticipated his remark that I had been in favour of such a committee to examine Suez. Quite rightly.

But let us take the comparison with the United States a bit further because this is the example; there has been a more recent war even than Suez. There was one in Vietnam. And we were told that this brilliant investigatory committee of Mr Fulbright's, I remember when it appeared on the television we were told, 'Oh, this is the way that Parliament ought to have conducted our affairs'. That committee sat on Vietnam some three years after the war had started. In the British House of Commons if there had been a war of that character, a British government waging a war without the approval of Parliament, believe me, there would have been a majority perhaps in the House of Commons raising that in the early stages, or, if not, a minority, a minority which from the first day would have had the chance to turn itself into the majority. *(Hear, hear)* Now, let me give two practical examples of why we say that to elevate investigatory committees above the House of Commons – because that's what we're arguing about, the most urgent need, that's what we're told about them – if that is argued what you would do is to suppress, or to injure at least, one of the most effective means of access to the House of Commons by minorities. Now let me give two examples. *(Interruption)*

RICHARD CROSSMAN: But before you give two examples, nobody on this side is saying investigatory committees should be elevated above the functions of the Chamber. *(Hear, hear)* What we are saying is precisely because we have an effective Chamber and we have got the chance of a debate on the Floor and it's very good, we think the balance now is that we are weak on investigations and strong on debate.

MICHAEL FOOT: You're saying that the most urgent need is to strengthen the investigatory Select Committees and we are saying that the most urgent need is to restore the power and authority of the Floor of the House of Commons. So don't let us dispute about the semantics of it. But let me give the examples. How, even in cases where Members were in small minorities, they had access to the Floor of the House of Commons but they wouldn't have had access to investigatory committees. The two prime examples of the century if you could put it that way. Churchill, in the 1930s; he didn't have the means of dealing with these matters through investigatory committees; it was because, even though in a minority of three or four of his own party, he had access to the House of Commons that he was able to state his case persistently and thereby led to the situation of 1940. Or Aneurin Bevan, in the 1950s. He would never have survived in a system if he had not had access to the House of Commons itself where he could state his case. You may say 'Ah, these are personal examples', but they are not; this is the history of our country. It is only because of the power and authority of the House of Commons, of the Floor of the House of Commons over the whole of the Palace of Westminster, that minorities have access to it and the ability to turn those minorities into majorities on major matters, major matters covering the whole field of politics. That is what Churchill and Co were judged on in 1940 and that is what Aneurin Bevan asked to be judged on. That is the glory of the House of Commons and we're not defending the *status quo*. We believe that the glory of the House of Commons has been greatly injured and impaired, much to the detriment of the mass of the people of this country.

JOHN JENNINGS: The Rt Hon Anthony Crosland.

RT HON ANTHONY CROSLAND: Mr Jennings, this is typical of Parliamentary debates at any rate in the sense that almost every speech is discussing something different. Almost all the speeches from the other side are about grand issues of principle, the great clashes of politics, whether they're bound up with an individual like Churchill or Bevan or whether they're clashes over new government policies, industrial relations, Europe, prices and incomes, whatever it is, the other side of the House are thinking primarily in terms of these great, national confrontations between parties or within parties that convulse the country as well as convulsing Parliament.

Now of course these are critical. Nobody on this side of the committee has for a moment suggested that in respect of these great confrontations the role, the authority, the power of the Chamber should be in the slightest degree diminished. But these great party confrontations are not what dominate the life of Parliament for 365 days of the year. Most of these 365 days of the year are spent in discussing housing policy, education policy, the social services, recently, issues like Maplin, Concorde, North Sea oil and so on.

Now these are not the sort of debates typically which attract Mr Foot and Mr Powell – even Mr Walden is occasionally found not to be present at these debates. *(Laughter)* But, as far as the ordinary lives and aspirations of the people of this country are concerned, these debates are critical. We have debated Maplin again and again in the Chamber, on the Floor of the House, and speaker after speaker has said to the Government, what is the case for a seaport at Maplin? It's never been made out. They have said to the Government, we now have new noise contours from Government sources, what reduction in noise around Heathrow would they actually mean if applied to that area? We have said we know we're going to have an eight-lane motorway from London to the new Maplin airport and seaport, where is this motorway going to go? It will destroy thousands and thousands of houses, where is it going to go? So what happens? *(Interruption)*

JOHN JENNINGS: Mr Powell.

ENOCH POWELL: We have carried the crucial question in the House of Commons against the Government.

JOHN JENNINGS: Mr Crosland.

ANTHONY CROSLAND: That is perfectly true. Of course the debate can influence what is a preliminary vote. That vote was not the main question, that vote did not destroy Maplin, that vote simply said that before Maplin finally went ahead there was to be another investigation – and it will be a cover-up one, incidentally. That vote was important but was not the end of the battle.

Now the only way of getting this information on Maplin, on the case for the seaport, the noise effects round Heathrow, what is going to be the access route for both the motorway and the rail, the only possible way of doing that is by cross-examination in a Select Committee. And Maplin is not the only example; I can give others, of improvement grants and the rest of it, where we've debated on the Floor of the House again and again what is the extent of the abuse of improvement grants. And of course, debating it like that, the Minister winds up at the end of a short period of time, or else you ask questions at Question Time and he can evade without the slightest difficulty. You cannot get the information. And this is why we want to add – we don't want to replace the Floor of the House by anything – we want to add to the present role of the Chamber an additional role for Select Committees.

JOHN JENNINGS: I now call the Right Honourable Reginald Maudling to sum up for the Opposition. The Right Honourable Reginald Maudling.

RT HON REGINALD MAUDLING: Mr Jennings, the actual wording of the motion is 'That the strengthening of investigatory Select Committees is Parliament's most urgent need'. This is what the proponents of the motion must seek to establish. I don't think so far they have at all.

I wasn't clear whether by strengthening they meant giving them more staff or having more committees. The question of giving people more staff, well maybe there's something in that. But I was interested in what Mr Crossman said about the fact that the information of expenditure on the atom bomb was not disclosed. Surely there was the whole apparatus of the Public Accounts Committee and the Auditor General and all the rest of them already there, and even then this great expenditure was hidden by a Government that wanted to hide it. Maybe these committees are not so effective as is sometimes said.

I think the major part of Mr du Cann's argument though was for having rather more committees and this I think is a fundamental conflict of this debate. As it's a simple fact that if you have more committees you do detract from the Chamber. Members cannot be in two places at once, nor can they expand the total amount of intellectual effort they give to their job. I'm quite certain that the real argument between the two sides in this committee at the moment is between those who give relatively greater or less significance to the Chamber itself, and I've noticed particularly in recent years how the Chamber is almost empty compared to what it was twenty years ago. Even for the winding up of an important debate on a three line whip the benches are relatively sparsely occupied and I believe this is a tragedy of Parliament. I believe this is what we want to put right first of all – I cannot for one moment accept that the most urgent need is more Select Committees. The most urgent need is a better, more effective Chamber, more attuned to the real requirements of the country. And I entirely depart from the attitude of Mr Mackintosh who spoke earlier when he said the primary function of Parliament is to make political rows. This is not the function of Parliament. It may be fun, we may enjoy having political rows, but the function of Parliament is to ensure that the country is being governed in the interests of the people as a whole and the measures taken by the Government are wise, well thought out and properly criticised. I think the first real and most urgent need of Parliament is to cut out a lot of what Mr Scott referred to as the 'political ping-pong', to get away from the sort of yah-boo stuff about

'You did it first anyway', or 'You did it worse than we did', and try and concentrate just a little bit more on what I'm convinced the public of this country want us to concentrate on, how to ensure the measures that are passed, the laws that are passed and the actions taken by the Government are in the real, true interests of the country as a whole. And we can only do this on the major issues if we really concentrate on making the Chamber work. *(Hear, hear)*

JOHN JENNINGS: Mr John Selwyn Gummer.

JOHN SELWYN GUMMER: Well Mr Jennings, I believe that the last speaker has, in fact, made precisely the point that we would have made in defence of this motion. The problem that we have is that the Chamber is not effective enough, not because we are all busy doing other things but because so often the debate is first of all not as informed as it ought to be and secondly, that instead of concentrating upon the real issues we are dealing with the ping-pong of party political differences which are bound to arise if you haven't got an intelligent argument to put forward. And, therefore, what we are asking is for the kind of investigatory Select Committees which would make it possible for those of us who are debating and who wish to debate – and after all, I spent ten years trying to get into the House of Commons, I'm already a devotee of that House, even though so recent *(Interruption* – John Jennings: Lucky man) – but the fact is that we believe that we want to make the Chamber more effective and we don't see how you can make it more effective by indulging in the kind of debate which we've seen, frankly, from the opposition to this motion today. It was very noticeable that both Mr Walden, and, indeed, Mr Foot, made precisely the kind of speech which we're complaining about. Mr Walden tried to lead us astray by a little gentle anti-American propaganda and Mr Foot tried to lead us astray by assuming that we meant that we wanted to close down the Chamber and open up the investigatory committees instead of having the kind of parallelism which we believe in on this side of the House. But it's very odd that when they actually come to look at the issues they are concerned with, they are on our side, and I would remind them that they are very often the people who are most concerned to make a fuss over the papers of the European Parliament and the European institutions. Who are the people who are saying we must have the facts, we must read the material, why hasn't the Government produced this material? It is Mr Foot. I've heard him again and again with enthusiasm if not with accuracy attacking the European institutions for not providing him with the information. Now they have a system for investigating at long last and we are pressing that system. What do we ask in the European Parliament? We want a system of demanding from the Commission the information we ought to have. *(Interruption)*

JOHN JENNINGS: Mr Angus Maude.

ANGUS MAUDE: Surely the question of seeking information about the European Commission and Parliament is a little irrelevant. What we are trying to get there is information about something which is being legislated on and decided about outside the House of Commons and outside our control. Inside, what is within our control in the House of Commons, we have the machinery of Question Time and so forth and the House of Commons can discover.

JOHN SELWYN GUMMER: And what we are proposing is that we want the information about that which is being legislated about in the House of Commons, that information which is not available at the moment. And I will give two examples of that: the first has been mentioned and that is that we have had a number of occasions on which it has taken the activities of outside bodies – and not always the Public Accounts Committee, it's sometimes in the *News of the World* – before we know about some of the things that are going on. And the other example is the Immigration Act. We've just passed an Act about immigration in which we have found a part to be retrospective[1]. Now I have no doubt that there are those who are wise after the event and who will say that they knew about that. But I would suggest that there was an example of an Act, debated on the Floor of the House of Commons, which did something which many Members of the House of Commons didn't know about and if they had known about would, in fact, have got up and complained about. And now why didn't we know that *(Mr Maudling rose)* . . . If I may just finish the sentence. Why did we not know about it? I suspect it is because immigration is another of those subjects which is

[1]The House of Lords ruled that the Immigration Act of 1970 applied retrospectively. Illegal immigrants who entered Britain before the Act was passed became liable to deportation.

either argued by extreme example, from extremists on both sides, or, in fact, by a cover-up job through a consensus operation between the middle on both sides of the House . . .

REGINALD MAUDLING: If Mr Gummer had been in the Chamber at the time of the Report Stage on this Bill, he would have heard me say precisely what the facts are about this. Either he was not there or he wasn't listening.

JOHN SELWYN GUMMER: The fact of the matter is that when Mr Maudling made that point, what was the result? Where was the Act changed? Where did it get into the press? How did we have an alteration? The fact is we are now in an extremely embarrassing position for Government and for Parliament. And the fact is *(Interruptions)* when we talk about the articulation of popular sentiment which Mr Walden said was the main purpose of Parliament, what he means by that, of course, is not the articulation of popular sentiment, it's the articulation of what he thinks popular sentiment ought to be. But I would suggest this; that there is a widespread feeling in the country at the moment that many of the issues that ought to have been raised in Parliament have not been raised, that Members of Parliament have been unable to raise them because their private sources of information have either been too limited or, in fact, have not been used sufficiently. And that, indeed, we ought to be discussing a whole series of issues which we are unable to because we haven't got the means to do it. All that we contend on this side of the House is not that the Chamber should be closed down – far from it – but that the Chamber should be enhanced by the fact that the Members arguing in that Chamber are better informed, more able to get information, more able to seek to cross-examine those who have information, in the conditions which can only be provided by an investigatory Select Committee. If we had such Select Committees I believe that the Chamber would be a better place to be in, it would be a hotter and more difficult place for Ministers, it would be a more exacting place for back-benchers, but it would mean that the public for the first time for a long time would feel that its interests were properly represented.

JOHN JENNINGS: Order. Order. At this point I propose to adjourn the debate. When we return we'll debate the third motion on the Order Paper and also the first motion will be re-opened on the final summing up which will be a general summing up on both sides on the first motion, plus the other two motions. Debate adjourned.

3

JOHN JENNINGS: Order. Order. The third debate is *'That legislative Select Committees are the only way to restore Parliament's proper role in law-making'*. I call upon the Rt Hon Anthony Crosland to propose the motion. Mr Crosland.

ANTHONY CROSLAND: Mr Jennings, I must bring the committee down from the rather giddy rhetorical level to which it has been accustomed so far, to the earthy and often dreary business of how we should examine legislation. And I shall speak entirely of major and highly controversial Bills and not of the run of rather small and non-controversial ones where for all I know the present system may work perfectly well.

Now what is the function of Parliament in respect of legislation? I take it that it has a two-fold function. For example, on the Housing Finance Bill, the first function, the function of Opposition, was to attempt to defeat the Bill, or if not, delay it. The second function, the function of the Standing Committee as a whole, was to examine in detail precisely how fair rents, for example, were to be defined and were to be applied, whether the method of doing so was as efficient and equitable as possible, given that fair rents were going to be imposed by the Government.

Now for the first function, that is to say the running political battle, the present system works tolerably well. Whether the Opposition actually succeeds in amending or delaying or defeating any part of the legislation depends of course on the determination of the Government, and on the Government's ability to retain the loyalty of its back-benchers. On the Housing Finance Bill, despite these endless sittings, the Opposition as such did not secure any major amendment of the Bill. What the Opposition did do was to delay the Bill to the point where a general increase of opposition outside the House of Commons compelled the Government to have some second thoughts, at any rate on the level of fair rents.

But for the second function, that is of proper scrutiny of the Bill, the present system is absolutely hopeless. *(Hear, hear)* Hopeless! For two reasons. First of all the formal procedure, which we have adopted here, of standing up and being called by the

Chairman and making set speeches. For the Opposition this provides an irresistible temptation, as Mr Maudling I think was saying in a previous debate, an irresistible temptation to make lengthy and repeated and innumerable Second Reading speeches rather than to get down to the detail of the Bill. This of course alarms the Government in terms of timetable, so Government back-benchers are then told by their Whips to shut up and not to speak.

JOHN JENNINGS: Order, order. It should be made clear that if that happens in a Standing Committee the Chairman should really call the Hon Member to task, on the question of making Second Reading speeches. He has got to refer to the amendment. I'm not taking sides, I'm merely rising to a matter of order.

ANTHONY CROSLAND: Mr Chairman, I am sure that what you say is absolutely right in terms of proper procedure. All I can say, Mr Jennings is, as we all knew already, you are a very exceptional Chairman. *(Laughter)* And the number of Second Reading speeches that in practice get through in most Standing Committees of course is enormous. And as I say, this then delays the Government's timetable, and the Government Whips tell their own back-benchers they can't speak. For example, we have my colleague on this occasion, Mr Scott, a well-known housing expert, who sat throughout this Bill and we were almost entirely deprived of his advice, alas, on the instruction of his own Whips. And the whole debate keeps going on a level of generality when it ought to be getting down to detail. Eventually, on major Bills, the thing is guillotined, and then large parts of the Bill never get properly discussed at all. That's one reason: this formal procedure encouraging generalised speeches.

The second reason is that we can't cross-examine expert witnesses, and in particular we cannot cross-examine the Civil Servants who have actually drafted the Bill, and this is a great weakness of the present system.

The Minister, if he is skilful, can evade questions that are put to him, as easily – not quite so easily perhaps in Committee as in the House of Commons, but fairly easily. If he is incompetent, as some Ministers, rarely no doubt, but as some Ministers are, then he can only answer the questions that are put to him by receiving bits of paper – he has his Civil

Servants, as you know, sitting near him, passing endless slips of paper to him which he then reads out, normally without understanding them himself. And of course they are impossible to digest under these circumstances. Scribbled bits of paper passed to him by his assistant.

The whole system is ludicrously inefficient, and means that vital points are neglected, hardly discussed at all, or else some superficial attempt is made to discuss them, but then the Minister evades the true questioning, and vital information dribbles out in little bits and pieces, late at night very often, after tedious debate, much too complicated to take in on the spot, without the possibility of coming back to it. And usually too late to affect the decision.

And I conclude from this that it is absolutely essential, with major and controversial Bills, to divide the process of examination into two parts. On the one hand, keep the present system, the present procedure, for major committee debates on the political and controversial parts of the Bill, but go over to a Select Committee procedure with Civil Servants present as witnesses for the detailed scrutiny of the complicated parts of the Bill. And this in my view, as I say, in moving this motion, is the only way to restore Parliament's proper role in legislation. *(Hear, hear)*

JOHN JENNINGS: The question is *'That legislative Select Committees are the only way to restore Parliament's proper role in law-making'*. Mr Angus Maude.

ANGUS MAUDE: Mr Jennings, I think the thing that has struck us on this side of the committee most is the remarkable hyperbole which has characterised both the motions which the other side have been moving today, and the way in which they have moved them. First of all we were told that investigatory Select Committees are Parliament's most urgent need. Now, that legislative Select Committees are the only way of restoring Parliament's proper law-making role. I am going to suggest that legislative Select Committees are not only not the only way to do this, but they are not even the best way, they are not a good way and in fact they are a bad way of dealing with the parliamentary processes.

Mr Crosland I thought half destroyed his case as he went, because he said to start with that legislative committees were defective where you were dealing with major controversial

Bills. And then as a sort of throwaway, he said of course the system of Standing Committees may work all right for the ordinary run of the mill of legislation. Well, the ordinary run of the mill of legislation – perhaps two-thirds, or three-quarters of the Bills which Governments bring forward – are in fact the ones on which most of the running of the country depends. And the Standing Committee system does work well. I don't doubt that Mr Crosland, an ex-Cabinet Minister, now a front-bencher, a Shadow Opposition spokesman, is too important to go to the kind of little Standing Committees on minor Bills which go on in the House all the time. The point is that very often in these Standing Committees you get a genuine give and take of argument and of information between the two sides, often with quite expert members present.

Of course, we know that in fact, as Mr Enoch Powell and Mr Brian Walden have already made clear in previous debates, what the people on the other side of this committee want to do is to produce a quite different kind of Parliament manned by a quite different kind of Member of Parliament from what we have now. What they want is something like the American situation. Now the point about the American situation is that it is the committees which virtually draft and produce and are responsible for the Bills. *(Interruption)*

RICHARD CROSSMAN: Since this is being said now again, is it really the contention of Mr Maude that we over this side, who after all are fellow parliamentarians, want to introduce a written constitution creating a division of power between the Executive on the one side and the legislature on the other? Because otherwise I don't follow his argument. That is the American system. We don't want it here.

ANGUS MAUDE: Of course we are not suggesting that what he wants to do is to introduce a written constitution on the American pattern. What he does want to do is to introduce here a kind of legislative committee which has been set up in the American political system because of their constitution and which is quite irrelevant to the needs of this country and to the functions of this Parliament. *(Interruption)*

ENOCH POWELL: If my honourable friend will permit me. At any rate Richard Crossman has got his written constitution already; it's known as the Treaty of Rome and the Treaty of Brussels. *(Laughter)*

RICHARD CROSSMAN: That was very unfair.

JOHN JENNINGS: Order, order! Mr Angus Maude.

ANGUS MAUDE: I really cannot allow an intervention from Mr Crossman to an intervention by my hon friend Mr Powell in the middle of my speech, nor do I propose to be side-tracked into Europe.

RICHARD CROSSMAN: Hear, hear.

ANGUS MAUDE: I want to make quite clear two things. As Mr Powell said in an earlier debate, the effect of this will not be, as Hon Members opposite purport to say and think, that this will strengthen the powers of Parliament against the Executive. On the contrary, it will in the end strengthen the Executive against the House of Commons, because everything will be pushed away into these committees. Ministers when they are questioned in the Standing Committee, or on Second Reading, will not answer any question. They'll say it has been sent to a committee which can examine the Civil Servants and the experts. That is where the work will be done and these hand-picked committees, selected by the Whips, will take over the investigatory functions of the House of Commons itself. And what they want to do is to produce a new kind of Member of Parliament, as Mr Walden said, the apparatchiks. They want busy experts continually dashing about the corridors of the House of Commons with large green boxes. Becoming themselves experts is not the job of Members of Parliament. The job of the Member of Parliament is to represent his own constituents and to see what is happening to them on the ground in his constituency in detail, as a result of the functioning of Government and the working of the legislation which the House passes. That is his job. Not to be in the Select Committee asking questions about the large issues of technical policy and so forth, but to see how it works out for his constituents.

JOHN JENNINGS: The debate is open. The Rt Hon Edward du Cann.

EDWARD DU CANN: Mr Maude made a great play with the words 'The only way'. I would say that to deal with some legislation Select Committees are the *only* way in fact, and this applies obviously with particular relevance to technical legislation of one kind or another. And to give one example to the committee, Mr Jennings, I suggest that tax is a field where the need for Select Committee examination is perhaps more obvious than any other. One of the unhappiest memories I have of my time in the House was when I found myself a member of the Standing Committee of the House examining the Finance Bill of 1968, I think it was. And the Government was acting – I make no complaint about this – to a necessary timetable, and we found ourselves, at the end of the proceedings of that Standing Committee – (you were not the Chairman, Mr Jennings; had you been I think it might have been all very different perhaps). But at any rate, there was the situation. We found ourselves with a great deal of that Bill wholly unexamined. Wholly unexamined. I believe half a dozen schedules and certainly a dozen or more clauses. Never was there a better case for an investigatory committee than in the case of tax legislation. To hear evidence from the experts, to cross-examine Ministers at great length, Civil Servants, Inland Revenue officials and the rest of them. Now Mr Foot and Mr Powell may well think that since we are, whether we like it or not, members now of the EEC and we have the Treaty of Rome and all the rest of it –

ENOCH POWELL *(Interruption)*: For the time being!

EDWARD DU CANN: For the time being, Mr Powell says. Very well, we're dealing with today and not tomorrow. They may think, perhaps more strongly than anyone else, that here is particular need for the most minute detailed and searching examination of legislation.

Sir, I have no hesitation in supporting Mr Crosland. There is no doubt that in technical matters in particular, this is the only way by which Parliament can do its job.

JOHN JENNINGS: The Rt Hon Enoch Powell.

ENOCH POWELL: Mr Jennings, I cannot help being struck by what wonderful friends Hon Members opposite are to the Executive. *(Hear, hear)* As, if I were a governmentalist, of course I'd be on that side every time. And I noted during Mr Crosland's speech that at least three major benefits which an extension of the Select Committee and the expert committee procedure on legislation would confer upon an Executive. He complains about repetition. Repetition is what governments fear most. When they're on a weak point they'd be only too glad for it to be disposed of at Second Reading. And for the Chairman to say 'Now now now now, we're only here to consider detail in Committee.' It is the fact that in Committee on Clause 1, Clause 2, oh the same point comes up and up again and again until eventually the Government gets rattled on it and the weakness of their case begins to appear. I happen to be sitting at the moment on a Select Committee on a Bill where the Government was defeated yesterday.

ANGUS MAUDE *(Interruption)* : Standing Committee.

ENOCH POWELL: On a Standing Committee on the Bill. Now that wasn't the first time that point had been raised. It had been raised, I imagine just on the edge of order, about half a dozen times before during the proceedings. And by the time the Government got to the particular amendment, they knew they were beaten. I very much doubt if they would have been beaten on it if there hadn't been that constant rattling process of repetition. Repetition, whether we like it or not, boring or not, is part of the parliamentary process and it's very effective.

Then there was his second point, that Ministers are often incompetent to explain their Bills. Quite true. And what's his solution? Why the poor dears, they oughtn't to be expected to. *(Laughter)* They ought to be able to bring their officials. But one of the effects of the parliamentary process is to show up the incompetence of Ministers. *(Hear, hear)* A Minister has no right to come before the House of Commons with a Bill if he can't explain the provisions of it. And he has no right to be allowed to say – 'Oh this is very complicated, this is a matter for experts.' After all he's making law by which people are to be bound; at least it's a minimum requirement that he should understand it himself. *(Hear, hear)* And in the committee we have the opportunity to show him up. And we have all of us seen Ministers whose career was ended by being pulverised because it was realised that they couldn't explain their own Bills. I want to keep them there, and there's no place for it like a Standing Committee, which is the microcosm of the House, and the House of Commons itself. *(Interruption)*

ANTHONY CROSLAND: Perhaps I could point out to Mr Powell that the Minister whose incompetence on the Housing

Finance Bill prevented any proper explanation of the Bill at all, has subsequently been promoted.

ENOCH POWELL: Well there are ways *(Laughter)* – there are ways and ways of dealing with – well – I don't want to use the word incompetence in a personal context. *(Hear, hear)* But I think the Rt Hon Gentleman has helped me to make my point. *(Laughter)*

And finally his notion was astonishing that you can separate the political parts of a Bill from the non-political part. Surely all of us know by experience that quite suddenly in examining an apparently innocuous clause, first of all Members discover that it means something different from what they've imagined and is more important, and secondly they realise there is a political intention behind it. That lurking beneath the apparent technicalities there was a political will. No, we're here to do a political job. We cannot shift that political job over (and it is one hundred per cent political) either to the interrogation of experts, nor can we delegate it to a committee of ourselves, whose business is not to be political but to be expert. And once again I say, this would be the dream of all Governments, to have an extension of this development. That is why we shall oppose it. *(Interruption)*

RICHARD CROSSMAN: Could we have one question?

JOHN JENNINGS: One question, Mr Crossman.

RICHARD CROSSMAN: I was just listening very carefully to the point about how you can't separate off what's called the political from the non-political. Now I am surprised at the gentleman saying this, because I had thought that the compromise we reached on the Finance Bill Committee Stage was broadly acceptable to people on the other side here, where we have in fact kept the controversial on the Floor of the House and put the less controversial into committee upstairs. Is he saying we have done a bad reform there, because I think it would be highly relevant to have that made clear?

JOHN JENNINGS: Mr Powell.

ENOCH POWELL: In my opinion no single change has been more disastrous to the House of Commons than the splitting of the consideration of the Finance Bill into four or five purely formal general debates – that is what they are – and an examination of what is called the detail, in Committee. And this is wholly on the Government's side, which is why one Government after another proposes and continues it. It prevents whatever time may be necessary being taken by ordinary Members of the House of Commons to discuss which clauses and which aspects they want to discuss. The all-night sittings, the series of all-night sittings on the Finance Bill, the fact that the Government couldn't guillotine the Finance Bill on the Floor of the House has been the strength of the individual Member and has been the strength of the tiny minority perhaps of members of the public who were affected by Clause 123. Because sure enough at three o'clock in the morning, when we were all groaning, nevertheless their case was going to get put. That case has no assurance, indeed somebody opposite said that, of being put under this system. *(Hear, hear)*

JOHN JENNINGS: One more speaker from the floor. Then I'll call the winding-up speakers. Mr Selwyn Gummer.

JOHN SELWYN GUMMER: Mr Jennings, I believe very strongly that our purpose is to represent our constituents. And it's very well for those who are oratorically inclined to be able to make a great deal of what they are able to say on the Floor of the House, and to show what their constituents at three o'clock in the morning think about something. But if their constituents then remain with their evils unremedied because of the system that we have, that is to the benefit of Mr Enoch Powell but not to the people of Wolverhampton. And I want the people of Wolverhampton to have their remedy actually found in the House of Commons. And I believe that that's more likely to be done if we are able to take the sensible decision, which is that there are many technicalities which actually can be seen as the way in which the Bill will work out in practice. At the moment many Bills get through Parliament unamended because everything is argued on the party political division and much which could have been improved, if we could have a system which enabled you to look at the matter more closely in technical terms, is not so done.

Now it was suggested, for example, that these systems we have at the moment, of Standing Committees, work very well. Well I sat for months on the Agriculture (Miscellaneous Pro-

visions) Bill, *(Hear, hear)* a matter of no argument at all between the parties. But there was a long speech, when we
were discussing slaughterhouses, on mink farms. Now I
agree, Mr Jennings, that you were not in the chair. But we
were discussing mink farms at great length. None of us knew
anything about mink farms. But the people who are concerned with mink farms would, I think, have been much
helped if we had been able to call some evidence, instead of
talking for a very long time about a point which turned out in
the end not in fact to be relevant to the Bill at all – which an
expert could have told us in two minutes.

And then I believe that it is true that the level of distortion is
directly connected with the level of ignorance. It is easy to
distort an argument if you know nothing about it, and one of
the great desires of some people in the House of Commons is
for us to be ignorant in order that they, by their oratorical
skill, can distort an argument.

ANGUS MAUDE: Would the Hon Member give way?

JOHN JENNINGS: Mr Maude.

ANGUS MAUDE: Is he really suggesting that it may be easy
to distort an argument to people who are ignorant? But there
is no person who is better able to distort an argument than the
man who is crammed with technical knowledge and pro-
ceeds to blind you with science. And you have no means of
knowing whether he's telling the truth or not.

JOHN SELWYN GUMMER: And therefore you do in fact need
a Select Committee in order to make sure that he can't, and
this is of course what Ministers do.

ANGUS MAUDE: You need to subject him to six hundred
Members of Parliament.

JOHN SELWYN GUMMER: This is precisely what Ministers
do. They get up and they bore the pants off us with long
series of technical arguments which we have no means of
checking . . .

ANTHONY CROSLAND: Absolutely right – quite right.

JOHN SELWYN GUMMER: . . . and which a Select Committee would enable us to check. And I believe that Ministers have increased the power of government very considerably in proportion to the level at which they've increased the boredom of Standing Committees, because what they have done is to enable people not to question them effectively on a whole series of issues which we ought to know about.

JOHN JENNINGS: I call upon the Right Hon Charles Pannell to reply for the Opposition. Mr Charles Pannell.

CHARLES PANNELL: If you take the terms of the motion, which we'd better get back to, 'That legislative Select Committees are the only way to restore Parliament's proper role in law-making', that almost leaves one breathless, because nobody seems to have glimpsed the idea of how far this business has gone already. I'd better give some of the figures of how far this disease has gone and wonder what time Members of Parliament have left. The total number of Members appointed to serve on Standing Committees in 1971/72 was 497 – rather bigger than my colleague suggested. The total number on Select Committees already in the last session was 250. There is a grand total of 747 appointments and there are only 630 Members of Parliament. So if they gave their full time to the Select Committees and the Standing Committees and bring all the brains and homework to bear they seem to have a busy time. We want rather more than a twenty-four hour day.

And now, the point really about Standing Committees – I'm surprised that somebody, Mr Crosland, didn't make that charge – that generally speaking the people on the Standing Committees of course are often dumb driven cattle, and . . .

JOHN JENNINGS: What?

CHARLES PANNELL: . . . people on Standing Committees are dumb driven cattle. I'm not referring to the chairman, but I'm referring to the members . . .

JOHN JENNINGS: As long as that's clear!

CHARLES PANNELL: . . . and this therefore has gone a long way. Now I've never served on a Select Committee or Standing Committee but what I haven't found that it's drained some of my interest away from the Chamber. There's another thing too. I notice that Mr Selwyn Gummer did not give way to me previously when I wanted to bring him back to the Immigration Bill. Now that is the case *par excellence*. On that case, we not only had a legislative Standing Committee, we had a Select Committee. And some members of that Select Committee do nothing else: they go up and down the country, they interview in our constituencies all sorts of organisations concerned with the coloured people and they do, I've no doubt, a first class job of work. But with all that they missed out the retrospective legislation. The combined brains of all of them had to be investigated and finally, I suppose, interpreted by the House of Lords to leave the monstrous injustice that we know is before us today. *(Interruption)*

NICHOLAS SCOTT: It strikes me he's totally missed the point about the motion that we're discussing now, which is that we need *legislative* Select Committees. We don't have a legislative Select Committee on race relations and immigration. It takes topic by topic and investigates that. Had the . . .

JOHN JENNINGS: Order, order, the honourable gentleman can make this point in his winding up speech. It's taking up valuable time.

CHARLES PANNELL: Well I think the honourable gentleman is confusing the issue. We had this raised previously. After all we had a legislative Standing Committee, nobody would doubt that, and we've had another committee which is a Select Committee. Doesn't matter whether it was a legislative one or not. We presumably had the ideal of the other side of two Committees and still the point was missed.

JOHN JENNINGS: I call upon Mr Nicholas Scott to sum up for the proposers. Mr Nicholas Scott.

NICHOLAS SCOTT: Mr Jennings, Mr Pannell's collection of statistics may not have added much to our argument but they were certainly a tribute to the research assistants that he has managed to acquire in some way . . .

CHARLES PANNELL: I did it myself.

NICHOLAS SCOTT: . . . well – to his own ingenuity! But I do

183

think he's failed really to understand what this motion is all about, and therefore I think much of his winding-up was very wide of the mark.

Now Mr Maude in opening this debate made great play, as others have in the course of our debates today, of the horror of some new breed of Member of Parliament who is going to be an expert, who is going to in some way corrupt the whole nature of Parliament by the acquisition of a new level of expertise.

Mr Maude went on to make claims for the good working of the present system and Mr Powell found some merit in the war of attrition argument, that simply repetition, repetition, repetition, will work, grind down the will of Government and make them accept amendments. But let's look and see for a moment, Mr Jennings, just how effective this process actually is. There was a study done by PEP which analysed every Government Bill during the sessions 1967/68, 68/69 and 70/71 and it looked at the way in which the Commons scrutinised and amended that legislation. The Commons spent over three and a half thousand hours looking at it and there were over 4000 amendments moved by people who were not Government Ministers. And the sum achievement of *significant* changes by the Commons in those three sessions were

nine amendments passed at Committee Stage,
nine amendments passed at Report Stage,
seven Government clauses defeated at Committee Stage.

And even if you add on, as it is right to do, the number of times that Governments listened to debates in Committee and then came back and introduced their own amendments at Report Stage, we only added 125 amendments to the total passed in those three sessions, and it seemed to me a pretty inefficient and wasteful way of seeking to amend Government legislation, persuade them to change their minds[1].

I would also think that . . . *(Interruption)*

BRIAN WALDEN: But if Mr Powell's argument is going to be rejected that easily, perhaps PEP has done a study on what happened to the House of Lords Reform Bill of Mr Crossman? Wasn't that ground down? Not simply amended but

[1]Mr Scott is here referring to Professor Griffith's study, other data from which are given on pages 124–127.

withdrawn and non-existent because of the process of attrition?

NICHOLAS SCOTT: No. The one thing that was absent there was any sort of will on the part of the Government. They weren't committed to their legislation and they weren't prepared to fight for it and so Mr Powell and Mr Foot were allowed to have a field day.

I think too that, as Mr Crosland said, the absurd chain of whispers and notes that pass backwards and forwards in a Standing Committee do Parliament no good at all. For brief periods on that committee, on the Housing Finance Bill Committee, I was asked to sit behind the Minister in the absence of his own Parliamentary Private Secretary. And as someone who was fairly new in the ways of Parliament, my life was rapidly changed because I suddenly saw the 'notes on clauses' that were produced by the Civil Servants that interpreted the real purpose behind amendments that were being moved by Ministers and analysed the motives of Opposition. And it made me aware for the first time really, just how huge was the gap in knowledge between most members of the committee and the Ministers concerned. *(Hear, hear)* And I believe that a Select Committee procedure would narrow this gap in knowledge and get a better balance of knowledge between the Ministers and those others who were taking part.

We've seen – I won't quote the Americans again, because that seems to offend Members on the other side of the House, but the Canadians who share our own system have, since 1968, been running a system of Select Committees on legislation and over three-quarters of the Canadian Members of Parliament who were polled on the results of that believe that it has improved their way of dealing with legislation.

I believe that I need no further convincing that the Select Committee would in the overwhelming majority of cases be an infinitely better way of handling our legislation at Committee Stage. And I therefore urge the committee to support this motion.

JOHN JENNINGS: Order, order. We now revert to the first motion.

Now I should be grateful if Messrs Crossman, Mackintosh, Foot and Powell would resume their original places on the front-benches – and I don't want that phrase to be taken any other way than procedural-wise! *(Laughter; MPs change places)*

JOHN JENNINGS: You'll remember that the first motion was *'That MPs are too ignorant to do their job properly'*. Now this debate which will take place, for another half hour or so, can include everything that's gone before in this committee, in other words it can include anything contained in the text of the three motions. Now the debate is open. Mr John Mackintosh.

JOHN MACKINTOSH: It seems to me that we have made some progress, though like most major debates in the House of Commons there has, I think, been too little answering directly of one speech by another. Nevertheless I think we have made some progress and I have the impression that one of the major arguments of the Opposition is that while they will accept the need for some Select Committees, and in fact they accept that we have them and that it has neither Americanised the House nor destroyed the House, they are arguing that having Select Committees damages the Floor of the House, the Chamber, the major debating function. And the only evidence they have tried to produce for this is the suggestion that if Members of Parliament are not in the Chamber, it is because they are in Select Committees upstairs. And that if there were fewer Select Committees these fellows would pour into the Chamber and there they would all sit listening to Mr Powell or listening to Mr Foot.

But what are the facts? Let us look at the situation. Last night in the House there was a debate on foreign affairs, one of our rare debates on foreign affairs. For the bulk of the time there were between eleven and sixteen Members on the Floor of the House waiting to speak. I checked at the time that there were four committees sitting with a total of sixty Members in attendance. And the suggestion is that the other 350 Members who were present in the building would have been in the Chamber if these four Select Committees weren't sitting? It doesn't hold at all. They were doing other things. And if those four Select Committees hadn't been meeting, there is no evidence that the sixty people there would have been in the Chamber. This does not arise at all. And in fact if you want to revive the Chamber you've got to give it the power to embarrass, attack, and damage the Government. And that is why I am with Mr Powell and Mr Foot when they say this is the fundamental task of the House. I want to equip it to do this task better.

There is a further point, that the House does not just consist of Chamber orators and Chamber listeners. There are many people with other abilities in the House and I think they are under-utilised. And we might also consider what the MPs themselves want to do. When in the last Parliament we asked MPs whether they wanted to serve on Standing Committees, Standing Legislative Committees, only nine per cent said yes. The vast majority said they were a waste of time and they had to be dragooned on to them. But over fifty per cent said they wanted to serve on Select Committees because they then could get biting on the subjects that mattered to them and they could really put it across the Government.

I was very interested in Mr Powell's two comments that if he was the Executive, if he were the Civil Servants and the Ministers, he would pile the place high with Select Committees. But you know they don't. They hate Select Committees, they detest them; it was because of the attitude of the Whitehall Civil Servants that the two Select Committees we had on agriculture and education were closed down. They kicked like mustangs when they were invited up to explain why. As for the idea that these committees shield an incompetent Minister, I can't understand how this suggestion could be made. It doesn't take a very able Minister to bat aside one supplementary at Question Time. But on the other hand if you have a Minister for an hour and a half before a Select Committee and you've already heard what his officials have got to say, he's then put through his paces in a way which never happens otherwise.

It's part of the task of Parliament to hold civil servants responsible, to make them explain themselves, to make them account for what they're doing and to make Ministers explain themselves, and doing this in only one place, on the Floor of the House, is grossly inefficient. This is what we did 100 years ago when we had a small Executive, doing very little. And if you've got four or five different committees beavering away, utilising the energies of Members who are not great Floor orators but can do the committee work, pestering and questioning and pointing out, who therefore have an occupation which is more important to them than becoming a Junior Minister – and that's very important – this is of vital value to the future of Parliament.

Occasionally they would strike oil, occasionally they'd get a really hot issue, and there we'd see the television cameras and people being grilled and what's wrong with that? What is wrong with other methods of holding the Executive responsible than just the Chamber?

We want now to have a Parliament which is as multi-equipped and has got as many methods of holding on to the Executive as the Executive have methods of dealing with the public. And until we have that, people's respect for Parliament will continue to decline.

JOHN JENNINGS: Mr Brian Walden.

BRIAN WALDEN: Mr Mackintosh complains that speeches don't always follow directly on each other – let me take him up at once, Mr Jennings, on – I don't know whether it was a slip, I rather suspect not – on what I regard as a quite crucial statement, much more important than anything else in what he just said. That it was the function of Parliamentarians to question *Civil Servants* about ministerial policy. It isn't. It's sometimes done and I'm not wholly opposed to the idea, but the principal job of Parliamentarians is to question *Ministers* about ministerial policy. And the principal function of Ministers is not particularly to be any more expert than the rest of us except in a very narrow area, but to be able to keep their wicket up under that kind of questioning and I suspect – I will give way – I suspect that at heart Mr Mackintosh doesn't like that system. *(Interruption)*

JOHN JENNINGS: Mr Mackintosh.

JOHN MACKINTOSH: I like the system enormously, but I just put it to you that you take one big Ministry like the Department of Trade and Industry – there are over sixty Assistant Secretaries making policy. They're not just advising the Minister. They're making policy. And if Parliament simply says, 'It is the Minister' it restricts itself to a tiny control over that department.

JOHN JENNINGS: Mr Walden.

BRIAN WALDEN: But if Parliament says that it isn't the Minister, then a vital link has been broken in the chain. The

Minister is responsible, that has to be our theory else we cease to be what we are. But I rose, Mr Jennings, to very briefly make two other points. One to slightly blot the escutcheon of these committees which are emerging more and more as the answer to all the maiden's prayers. I want to say a word or two having served on one, about a few of their failings which haven't been mentioned. And secondly to say a brief word on this vexed subject of oratory which is already deeply concerning Mr Crosland and Mr Gummer – plain, witless men who obviously would never dream of using oratorical devices – and is even beginning, apparently, if we judge his last remarks, to concern Mr Mackintosh. First of all . . . *(Laughter)*

The picture that is being given of one group of earnest plain men who are doing their homework and wish only to contribute to the legislative process, as against a group of demagogic orators wholly without the power of analysis who nevertheless demoniacally grip their colleagues' imagination, is a farce. And the other side of the committee knows it's a farce. *(Hear, hear)* The truth is that the other side of the committee though, as we do, recognising the value of interrogation and knowledge, will not accept the value of what goes on in the Chamber. *(Interruption* 'Not true'*)* However much they deny it, basically they despise the whole theory behind a Minister having to prove himself in the Chamber. And for that matter a Member having to prove himself in the Chamber.

JOHN JENNINGS: The Rt Hon Enoch Powell.

ENOCH POWELL: I only want to make one point briefly, Mr Jennings, but it is I think the crucial one and is the test question. I just put this question. And I put it with confidence to Honourable Members on both sides who have been in office themselves. Of what is it that a Minister and the Cabinet are most afraid? What test is it that they have in their minds, other than that of the next election, when they elaborate policy and legislation? Do they say, what if a Select Committee were to get at this? Do they say, what would *(Interruption)* . . . yes, but what are they afraid of?

RICHARD CROSSMAN: Being found out.

ENOCH POWELL: Being found out – and where are they afraid of being found out and exposed?

RICHARD CROSSMAN: In the Select Committees.

ENOCH POWELL: No, the Right Honourable gentleman cannot say that. That is the test about which – *(Mr John Selwyn Gummer rose)* – the Honourable Member needn't intervene. He hasn't got this experience. I am putting this to those who have experienced it. Of what is it that Governments are most afraid? I say they are most afraid of the House of Commons and it is only the House of Commons that ever destroys a Minister or – outside an election – an administration.

JOHN JENNINGS: I now call Mr Michael Foot to sum up on behalf of the Opposition for the whole debate. Mr Michael Foot.

MICHAEL FOOT: Mr Jennings, if I may, could I seek to approach this question obliquely from the start. It appears maybe that we have been discussing questions of procedure in the House of Commons, and complicated matters of that nature, but we are in my opinion discussing something which affects the health of democratic politics in our country as a whole. And, although great, important freedoms may be embodied in procedures, we are seeking to discover how we can make democracy work properly in this country. It would be futile for us, in my opinion, to conduct the debate solely on the basis of saying – we on this side are in favour of all power to the Floor of the House of Commons and no power to committees and that Honourable Members on that side of the House should take exactly the opposite view. That is not the case. There is a balance. It is a kind of see-saw and what we are saying is that when you put such almighty weight on investigatory committees or Select Committees as is proposed by the proposers of this motion, then the see-saw will tip up and the Floor of the House of Commons will lose its authority and lose its influence. Indeed part of my contention certainly is that this has already occurred on a very serious scale. I am certainly not a defender of the present *status quo*. I do not think it is satisfactory at all. I think there have been a whole series of developments which have gravely injured the power and authority and the affection of the British House of Commons among the people of this country.

Some examples were given in some of the cross-examinations in the first discussion [pages 111–115], how in fact a Government has made such complicated and detailed arrangements and commitments to outside bodies that when they came to the House of Commons and to the Standing Committees, their hands were tied. That is an intolerable situation. One which only a few years ago would have been absolutely abhorred. Aneurin Bevan, who introduced that huge Bill, the Health Act, into the House of Commons, refused to make any detailed commitment whatsoever and explained to all the outside bodies that he must hold himself free when it came to the House of Commons to change his mind or to listen to what the House of Commons had to say. And we should seek to restore that. I also say as an example, I think one of the most serious threats to the power of the House of Commons is the notion which is growing up that you can have a meeting in Downing Street of the Executive and the CBI and the TUC who make an agreement that is binding and when it comes to the House of Commons the House of Commons has not the power, as is inferred, to tear that bargain apart. Now that, that is the kind of danger that we have to guard against. Also I don't propose to go into the details of it, but by far the most wide-ranging and calculated surrender by the House of Commons of its powers was of course the Common Market Act which has not merely given away powers to institutions in Europe but has given away powers from Parliament to the Executive here on a scale that is only now beginning to be conceived by some of those people who were responsible for doing it. But what I am trying to underline in this sense is: if MPs don't do their job – and very often they neglect it – it's not because of the institution itself, it is because of the way in which the institution and the machinery have been used.

Indeed one of the great virtues of the House of Commons is it's so flexible, it is so little dependent upon any written rules, it gives so great leverage even to single members. And by the way it's not only a question of orators. Some of the most effective Members of Parliament over the years have been crashing bores: precisely because of their persistence the House of Commons gave them access to itself.

And so the whole system depends on access to the House of Commons, whatever other means you may say they must go through first. Mr Mackintosh at the beginning of these proceedings, tried to make the argument as if it was one between those who wished to have facts at their disposal and those who believed in something else, and he recalled some occasion when I'd said that I didn't want the facts to interfere with my argument. I'm sorry that this instructive hyperbole fell on such stony ground. (MACKINTOSH – *Interruption* – 'I believe you'). But it happens to have a great deal of virtue in it because if you have too many facts, it destroys the argument, and it is the argument which people want to hear. The business of Members of the House of Commons of course is to equip themselves properly, not merely by Select Committees but by every available means, to acquire the facts, but their main business is to judge one set of facts as compared with another set of facts and all the time to be suspicious and sceptical of what experts in particular sets of facts or experts in particular Departments happen to say to us. The whole complication of modern government is how by democratic means you can have a body debating who will be able to discuss these complicated measures and to put them into some kind of coherent form, so that the nation can understand what people are saying here and so that the nation can say to the people here what they want to say.

And it is this process that I say would be so gravely injured if we go so much further along the road of transferring the effective influence and power away from the Floor of the House of Commons to many of these cosy committees. We were told about jamming the pipeline and that some mischievous people had been trying to hold up another Bill because they objected to the Government's programme in general. What's wrong with that? There's nothing wrong with that at all. That is the way for an Opposition to succeed, if it's got the command of the nation behind it, to burst the pipe, and that's what they try to do. They don't always succeed – they don't always succeed in doing it, but they've got a perfect right to do it. Now, I know the remedy, but he suggested, Mr Crosland suggested, 'Oh, you must make the debates orderly, you must make everything go according to the time-table.' Oh yes, that's what he's suggesting. If you remove the sanction of long debates, repetitious debates, boring debates, you would remove all the sanction about time. Indeed these gravediggers of debate, they would produce the tidiness of the tomb. That'll be the result of such measures. *(Interruption)*

JOHN JENNINGS: Mr Crosland.

ANTHONY CROSLAND: This is a straight factual misunderstanding. My point was that the Committee Stage of a Bill should be divided into two separate procedures. One would be the Select Committee procedure for the highly technical parts of the Bill. The remainder, the political and controversial parts of the Bill would go as now on Standing Committee lines and as far as I'm concerned I agree with Mr Foot on this: the Opposition can delay for as long and as long and as long as it likes.

MICHAEL FOOT: I think that that has already been dealt with on the question of the Finance Bill. The more you have the division between the parts of the Bill that are supposed to be major and the ones that are supposed to be minor, you give again to the Executive and its majority in the House of Commons the power to choose which is to go into one area and which is to go into another and there's no doubt that this can gravely injure the way in which such debates proceed.

But I conclude with this because there's hardly any time left: what we are concerned about is maintaining the party battle, the conflict of clash of interest. And the real issues must come out into the House of Commons. All the remedies that are proposed on the other side would reduce the party struggle, would reduce the clash of interests, would reduce the clash of politics generally. It would reduce it to a technical affair. I don't say they want to imitate American methods. I think many of them want to imitate many of the methods used in the Common Market. This is coalition politics. That's the way they run their politics there. We don't believe in it in this country and most of the measures that are proposed as a remedy by speakers on that side of the House would thrust, plunge us into the kind of coalition methods which would destroy the real clash and battle of democracy in this country.

JOHN JENNINGS: I call the Right Honourable Mr Richard Crossman to sum up for the proposition on the whole debate. Mr Crossman.

RICHARD CROSSMAN: I have a little difficulty, Chairman, in really winding up the debate. Already as the result of debating in this House of Commons form, we have become artificially turned into two blocks. Of course I agree with Michael about Europe, and with Enoch about Europe, and we have divisions of every kind between us. But I've noticed, we don't need the whips here almost: we're lined up now, we have passion here, we're artificially divided. And this of course is what happens in politics. It is absolutely essential it should happen, but it's also essential one should be able to regain one's sanity when one leaves the Chamber. *(Interruption)*

JOHN JENNINGS: That's what I'm here for.

RICHARD CROSSMAN: I don't think myself, Chairman, you can induce sanity, or what we would call sanity, into the debate. I don't think we can. I think we're stirred up and we go back.

Of course Enoch Powell – he always does – I must answer him first direct. This first key issue is one which he and I, with some ministerial responsibilities both of us, I think we genuinely disagree about this. I was the Leader of the House when we first introduced these specialist committees. I can never forget the passionate opposition of most Members of the Cabinet, briefed by their Permanent Secretaries. *(Interruption* – POWELL: 'They had to take the brunt of it –'*)* They hated it. I'm only saying the idea that Whitehall wants to be pulled out and cross-examined is a delusion. If anybody here thinks the Executive, in terms of the officials liked it, of course the answer is not – they detested it. They may have partly good reasons for wanting to remain anonymous, but there's a great resistance to investigation.

I think on balance the existence of it or the increase of it will in fact be alarming to an Executive and really I feel a certain one-sidedness about the opposition. All I am saying to the opposition is that cross-examination has a place in parliamentary affairs as well as debate. We need to cross-examine, we need to debate. We need debate more on certain subjects such as the big confrontations. The major issues are much better debated on the Floor. There are areas where cross-examination is even actually I think more important than debate. *(Interruption* – MAUDLING: 'Of Ministers or Civil Servants?'*)* Of both. Of course both. I think a Minister is subjected to a far greater test by a Select Committee in a couple of hours. I only had one experience: I had to work far harder to prepare my position on population, as a matter of fact, when I was cross-examined on it by a Select Committee, than I ever had to bother about Question Time; I mean we all know that the usual parliamentary devices for testing Ministers are weak compared to the power the Minister has, unfortunately, through the Whips and through his unusual authority and his information. And therefore I do think it's unwise to rule out the importance of cross-examination if it's used on the right thing.

Now here we come to the second thing. I don't think I agree with Michael Foot entirely, our institutions need improving. Our debating institutions are pretty good but the committee system I think, especially the Standing Committee – Mr Crosland's absolutely right – is intolerable. I don't agree with his particular solution and I won't go into it. I would be much more drastic. I would go for the Select Committee the whole way through and banish the whole confrontation technique in a committee upstairs. But I do really believe in cross-examination. I happen to delight in being cruel to wickedness, in hunting it out and exposing it. And I know that a Minister will be weakened far more and tested if he's put up against it morning after morning. I think myself that what's going on in America proves that all right.[1]

Now I suggest we want to send certain parts of legislation to Select Committee, to take it off the Floor. Now we heard all this praise of the Floor and admission that it's empty most days. I'll say why it's empty. Because it isn't worth listening to. Because most of what is discussed on the Floor is unsuitable for general debate between 625 people, because it's better discussed in small areas. Of course we've got to make sure of the ultimate right for the House as a whole or the individual to get at a thing on the Floor. But I would try as far as possible on a whole mass of legislation, parts of Bills, whole Bills, to see that most of the work is done upstairs, because there's really basically not so much to debate, and leave more room on the Floor for the things which ought to be debated: the great issues of politics should have more time on the Floor. And the reason it's empty is because the Floor is so often irrelevant to the needs of the people. Now that's why I think myself that the main thing we've got to face is that the wrong things are debated on the Floor. The wrong things are debated there constantly. You have the details of Bills, the business of Standing Committees; four-fifths of them are unsuitable for debate and therefore we people don't sit there.

Now Enoch Powell, he loved the old days, the day after day in the summer of the Finance Bill. If anything made the public

[1] The debate took place at the time of the Watergate hearings.

think we were idiotic it was the day after day of all-night debates, sitting about, sitting and boozing in the Smoking-room or walking up and down the Terrace, none of us in the Chamber, except one or two. This was a fine old idea and it was a delicious thing. I like to remember I was part of it, but I'm very proud that I reduced the amount of all-night sittings because I think on the whole they should not be necessary.

And now I come to the final point I want to make. That is that the other need for investigation is to ensure that we get things debated in Parliament in time. Very often there are great issues which remain undebated year after year and then we have to rush legislation through at the last moment. Think of local government corruption. Now we leave this to the Attorney-General and the Public Prosecutor and say because there's a prosecution on therefore we close our mind to the whole area. But we can't debate that effectively on the Floor. We need first to investigate it. Yes, and MPs should go and interfere and look inside local government and see what's going on. I would like to see that investigated in that way.

I'll tell you another one – National Assistance and the whole question of supplementary benefits, where legislation is urgent and necessary. We put up a Departmental Committee – hope-less. Send the MPs out to see what's going on and see how much corruption there is. Let them go round and see the things, be seen seeing it, be seen in the press, be seen on tele-vision. That I think is the way to make Parliament relevant and make our debates relevant as well. *(Hear, hear)*

JOHN JENNINGS: Thank you. That brings us to the end of the debate. This committee is now adjourned.

A brief look at the Granada Survey

by David McKie

Reprinted from *The Guardian* with additional tables

A full report on the Granada Survey of public attitudes towards Parliament, prepared by Ivor Crewe of the Department of Government, University of Essex, is due to be published by Macmillan in 1974.

DAVID McKIE on new poll findings which restore MPs' good image

Political cynic cure

Two weeks after one opinion poll found widespread disillusion with politicians and their works, another poll has given them a relatively favourable bill of health. The picture of MPs as 'the untrusted men who don't run Britain' – to quote the *Sunday Times* headline on its report of an Opinion Research Centre poll for the *Sunday Times* and BBC, is not borne out by the findings of the second poll which was carried out by National Opinion Polls for the Granada TV series, *The State of the Nation* which starts tonight.

The Granada poll, too, was a more sophisticated operation than the BBC's. There was a larger sample (NOP used a random sample of 2,000, ORC a quota sample of 1,000) and a longer list of questions. But the Granada exercise also sought to go beyond snap answers to simple questions, attempting to draw out the underlying attitudes of mind of the respondents.

The BBC poll found that 58 per cent of the sample believed that 'MPs are there for their own gain or ambition'. The Granada poll put a similar contention – 'politicians are in politics for what they can get out of it' and found that 39 per cent agreed while 33 per cent disagreed. But when they asked 'Why do you think people become MPs?', by far the most popular single answer was 'to serve the people' (mentioned by 29 per cent). Runners up were: 'to do something for the country' mentioned by 19 per cent, 'because they are interested in politics' (15 per cent), and, first among the cynical responses, 'for the money' (13 per cent).

The Granada findings showed, as did the BBC-*Sunday Times* ones, that MPs were thought to have little real power in running the country. But figures in the Granada poll suggest that they are not accordingly judged to be ineffective. What the Granada survey seems to show is that people do not send MPs to Westminster to see them running the country so much as to prosecute causes and get rid of grievances on their behalf.

The respondent was asked to imagine three possible situations. First, a motorway was about to be built next to his house. Second, he might wish to change the laws on crime. Third, he might wish to have old age pensions increased. To whom, in such situations, would he turn for help?

In each case, the MP was named far more often than the local councillor, government department, local authority department or anyone else.

People were also asked: is your MP doing a good job? A fair job? Or a poor job? It was immediately noticeable that the blanket criticism which seems sometimes to be applied to MPs as a breed was not reflected in judgments of individuals. Responses were: a good job, 26 per cent; a fair job, 35 per cent; a poor job, 8 per cent; don't know, 30 per cent.

A similar pattern emerged from responses to two linked questions, one asking how valuable to the community the respondent believed certain jobs to be, the other asking how much influence each job had in making decisions affecting the community. MPs were rated as having little influence but considerable value.

The image of the MP (in Table A) as the devoted servant of his constituents' direct interests and as a kind of public leaning post in times of affliction is not one they themselves necessarily cherish. Some like the role of constituency ombudsman and free aid service which is wished upon them; others resent it as a distraction from their real purposes in life.

How cynical are the British public about politicians? Table B shows a surprisingly balanced result: on three out of five questions, about as many express views that are positive or favourable as cynical or negative. Only one question in the Table drew an extreme adverse response from a substantial majority: faced with the statement, 'MPs will promise anything to get votes,' 64 per cent agreed (the negative response) and only 24 per cent disagreed. But perhaps this does not indicate cynicism so much as a realistic understanding by the public that the first job of an MP is to get himself elected.

An overwhelming majority (66 per cent) say that the MP should first represent the views of his constituents. (Table C). Electors aged 18–24 (72 per cent) and the middle class (71 per cent) produce the largest majorities for this choice. The *local* party's views come second among the total sample's priorities;

all groups agree that the MP's own views should be considered least. However in response to an earlier question, 57 per cent agreed that 'MPs should use their own judgment, even if they go against public opinion'. This apparent contradiction may be explained by the fact that a single question which offers no guidance as to the possible alternative answers is likely to be less significant than a question which invites the respondent seriously to explore a range of possibilities.

The successes of the Welsh and Scottish Nationalist parties in both local and Parliamentary elections caused the Labour Government in 1968 to set up the Royal Commission on the Constitution to devise ways of sharing power with these apparently discontented distant regions.

It might be expected that public hostility to Parliament would be stronger in Scotland and Wales than say in the Home Counties. The finding of the Granada survey is therefore significant: the attitude of the Scots and the Welsh is not substantially different from that of the English. The English, the Scots and the Welsh feel equally strongly that their local MP is doing a good job, the Welsh are only 5 per cent less inclined than the others to believe Parliament works very well. Respondents of all three nations are equally convinced that the MP's chief responsibility should be to represent the views of his constituents.

Some differences are revealed, although the smallness of the sample in Scotland and Wales makes them of doubtful validity. What is happening in Parliament is a more popular topic of conversation in Scotland than it is in England or Wales and the Scots score markedly better on Granada's Parliamentary knowledge index: 13 per cent of Scottish respondents come in the high knowledge group, compared with 7 per cent of the Welsh and 8 per cent of the English.

However, the average Welshman is more likely to consider himself knowledgeable about Parliament than the others. He is certainly more interested both in Parliament and politics: 83 per cent (compared to 71 per cent of the sample as a whole) say they are very or fairly interested in Parliament; 65 per cent (compared to 59 per cent of the total sample) say they are very interested in politics. This result is particularly striking, because the Welsh tend to consist of working class Labour supporters, a group who elsewhere generally express lower interest than most in Parliament. The high expressed interest seems genuine as Welsh respondents are more conscious than others of recent Parliamentary activity affecting them, and more likely to be active in political affairs. Also they are more likely to recall their MP's name, his specific constituency activities, and are twice as likely as the others to have had some personal favour from him.

The results of the poll were something of a blow for the Granada team presenting *The State of the Nation* as they had originally intended to set their discussion of Parliamentary reform within the context of public disaffection with MPs.

But the poll failed to demonstrate the extent of disaffection they expected. So in the end they discarded the poll and used the dissatisfaction of many MPs and Civil Servants as their framework. The Granada survey is said to have cost £8,000.

TABLE A

How valuable to the community do you consider these jobs? How much influence does each job have in making decisions that affect the community?

(Answers in %)	Very valuable	A great deal of influence
Doctor	91	32
Judge	76	43
Government Minister	52	58
Ordinary MP	41	17
Managing director of a major company	33	20
Trade union leader	28	33
Senior civil servant	24	15

TABLE B   Cynicism about politicians.

Could you tell me whether you agree or disagree that . . .	Agree %	Neither/ don't know %	Disagree %	Size of majority taking a favourable attitude to politicians %
Most politicians will promise anything to get votes	67	14	19	—48
Politicians are in politics for what they can get out of it	39	28	33	—6
It doesn't matter who you vote for, politicians are all the same	47	6	47	0
Politicians are all talk and no action	35	27	38	+3
Politicians do care what people like me think	48	21	31	+17

TABLE C

Whose views do you think the MP should represent

	First %	Second %	Least %
His constituents'	66	16	1
His local party's	11	33	5
His Parliamentary party's	7	18	10
His party's as expressed at the party conference	5	11	13
His own	7	15	54
Don't know	4	7	15

TABLE D

Electors aged 18–24 compared with all electors . . .

	All electors %	Electors aged 18–24 %	Difference %
Say that they are not interested in politics	41	61	20
Say they are not interested in Parliament	28	44	16
Say they have discussed Parliament in last month	25	9	—16
Say Parliament works very or fairly well	55	42	—13
Say the local MP is doing a good job	26	14	—12
Are in the low knowledge group	15	25	10

SOME ADDITIONAL TABLES FROM THE SURVEY
(i.e. not published in *The Guardian*)

Knowledge about Parliament and MPs	Acceptable answers	Correct answers %
How many MPs are there in the House of Commons?	600–699	22
What is the maximum period between General Elections?	5 years	60
Is Parliament meant to pass laws?	Yes	90
Is Parliament meant to appoint the Cabinet?	No	25
What is the party of your local MP?	Various	78
What is the name of your local MP?	Various	53

Representativeness of MPs.

Do you agree or disagree that . . .	Agree %	Neither/ don't know %	Disagree %
MPs are in general in touch with the people in their constituency?	44	18	38
An MP cannot do a good job of representing me if he comes from a different social class?	34	10	56
There should be more women MPs in Parliament?	64	17	19

Which two or three of the following institutions do you think . . .

	(1) are most important in law-making? %	(2) best looks after individual rights? %	(3) are most interested in ordinary people? %
Local council	8	6	33
The police	25	32	23
Trade unions	10	24	27
PARLIAMENT	63	18	7
The courts	28	18	5
Newspapers and TV	2	14	24
Ombudsman	5	9	3
Political parties	23	9	9
Church of England	3	5	18
Civil Service	6	4	4
Cabinet	24	3	1
Queen	6	2	3
None/don't know	4	10	11

NOTE: Other institutions – the armed forces, big business and the City and international bankers – were in the original question but have been excluded from this table since fewer than 5% of respondents chose them.

What is the most effective thing to do if . . .

you discovered that a planned motorway would pass right beside your house?	you wished to change the present laws against crime?	you wished to have old age pensions increased?
Contact MP (39%)	Contact MP (49%)	Contact MP (46%)
Contact local councillor (32%)	Contact Home Office (22%)	Contact Dept. of Health & Social Security (26%)
Contact local planning department (29%)	Contact local police (14%)	Contact local political party (12%)

NOTE: 17 choices were presented to respondents and some picked more than one.

What the press said

The makers of the law

The TV event of the week could be Granada's three-part *The State of the Nation* (10.30 ITV). Brian Lapping spent eighteen months, before filming, preparing this major investigation into Parliament's relationship with the Executive. Tonight's 100-minute film is followed by a 105-minute Inquiry (Tuesday) and a 130-minute Debate (Wednesday). Lapping regards it as a 'Royal Commission of the Air'; a grand overstatement, but you can see what he's getting at.

For tonight's film 'A Law in the Making' director Roger Graef concentrated on two clauses in the Government's Fair Trading Bill. From January to April, during the Standing Committee's discussion of the Bill, he followed the MPs and Civil Servants who were involved, together and alone, in the Commons and Whitehall. Parliamentary practice excluded the film crew from the committee room itself; but it was able to film in the Commons' basement where the two Parties held their own meetings on the Bill, and in the Department of Trade and Industry where Civil Servants and Government MPs held regular briefing sessions.

The two clauses, about the powers to be given to the new Director General of Fair Trading, proved more troublesome than expected. At the end, neither side appears satisfied. The Civil Servants were plainly confused and a bit fed up; even halfway through, one picks up the Bill at arm's length before dropping it with distaste in his out-tray. Another: 'I wouldn't mind doing this in the war; but why shorten your life?' The Minister, Sir Geoffrey Howe, is not much more optimistic: 'It's very very difficult to believe we have the general line accurately defined.'

Roger Graef has directed 'A Law in the Making' as he directed his 'Space Between Words', emphasising the collective aura of committee work, where nobody seems to speak directly to anybody else. One long shot deliberately stays on a listener, resisting the temptation to swing round to the speaker or the probable answerer. His elliptical style gives a variety of insights into the frustrating work of a Commons committee; again and again, you are reminded that the Civil Servants have already done most of the work and the committee has little room for manoeuvre.

The second part of *The State of the Nation* (10.30 ITV) is an inquiry: 'Has Parliament Lost Control?' Five MPs (Edward du Cann, Michael Foot, Reginald Maudling, John Mackintosh and Nicholas Scott) conduct a quasi-Select Committee inquiry into the Commons control (or lack of it) of law-making and public money. They question MPs and Civil Servants, including Sir William Armstrong, Head of the Civil Service, and Sir David Pitblado, Comptroller and Auditor-General.

Under-Secretary Dennis Lawrence discusses his preparation of the Sound Broadcasting Bill, and Phillip Whitehead MP, discusses his opposition in Standing Committee. Lawrence admits that Commons committees 'are not always frightfully relevant' to his work; and he reveals a dislike of consultation. Phillip Whitehead says his 'time was totally wasted'. Reginald Maudling sums it up: 'So the politicians go on bashing one another while the Civil Servants get the legislation right.'

Best talkers in the House

Early on, the production team of *The State of the Nation* (10.30 ITV) realised that MPs' arguments about the role of Parliament could be summed up in one issue. The more traditional members believe the Commons functions best as a debating chamber; the 'progressives' that MPs are best employed in investigatory committees. Producer Brian Lapping asked several MPs and lobby correspondents to name the MPs they most preferred to listen to (apparently, their choices were almost unanimous) and invited twelve of them (including Powell, Foot, Maudling, Walden, Crossman, Crosland and Mackintosh) to debate this basic motion: 'Are MPs too ignorant to do their job?'

MPs are undoubtedly happiest when they are talking about their common concern for the most exclusive club in Europe: it stimulated a remarkably matey and amusing debate, and a welcome change from their normal TV appearances (and, if it could continue, an unanswerable argument for the televising of Parliament). Both sides are persuasive; although the progressives probably win the day. John Mackintosh, especially, displays a powerful combination of logical reasoning and anecdotes – Michael Foot, he says, once told him, 'Facts confuse my argument'. But, like the rest of *The State of the Nation*, this debate is most useful for the endless revelations about how politicians, both particular people and in general, behave when they are at home in Westminster.

Politics by TV

by J W M Thompson

The debate on Parliament's effectiveness, or lack of it, in modern conditions is likely to be transferred from the confines of Westminster to a wider public this week, as a result of an unusual and in some ways remarkable piece of television.

Those fascinating Sunday night political discussions on sound radio have recently demonstrated that political broadcasting need not consist solely of party bickering. Granada has now done its bit to extend the range so far as television is concerned with a *State of the Nation* marathon (tomorrow, Tuesday and Wednesday) which offers, to those viewers able to take nearly six hours of it, an unprecedentedly intimate view of the workings of the political process.

Not the least of the programme's achievements was that of obtaining such extensive co-operation from Government and Civil Service. Tomorrow's instalment, for example, shows a film of the behind-the-scenes working of the legislative machine on one Bill, the Fair Trading Bill, as it progresses slowly and with difficulty towards the Statute Book.

Cameras were allowed in such normally inaccessible places as the Civil Service offices where the struggle to get the Bill through was directed, and they also recorded the Ministerial briefings and the Opposition's private conferences. Later, such usually unseen men of power as Sir William Armstrong, Head of the Home Civil Service, submitted to interrogation.

The thread which connects the various episodes is really a question: Have MPs lost much of their control over the Executive, and should they attempt to regain it by such means as the development of investigatory committees on the American pattern?

After seeing a preview of the programme, it seemed to me a safe bet that most viewers will think the answer to the first part of the question, at least, is 'Yes'.

Furthermore, the large part played in the legislative process by Civil Servants, flanking their Ministers in battle with Opposition MPs and rebels from the Government back-benches, can never have been so plainly displayed to the public view.

As the Fair Trading Bill is slowly manoeuvred through its committee stages, there are riveting glimpses of the stresses behind closed doors. The junior Minister, Mr Peter Emery, for example, contemplating in horror the prospect of a series of Government defeats in committee as Tory rebels press for an unwelcome amendment; or Miss Elizabeth Llewellyn-Smith, Assistant Secretary in charge of co-ordination of Civil Servants on the Bill, sternly counselling firmness with a classic Whitehall dictum: 'If we begin by crumbling on these things, there's no end to the trouble'.

Many of the MPs taking part in the discussions do indeed convey a certain sense of impotence. Mr Phillip Whitehead, a Labour MP, provides some sour reflections on his work in committee on the Sound Broadcasting Bill: four and a half months of talk, embalmed in two fat volumes of print, during which radical alterations were made in the Bill – after which the Government used its majority in the whole House to wipe out almost every change. 'Totally wasted time' is how he describes his labours.

But when the clash is on strictly party lines the Opposition is likely to feel frustrated. The more subtle, and more important, question concerns the control exercised by the House as a whole over the doings of the Executive.

Sir William Armstrong, with his unrivalled authority in Whitehall, emerges as clearly believing that the House has lost some of its effective control. He remembers when Civil Servants frequently warned Ministers against certain courses of action because Parliament had not yet voted them the appropriate powers. Nowadays Ministers don't feel they have to wait. They assume Parliament will dutifully back them up. Some 'loosening of control' may be inevitable in view of the immense growth in the volume and complexity of Government business, but Sir William feels the loosening has gone too far. He, interestingly, actually favours more scrutiny by small expert committees of MPs.

Mr Michael Foot puts the contrasting view that Parliament 'still has enormous powers against the Executive if they wish to use it'. Sir William gently inquires: 'If they wish to use it – but who are they?' Government MPs support Governments. In practice, Parliament carries out the will of the Government almost invariably.

This very long piece of television may or may not be a winner

with the ordinary commercial television public, but it consti-
tutes a fascinating archive for anyone interested in the present
stresses and strains of the Parliamentary machine. It also
makes one envy future historians. If only we had this sort of
material about Parliament at the time, say, of Walpole, or
Disraeli, or even Churchill!

THE GUARDIAN Tuesday, 24 July 1973

Television
by Nancy Banks-Smith

. . . The Civil Servants in 'A Law in the Making' showed
understandable and endearing signs of humanity and humour.
'Why should one shorten one's life?' grumbled Elizabeth
Llewellyn-Smith. 'Is this not giving him more freedom to do
nothing than he already has in the Bill?' asked Brian Armstrong with knife irony.

How slim yet sensitive like a cat's whisker, were the gradua-
tions of meaning in the wording of a Bill. The delicate distinction which, apparently, exists between 'rebutting' and
'resisting', between 'looking at again', 'keeping under review', 'taking note of' and 'expressing a willingness to listen'.

Yet watching other people work is always irresistible and I
am positive that this is the best kind of television. Not explaining the working of politics in a studio with maps and
graphs and models and middlemen, but watching the politicians at work.

It was no fault of Granada's that both the grind and the glitter
of politics were slightly sham. No part of the parliamentary
process may be filmed so the Standing Committee never
exactly sat but was filmed fragmented: the Minister with his
advisers, the Opposition, the pressure groups. And 'Tomorrow's a Debate' is, of course, a staged performance outside Parliament. But this most unobtrusive, faithful (and
flattering) programme is an excellent argument for televised
government. Almost ceremonially, as it does Black Rod,
Parliament has repulsed television quite long enough.

DAILY MAIL Tuesday, 24 July 1973

by Peter Black

With the eager co-operation of most MPs, television has

contributed more than any other thing to the general soiling of their image.

They've always regarded it as the key to the voters' brains, or whatever part of the equipment we're supposed to vote with.

They've rushed to exploit the medium with obviously unattractive motives: to keep the party in office if it's in it, and to get it back if it's not.

Granada's series on the working of Parliament *(The State of the Nation)* persuaded MPs to collaborate in an attempt to rehabilitate themselves.

In so doing, it proved what some of us have been arguing for years: The best way to present politicians is to show them at their real work, in their own place, not in television's.

Producer-editor Brian Lapping ingeniously chose as a peg the Fair Trading Bill, in which, as consumers, the public's interest might be stirred.

Last night's programme took a couple of clauses concerning health and safety, and the powers of the Director General of Fair Trading: Should he or should he not be able to define what goods are shoddy?

It edited down, from four months of filming (by Roger Graef), the private goings-on that accompany a Bill through Parliament.

The Ministerial meetings with the Civil Servants, who feed them with advice on drafting and debating; the informal party sessions where the sides discuss strategy.

It was all no less comforting than absorbing. The two most clearly formidable Civil Servants, Elizabeth Llewellyn-Smith and Cyril Coffin, seemed almost luminous with authoritative intelligence, like Bertie Wooster's Jeeves after a plate of fish ('Resist, but indicate willingness to look at again', Miss Smith crisply minuted the Minister); and the party men (the Tories thought fools shouldn't be protected – the Socialists that prudent buying was impossible without adequate information) really seemed concerned with the public interest.

Tonight's programme follows on by asking five MPs to conduct, in the normal language and procedure of a Select Committee, an inquiry into Granada's question: Has Parliament lost control of law-making and public spending?

The third programme (I've seen a preview) is a debate as it might occur in one of the Westminster committee rooms.

Here the question is whether MPs are too uninformed, whether more Select Committees would improve their equipment as watchdogs.

Once again, the fascination and reassurance is in the minds it shows at work.

The Opposition, led by Michael Foot and Enoch Powell (and there's a partnership for you) argues in essence that politics ought to be an art not a tidy science – that too many facts might endanger an MP's natural bent for penetrating to the root of things by the mere exercise of moral purpose.

It may seem to you that the other side's citation of such calamities as Concorde proves its case.

Granada deserves all the compliments we can shower on it for a most valuable and interesting piece of public service TV.

It not only refurbishes MPs. Its responsible and successful editing must knock the last support from the ban that keeps TV out of Parliament.

DAILY EXPRESS Tuesday, 24 July 1973

Corridors of boredom
The State of the Nation – ITV
by Mary Duffy

Worthy intentions can often be the shortest road to television ruin.

But, and it's a big but, I doubt if there were enough to keep many viewers awake all through Granada's *The State of the Nation* last night.

For although the company decided to deal with Parliament in action in greater depth than I have seen the subject handled before, it proved too complicated a course to follow and, no doubt, had many viewers yawning long before its 90 minutes were up.

You just cannot expect the viewing population to be on their intellectual toes at 10.30 pm, an hour when they are usually sipping their bed-time cocoa.

Add to this the drugging effect of a gaggle of top Civil Servants talking permanently over most people's heads and you get an instant cure for insomnia.

'The Story of a Bill', part one of this three-part series, dealt with the complicated cut and thrust in the Corridors of Power that make up the drafting of a parliamentary Bill.

This is the behind-the-scenes operation where back-benchers from both sides of the House put forward amendments to the Government's proposals.

Surrounding the Minister is a regiment of Civil Servants, weighing the meaning of every word, anticipating every loophole, and generally bringing their experience to bear on the important job of saving the Minister from committing himself without a fight.

In this case, the Bill being drafted was the Fair Trading Bill, steered through by Sir Geoffrey Howe, Minister for Trade and Consumer Affairs. It is a document with 123 clauses, numbers two and three of which took as long to get through as the rest put together.

The programme ended up as a huge welter of words, a mystifying conglomeration of discussion. At times it came as a shock to remember that the purpose of the whole effort was to bring some degree of fairness into the consumer's life.

Parts two and three follow tonight and tomorrow.

DAILY MIRROR Tuesday, 24 July 1973

What a crashing bore!
William Marshall's view

There was a stunning demo on TV last night on how to take a long, boring, frightfully dull subject and fashion from it a long, boring, frightfully dull documentary.

It was the first of a three-part Granada series *The State of the Nation; Parliament* (ITV).

The idea was to show the drama – that's a joke – in Westminster and Whitehall as the new Fair Trading Bill was being hammered out.

What a crashing, stupendous yawn it all was. We were bludgeoned by the blather on amendments to the amendments, inserts in paragraph four, deletions at the top of page six, etc, etc.

We were privileged to sit in on conferences held by Sir Geoffrey Howe, Minister for Trade and Consumer Affairs.

It was the first time TV cameras have been allowed in. But it didn't matter a damn for all we heard.

We saw the MPs and committees surrounded by forests and acres of paper, and when things got to the stage where you were almost screaming with the pain of it, the camera would focus in on someone's earhole or a blotchy, off-white neck.

My favourite shot was of the Minister lighting yet another cigarette.

He has an amazing way of inserting it in his chubby little mouth, and you think he's not inhaling until you spot the thin trickle of smoke oozing out of his nostrils.

It was that sort of programme. You were looking out for highlights all the time.

And all this went on for 100 minutes. There is more tonight, and more the next night. It can only improve.

The birth of a bill, they called it. More like hard labour.

Granada, who do so many good things, told me that the programme had been shot with hand-held cameras and no lights.

They should have shot it without cameras as well.

THE DAILY TELEGRAPH Tuesday, 24 July 1973

Give-and-take of law-making well shown
by Peter Knight

Despite all the facilities that were made available to Granada for its massive and impressive study of Parliament at work in *The State of the Nation* (ITV), it was clear from the first programme last night that many irritating and insurmountable objects were still left in its way.

Opening the three-part examination, which will take up nearly five hours during the next couple of nights, the programme followed the tortuous progress of two contentious and controversial clauses in the Fair Trading Bill.

For the first time cameras were allowed into Government and Opposition meetings to observe and record the strategy of each side being drawn up.

But the confrontation between them when they met in meetings of the Standing Committee on the Bill and, of course, in debate in the House, never materialised because the cameras were banned.

It was all rather like watching two boxers training for a fight only to be denied access to the actual encounter. Admittedly we got inter-round summaries from each side as they met to consider counter moves being made by the other, but it was a poor substitute for the real clash.

The sheer length of 100 minutes, mostly consumed by the constant chatter of committees at work, may well have put off many viewers but it was clearly the intention of the programme's editor, Brian Lapping, to use it to show the ponderous machinery of government in its day-to-day workings.

By allowing such large chunks of his programme to be taken up with meetings, which often trod tediously over ground already well covered, he was able to convey the thoroughness with which each sentence, word or comma, is studied before a Bill is allowed to become law.

What eventually emerged was the give and take there is among the opposing sides. Each weighs carefully just how far it can push the other, what concessions it can trade in return for points gained and how far it is prepared to retreat before reaching the politicians' holy land of compromise.

Perhaps the most revealing part of the programme was the role of the Civil Service, so often regarded as the faceless men of power behind the Government. Here they were shown as sincere, dedicated, hard-working people drawing up the guidelines for their Minister, swiftly papering over the cracks in his case and trying to anticipate every pitfall he might encounter.

Its unavoidable deficiencies apart, the programme remained the most comprehensive and detailed study yet shown of government at work. Granada may win no mass audience with it, but at least a word of commendation is thoroughly deserved for its enterprise and industry in tackling such a project.

MORNING STAR Wednesday, 25 July 1973

What a long, long way from Watergate!
by Stewart Lane

Is there adequate control of the Executive? Not a question being discussed by the US senate committee on Watergate, but the issue before last night's second instalment of Granada's mammoth *The State of the Nation*.

While this exercise in examining how our Parliament works

may be instructive to some degree, what needs to be brought out in relation to the operation of Parliament and the Civil Service is the common class basis.

In his book 'The British Political System', John Gollan stressed that 'the British ruling class has forged, in the upper administrative class of the Civil Service, a unique, powerful and loyal instrument of capitalism for ensuring its permanent grip on the State administration, no matter what Government is in office.'

The members of last night's 'select committee', with Tory Edward du Cann in the chair, were Labour's Michael Foot and John Mackintosh and Tories Reginald Maudling and Nicholas Scott.

Here were no TV cameras, no members of the public; and giving 'evidence' in the quiet of the mahogany-panelled room were top Civil Servants.

Sir William Armstrong, Head of Home Civil Service, not surprisingly repudiated any suggestion that the Civil Service ran the country and stressed the influence a Minister can have on a department.

But if a 'strong' Minister made for a strong department, did the same maxim apply for a 'weak' Minister? I doubt it.

The fact is that, while final decisions rest with Ministers, high-ranking permanent state officials play a vital role in policy-making.

As H R G Greaves wrote in 'The Civil Service in the Changing State', Civil Servants come, with rare exceptions, 'from the wealthy and professional classes.' They therefore, broadly speaking, have a vested interest in maintaining the *status quo*, i.e. the capitalist system, no matter what Government is in power.

Monday's programme, tracing the progress of the Fair Trading Bill, was of greater, more detailed interest, displaying much of the machinery of government, and top Civil Servants like Elizabeth Llewellyn-Smith and Cyril Coffin in action.

Certainly *The State of the Nation* is a commendable achievement and provides an argument in support of televising Parliament. I will be interested to learn what proportion of viewers actually stayed with it.

Salutary insight into problems of MPs
by Sean Day-Lewis

Let it be said without equivocation, Granada's *The State of the Nation* (ITV) is the most important television investigation of Parliament in the present decade, as much for what it shows of the untapped possibilities as for what it achieves.

Part two of Brian Lapping's five-hour enquiry, shown last night, asked whether the House of Commons back-benchers have lost control of law-making and public expenditure and demonstrated that, in large measure, they have.

Denied the uncluttered technique of Roger Graef's 'fly on the wall' tele-verité, which so illuminated part one, the second instalment was more generalised in its approach, and more interrupted by editing and the resounding explanations of Mike Scott.

Nevertheless the directors, Peter Mullings and Royston Morley, got nearer the heart of the matter than a hundred party political broadcasts, studio interviews or confrontations, by letting the MPs do their own investigation, in the polite manner of a Select Committee.

As my colleague Peter Knight pointed out after part one, the rules against showing Parliamentary procedure itself make the exercise, in some ways, like 'watching boxers training for a fight only to be denied access to the actual encounter'.

This is not without value. Fighting is a well-publicised segment of Parliamentary work, hiding many things like the pacific but all-important work of Civil Servants. Also, the restrictions led to such ironies – for example, the use of the Greater London Council offices for the 'mock' Select Committee – that the beginning of a new campaign to end the ban on television must surely be hastened.

The failure of ITV to clear an entire evening for the inquiry, and the insistence on 'throwing it away' in July, has been noted. Yet even the timing has its value, not simply because it follows close on the recent uncharacteristic hint from the BBC that it is incapable of governing either itself or political debate.

The general impression after the first two programmes is that most MPs are honestly if unsuccessfully working to control a

Heath Robinson (or Heath Armstrong machine), and use it for the general good. At a time when public mistrust of politicians is apparently at its height this is a salutary insight.

THE FINANCIAL TIMES Wednesday, 25 July 1973

The State of the Nation
by Chris Dunkley

Granada Television can claim three major achievements for their massive three-part programme, *The State of the Nation,* which ends this evening: they have proved that it is quite possible to present politics and politicians on television outside the realms of both the acrimonious studio debate and the somewhat absurd party political broadcasts, and to remain serious and interesting; they have shown that television can still be immensely exciting; and they have provided the best case yet produced by television itself for the televising of Parliament. In all this it is no surprise that the company involved is Granada. They have a long tradition of which they are justifiably proud as self-appointed leaders of the broadcasters' attack on the obscurantism which is such a strong feature of British political organisations.

In 1955 when commercial television was opened in Britain, the Government introduced the '14-day rule' which (astonishingly, as it seems now) prohibited broadcast discussions on any subject due for debate in Parliament in the ensuing fortnight. Granada were in the vanguard of those challenging the rule, and by the end of 1956 it was revoked. Two years later, at the Rochdale by-election, Granada set out to make detailed daily reports of the event including interviews with the candidates; an approach which many people considered not only undesirable but even illegal under the Representation of the People Act. Granada challenged that view successfully too, and as a result the General Election in 1959 was more thoroughly covered by television than any before it – not only by Granada (who offered every Parliamentary candidate in their region the chance to state his case, and were taken up on the offer by more than 200) but by the BBC.

Then in 1962, deciding that the Annual TUC Congress and party conferences were badly under-reported, they took outside broadcast units to the meetings and televised practically the entire proceedings live. Once again other organisations, including the BBC, followed where Granada had led – and now a team from the same company, headed by Brian Lapping, the editor of *The State of the Nation*, has marched up Whitehall and succeeded in carrying its cameras and microphones inside a Ministry for the first time to make a film of a Government Bill being thrashed out between Ministers, MPs, pressure groups and, perhaps most significant of all, Civil Servants. Additionally in programmes two and three they have shown the precise workings of Select Committees and Standing Committees of the House of Commons; bodies whose work is normally seen by perhaps one member of the public in a million. Finally they have not only brought to the screen an illustration of the form of these bodies, but by inducing the MPs who sat on them to discuss – instead of airports, white fish or play schools – the contemporary difficulties facing Parliament itself, they have provided a national teach-in on the large and vital problems surrounding the British form of government, and in the process made available some of the best political debates ever screened on television in this country.

Collectively it is a huge achievement, and looking back over Granada's history it is impossible to accept that the programme will simply be left to stand alone as a monument to the research and negotiation techniques of Lapping, Norma Percy and Maureen Tomison, who talked her way (and that of the film crew) into the Department of Trade and Industry. Certainly it *is* such a monument but one feels that the most significant aspect of the programme is still to be seen: the future programmes which will have been made possible primarily as a result of the initiative taken by *The State of the Nation*.

Whatever these programmes turn out to be, and whatever else happens in the interim, one thing is certain; one day cameras will be regular features of Parliamentary committees, and sooner or later they will be installed in the Houses of Parliament themselves. When this battle is won, it will be impossible to look back and trace the path towards the achievement without noticing that one of the biggest blazes on the trail was marked by this series . . .

Starting with the widely believed notion that the public is discontented with Parliament, they commissioned the biggest survey of public attitudes on the subject ever attempted – and to their astonishment discovered that the majority of people express a consistently high level of satisfaction with Parliament and their own MPs; that the Scots and the Welsh are just as happy as the English; that trade union members are just as happy with Parliament as the rest of the community; and that in general the power of Parliament is not over-estimated but its value is recognised nonetheless.

. . . Having discovered from their poll such surprising reactions from the public, the Granada team wondered whether to drop the whole idea. But then they found that however happy or indifferent the electors might be, many MPs themselves, Clerks at the House of Commons, Civil Servants and academics were far from satisfied and were concerned that much was wrong with Parliament. Since the survey showed that the public did not realise this, the obligation to inform them was all the greater they decided. So after conversations with about 60 MPs and 20 academic experts, followed by a long series of dinners with groups of Labour and Conservative MPs working over a prepared agenda, and finally consultation with David Watt, the political editor of this newspaper, two major subjects were chosen for the programmes: legislation, and oversight of Government policy.

(Chris Dunkley will discuss 'The State of the Nation' again next week.) [See Wednesday, 1 August, below]

THE TIMES Thursday, 26 July 1973

The 'Ring' of MPs
The State of the Nation: Parliament (Granada)
by Michael Ratcliffe

'*Resist*', dictated the lady Assistant-Secretary firmly, 'but indicate a willingness to look again.' After a further conciliatory passage she concluded her memorandum with the date and a final reminder to her colleague in the Department of Trade and Industry, to *resist*. You could almost hear the ranks closing: the Government was at its business.

Miss Elizabeth Llewellyn-Smith was following the official line on Amendments at Committee Stage – one by Labour Members and one by a Conservative back-bencher, Mrs Sally Oppenheim – to clauses 2 and 3 of the Fair Trading Bill early this year. In the whole of Granada's amazing parliamentary *Ring*, which has stretched across the past three evenings, nothing was more coolly breathtaking than the observed process by which the Government set about getting its own way whilst ensuring that the processes of scrutiny and debate were decently observed. None of this had been televised before.

The Labour amendment was squashed by force of numbers, whereat the Labour Members appended their names to Mrs Oppenheim's amendment, thus ensuring that it was properly discussed in Committee but also that it became, in Party terms, a Major Embarrassment, and therefore meat for the doctrinal knife. There was a show of force: the Minister himself persuaded the committee to reject the amendment, and the Parliamentary Under-Secretary cornered Mrs Oppenheim in the Division Lobby and made her an offer she couldn't refuse. Neither of these decisive meetings did we see.

The Minister's carrot was the reconstruction of Clauses 2 and 3 to accommodate Mrs Oppenheim's provision – in the knowledge that the Ministry of Agriculture and Fisheries could be relied on to shoot them down later since, arguably, they would invade territory already patrolled by them. Sure enough MAF's veto struck, and the clauses went forward more or less as the Government originally intended, but with enough minor adjustments of wording for the Labour Members and the Consumers' Association to chalk up a small victory. Very small.

Such was the content of the first evening in *The State of the Nation: Parliament*. It was directed by Roger Graef; edited by Terence Twigg to 100 minutes from an astonishing 50 hours of film; shot over four months, by Charles Stewart, without extra lighting in small, crowded rooms. I have stressed it in some detail because it was the most valuable, the most disturbing and the most genuinely historic of the three evenings and raised most graphically the major issues behind the whole enterprise.

Has Parliament lost the power to influence legislative decisions? Is the Executive too powerful? Are MPs sufficiently informed to do their job properly, in particular as to how public money is going to be (as distinct from has been) spent? Does the regular committee process offer a genuine scrutiny or is it, in the end, merely a continuation of the Party battle? Mr Phillip Whitehead, a Member of the Standing Committee on the Sound Broadcasting Bill, bore witness to the examining committee of fellow MPs on the second evening that none of the major committee amendments on that Bill was accepted by the Government, which sent it forward in virtually its original form. 'So you felt that your four and a half months were wasted time?' Mr du Cann asked him. 'Totally', replied Mr Whitehead. The shadow of Maplin must have crossed many minds. Is the machinery of restraint a joke?

This second evening – Brian Lapping, the overall Editor, asked us to consider *The State of the Nation* as one programme in three parts – was cast like a Select Committee of the House of Commons and elicited information from expert Civil Service witnesses on the vital issues facing the future of Parliament as a decisive law-making body retaining the confidence of the electorate. The third evening simulated a debate in the Commons itself, in which MPs chosen for their eloquence discussed the whole question of Parliamentary reform, in particular the need (or otherwise) for strengthened committees as a means for keeping MPs sufficiently informed.

The choice of imitative procedural formats on both these evenings – suggested, of course, by the camera's continued exclusion from the Chamber itself – was, I think, a mistake. It led to an artificiality not present on the first evening, where the initially camera-shy blossomed into a revealing forthrightness and even wit long before the four months were up. The Select Committee was chaired by Mr du Cann with the kind of suffocating civility which, if it does not send me to sleep, always has me itching for the services of my friendly neighbourhood *tricoteuse*. We weren't half made to feel how jolly lucky we were that these functionaries were blinking up into the light – *our* light – for the first time; yet, genial though they mostly were, none of them equalled the immediate political impact of Mr Whitehead's 'Totally'.

The debate was equally polite and old-chumsy. Members discussed the very nature of their function and existence with something less than passion, though it should be recorded that Messrs Powell, Foot, Walden, Mackintosh and Selwyn Gummer all spoke well and would probably have been asked to form an executive junta on a free phone-in vote.

The State of the Nation: Parliament was originally envisaged by Mr Lapping as 'a kind of Royal Commission of the Air'. It aimed, therefore, at exhaustive investigation, yet, unlike a Royal Commission, it did not recommend. If some of it was boring – and it was – this at least reminded us that the greater part of Government and administration *is* boring, which is why so many complacent people are willing, and allowed, to take it up. It was Mr Powell, a firm believer that proliferating committees will only weaken the forum of debate on the Floor of the House, who reminded us that it is often at such moments of repetitiousness and boredom that Governments drop their guard, surprise attacks can be made and famous victories won. (The 3 am Theory.)

But do we have time for this kind of carry-on any more? It has worked well enough for patient and brilliant opportunists like Joseph Chamberlain or Mr Powell himself, but what of most Members, crushed by the guillotine, by the huge growth in Government business, by the inevitably inadequate provision for debate in the House? Is there no way of stopping the Party in power? All these problems have been raised before probably a larger audience than ever before.

The State of the Nation: Parliament took its responsibilities very seriously and more than justified the immense trouble taken, up to Cabinet level, to get it on the air at all. But when solemn Mr Whitehead appeared, or Mr Mackintosh briefly flared with a reference to the Prime Minister's extra-Parliamentary 'deal' with the TUC, I realised that I was most missing the real anger and enthusiasm without which politics remains a tactical exercise. Maybe that was the whole point, but at five hours it was an unduly protracted one.

NEW STATESMAN Friday, 27 July 1973

by Ian Hamilton

... My own feeling is that however many cameras you wheeled into Westminster the real work would still be done in secret and the debates would become even merer (and direr) formalities than they are said to be at present. But all the same I must say I was surprised at how little staginess there seemed to be in these discussions, especially on the Government committee, how little apparent effort to disguise the boredom and expediency. Thus, during the dullest exchanges, it was possible to focus with genuine eavesdropping zeal on the humble human details; the way in which juniors blossomed into firm-jawed decisiveness when their superiors were absent and sagged again into subservience when they returned (Emery in particular became a new man when Geoffrey Howe hadn't turned up, which was fairly often), the minute flickers of envy or irritation that now and then afflicted the haggard faces of the Civil Servants when some colleague was hogging the stage. It is a tribute to Granada's stealth that one didn't particularly feel that this kind of thing would have been more overt and entertaining if the cameras had not been there.

THE SUNDAY TELEGRAPH 29 July 1973

by Philip Purser

No need to be grudging about Granada's *State of the Nation*, on Parliament, which as a properly thought out, inventively executed, adequately roomy exercise in public service left most political programmes looking like scribbles on the wall.

My only reservations are that it was silly and will one day look very shortsighted to have left the Liberals out[1], and secondly – though this is directed against television in general rather than Granada in particular – the timing of the three instalments, none ending before midnight, was outrageous. The tendency to exile almost anything of interest to the end of the evening means a blearier and blearier audience for it; it is also killing the wedded bliss of television critics.

Note how the overall editor, Brian Lapping, cunningly housed the substance of each programme in the convention most suited to it, like declaiming in verse to describe poetry or staging a battle to explain war. Thus the workaday business

[1]Brian Lapping writes: We had no Liberal in our programme for a succession of reasons:

1. In Part one, the film on the Fair Trading Bill, no Liberal was on the Standing Committee on the Bill, nor did any Liberal take an active part in the debates on the clauses we happened to follow.

2. In Parts two and three, we tried to follow normal House of Commons procedure in selecting our committees of MPs. According to the Procedure Committee of the House of Commons, no Liberal is normally appointed to a committee of less than 30. Our committees had respectively five members and twelve.

3. In spite of 2 above, we decided to include a Liberal. We asked Jeremy Thorpe and David Steel. Both were unable to take part.

Complaints from Liberals arose largely because our programme was transmitted on the eve of the Ripon and Ely by-elections. Leading Liberals argued that by excluding Liberals we damaged the Party's chances. The Liberals won both by-elections.

of chipping away at the clauses of a new Bill in committee was followed through using the fly-on-the-wall or visual bugging approach which Roger Graef demonstrated in the 'Space Between Words' two years ago but which rarely yielded as illuminating a result as he obtained here.

Then to look beyond the machinery of Bill drafting and wonder how really effective the committee process was, and whether outside pressure groups were not now exerting more influence, Lapping (and directors Royston Morley, Peter Mullings) threw the question to a select mob of MPs who pretended they were a Select Committee inquiring into this very question and called for Select Committee-type evidence from themselves and from Civil Servants. A star witness was Phillip Whitehead MP, who testified that at hearings of the Standing Committee on Sound Broadcasting, on which he sat, a fellow-Member wore ear plugs the whole time.

Finally came a mock debate on Standing Committee lines as to whether the whole institution of Parliament needed modifying to the American pattern, or was it better left as it is. Much the same star-studded lot took part, with Enoch Powell outglittering most of them, but no viewer of reasonably generous spirit will have failed to conclude that on the subject of politics itself our politicians are wiser, more eloquent and better informed than is popularly supposed. The snag, of course, is that sooner or later they have to deal with things in the world outside Westminster.

THE GUARDIAN Monday, 30 July 1973

'The great need is to develop more forms of discourse, not limit them'
by Peter Fiddick

There are times when a television critic of less than total monomania might take fright and never put mind to paper again, and the wake of *The State of the Nation* is one of them. On 'Open Night' this weekend the reactions of the cross-section audience ranged from 'complete balderdash' to 'magnificent effort'. Elsewhere there have been opinions ranging from those who aver that television can do few things better than showing us others at work, to the Rt Hon Richard Crossman MP, PC, journalist, and former Cabinet Minister, who admitted to going to sleep after half an hour.

Amid this confusion, I suspect one of the most desperate moments for the editor of the project, Brian Lapping, must have come on 'Open Night' when it was not a member of the public but David Steel, Liberal MP, who suggested to him that the debate in part three of the series would have been more interesting had the subject been something not connected with Parliament itself.

It was just about the one touch we needed to crown this week in which the relationship of television and politicians has returned to the headlines. While the BBC has been rushed by its governors into a fake confrontation with MPs, the other network has devoted some five hours to helping them examine the strengths and weaknesses of their own position in serving and governing the country.

Unfairly hammered

One is sorely tempted at such moments either to cry 'pox' to the lot and retire or to smack a few knuckles with the ruler and resort to magisterial generalisations about the nature of the medium. Such as that there are no generalisations. Or that the single most important quality of the television audience is its diversity, so that, for instance, if the Governors of the BBC would examine the 'Open Night' discussion with care they would find that some ordinary viewers see value in a free-for-all now and again, and would rather judge for themselves whether some specialist is being unfairly hammered by the public than endure yet again him toying with the truth (as they see it) out of reach. The voters of Ely and Ripon have television. The great need, not just of television, but of newspapers, and come to that of politics too, is to develop more forms of discourse, not to limit them, and broadcasters have probably made more efforts in this direction in the last five years than any of the others.

But in moments of stress what we need is not assertion but description, to add to the store of information rather than that of myth. It is clear that some people will never have switched on *The State of the Nation*, some will have switched off, others been absorbed in varying degrees, and that neither intelligence nor active political interest will necessarily have had much to do with it. The useful question would seem to be not 'Was it good or bad?' nor 'Would it have got a bigger audience done another way?' but 'What was gained by doing it this way that other programme forms do not give us?'

This was not a beginner's guide to government; its assumptions were pitched higher than that and it is no objection to say that some viewers might not have cottoned on. Nor was it, I thought, a case for reform, whether in the Civil Service or in the organisation of Parliament. I was surprised to see Brian Lapping suggesting quite so vigorously on 'Open Night' that the Civil Servants were making policy, since the film of their operation did not seem to lend itself to that conclusion, though it certainly showed the potential.

Clear contrast

Indeed, I thought it a merit of the series that it was strong on information and that the forms Lapping had chosen for each part added to the informing process and got in the way of prejudgment.

The committee on committees in part two, and the debate about the role of the Chamber in part three, similarly added to our information in a way that neither a journalist's report nor a round-table discussion could have done. At primary level the contrast was clear: the committee coolly asking its questions, giving time for answers, coming back again, appeared clearly a more useful instrument than the debate with its prepared positions, its wit and wisdom deployed to achieve no significant movement, its attendant theatricals in which all behind the speaker smile confidently while all opposite look solemn or whisper.

Yet, by the end, we were left pondering complexities. Offerings like those from Professor Griffith, on the pathetic number of committee amendments left standing after Report, or Phillip Whitehead on the screws a Party can apply to its own Members of a committee, defied tidy conclusions. Yet the debate, for all its surface brilliance, left as many questions untouched (rigged question-time, absent Ministers) about traditional methods.

And right on cue out comes the mighty Public Accounts Committee's asterisked report on Concorde. The debate goes on. I cannot believe that anyone who watched *The State of the Nation* will not have a clearer idea of what they are up against.

THE FINANCIAL TIMES Wednesday, 1 August 1973

The state of Parliament
by Chris Dunkley

Two techniques were used in making Granada's three-part

television series about Parliament, *The State of the Nation*. For programmes two and three mock committees were set up in the GLC buildings and MPs discussed topics – chosen by the television team – in exactly the manner that Select and Standing Committees normally proceed. There was, in fact, a degree of unavoidable artificiality or even dramatisation involved, though this was kept to a minimum. In contrast the first programme, subtitled 'A Law in the Making', was directed for Granada by freelance Roger Graef who in his BBC series 'The Space Between Words' proved that he had discovered how to use the knack of merging his team into the wallpaper in order to achieve a highly efficient system of verité reportage.

Having failed to get special dispensation to take their cameras inside the Palace of Westminster – even to film MPs talking in a bar – the team attacked another taboo and, after winning the agreement of the Cabinet, succeeded in a different innovation: they were given permission to film the work inside a Ministry while a Parliamentary Bill was being argued out between Ministers, MPs, Civil Servants, and pressure groups. For four months they did precisely that as the Fair Trading Bill was drafted. Cameraman Charles Stewart (who shot much of 'The Space Between Words') worked entirely without lights or even a tripod, and sound recordist Iain Bruce used a miniaturised microphone clipped to the tip of a telescopic car aerial. Frequently they were the only television personnel in the room, and watching the programme carefully there can be no doubt that they succeeded almost entirely in persuading the officials to take them for granted. During the one-and-a-half hours of broadcast discussion – rendered down from the 50 hours actually shot – there was only one statement which was clearly aimed consciously at the viewing public beyond the camera.

Having been denied the opportunity of filming the central discussions about the Bill in the Standing Committee and in the Chamber of the House during the Report Stage (as though it were some sort of masonic rite or State secret they were trying to broadcast, rather than the drafting of a law to protect consumers) Graef and his team trained their cameras on every other aspect of the Bill's progress which they could find: the Labour and Conservative sides of the committee separately discussing amendments and tactics for forthcoming meetings; the Confederation of British Industry hearing reports from their committee observers on the progress of the Bill and planning their own lobbying for amendments – likewise the Consumers' Association – as well as the Civil Servants advising Ministers and discussing drafting details among themselves.

The results for the home viewer were complex and remarkable: every member of the public who saw the programme learned more about the various preparations for the Bill than any person actually involved could ever have known, since the Labour committee members did not see the Tory members' preparatory meetings; the Civil Servants were not party to the meetings of the pressure groups and so on. (There were occasions when the ubiquity of the crew during the making of the film produced odd situations: at some meetings they were alone in knowing the answers to certain questions, but being strictly silent observers, could not enlighten the officials.)

As a former reporter who has followed other Bills through their long and strenuous passage to Royal Assent, the collective process was not entirely novel to me yet the paradoxical effect of concentrating the entire business into $1\frac{1}{2}$ hours was to emphasise the enormous amounts of time and energy which are put into achieving minor – almost meaningless – compromises. What I had never seen before was the Civil Service at work, and this was an education; those who fear that the Commons dog is in danger of being wagged by the Executive tail would seem from this film to have at least some reason for their misgivings. More important, perhaps, in the long run is the question which the programme raised more urgently in my mind than ever before: the extent to which the political leanings of Civil Servants (individually or in groups) can influence the success or failure of legislation. It is clear that not all Civil Servants are going to be politically neutral, and from the example of Elizabeth Llewellyn-Smith in this programme it is also obvious that some of them at least are very intelligent, able and tough. The programme which explores and resolves that situation will indeed be a dangerous one, and it will need to be as well made as Roger Graef's – which will be extremely difficult.

The second programme, 'Law-making and Public Money: has Parliament lost control?' was the least successful of the three – though not through any fault of directors Peter Mullings and Royston Morley. It is simply that the form of a Select Committee is less intrinsically dramatic than either a verité film or a Standing Committee, and the subject matter was more esoteric than that of the other programme. Undeniably, however, the *facts* brought out in this section were the most worrying of all. Edward du Cann chaired the committee, which was manned by Michael Foot, John Mackintosh, Reginald Maudling and Nicholas Scott, taking evidence from a succession of people including four whose views are very rarely heard in public: Sir William Armstrong, Head of the Home Civil Service; Sir David Pitblado, Comptroller and Auditor-General; and House of Commons clerks Frank Allen and Michael Ryle.

But interesting as their evidence was (Sir William said that during the last 20 years Parliament's control had slipped, and later suggested a return to the 19th century habit of including outside experts on Select Committees) the most alarming facts were presented by J A G Griffith, Professor of Public Law at London University, who studied three sessions of Parliament between 1967 and 1971. He found that during that time the Commons spent 3,250 hours scrutinising Government legislation; that MPs not in the Government moved more than 4,000 amendments; and that of these nine were passed at Committee Stage and nine at Report Stage, seven Government clauses being defeated at Committee Stage, and 125 amendments being introduced by the Government at Report Stage to institute back-bench amendments moved in committee and withdrawn on Ministerial promise to redraft or re-examine the clause. Professor Griffith told the committee that in controversial Bills all that occurred in committee was a repetition of the known political arguments, division along Party lines, and virtually no changes ultimately.

His view was reinforced by another witness, Phillip Whitehead MP, who sat on the committee considering the recent Sound Broadcasting Bill which introduced commercial radio to Britain. Asked 'Would you say your work was effective?' Mr Whitehead replied: 'No. Quite the contrary. All our main alterations were struck out, and the clause that *we* struck out was replaced at Report Stage.' All the witnesses on this programme submitted written as well as spoken evidence (as occurs in reality) and one piece of Mr Whitehead's written evidence was conveyed to viewers by Mike Scott, who made an admirable anchorman for all three programmes; he wrote that most back-benchers on the committee showed little interest in the business 'and one even wore earplugs throughout'.

Though it was neither visually nor verbally particularly dynamic, this sort of evidence – showing the extraordinarily ineffectual nature of so much Parliamentary business – was potentially one of the most important aspects of the entire series.

The final episode of the programme, subtitled 'Are MPs too ignorant to do their job?' directed by Eric Harrison and Peter Mullings, was – in the very best sense – the most entertaining. Three birds were killed with one stone: by mocking up a Standing Committee it was possible to give an example of that particular structure and, since procedure in Standing Committees bears a close resemblance to that in the Chamber of the House, also to give a very accurate idea of a genuine Commons debate; in addition, once again. Granada's choice of Parliament itself as the subject for debate ensured that the form was complemented by the content (or vice-versa).

The content was a complete re-run of the ageing, but increasingly important argument between those who believe that in an age of increasing specialisation more business must be done in Select Committees so that – as John Mackintosh said – MPs will gain a greater knowledge of affairs at an earlier stage, and thus have greater effects upon legislation; and those such as Enoch Powell (allied again with Michael Foot) who believe that the proliferation of committees takes business away from the Chamber and that 'Everything which diminishes true debate on the Floor of the House of Commons strengthens the Executive and weakens Parliament.' Since this debate actually took place on television, it was odd that nobody made the point that the presence of cameras in the Chamber might very well encourage better attendance, more enthusiastic participation, and better preparation by MPs.

That the cameras *do* have remarkable power could hardly have been denied, since this very programme succeeded in collecting for one debate John Mackintosh, Charles Pannell, Angus Maude, Nicholas Scott, Anthony Crosland, Reginald Maudling, Brian Walden, John Selwyn Gummer and Edward du Cann as well as Messrs Powell and Foot – many of the leading orators in the House, and brought together in a concentration which would be very rare for any real debate. This was both the programme's strength and its weakness; such an assembly of talent showed the Commons in its best light and made a dramatic advertisement for the televising of live debates. Yet anyone who knows the House realises that such an assembly occurs in the Chamber once in a blue moon – and such good manners are only a little less rare.

These, however, are considerations for politicians. For the public *The State of the Nation* proved that opposition to the use of television cameras inside the Houses of Parliament is now as outdated and as anti-social as would be opposition to the use of a shorthand notebook.

What the viewers wrote

At the end of the third part viewers were invited to write in and give their opinions about the programme. Nearly 400 letters were received, most of which dealt with the points raised in the last part. The majority of the letters were congratulatory, although one correspondent said that Granada had no right to bore their viewers with long programmes on Parliament. Another complaint concerned the time of transmission.

The correspondence covered five main topics:
1. Members of Parliament
2. Civil Servants
3. Parliamentary organisation
4. Party politics
5. Electors

Complimentary as they are, the letters which have been selected for inclusion here are a fair representation of those which came in.

1. Members of Parliament

Several writers suggested that MPs should be full-time employees, with adequate secretarial and office facilities and that they should also have access to any specialist information that they needed, e.g. a larger House of Commons library. This point was enlarged upon by one correspondent who wondered whether more MPs should be specialists in certain fields.

Certain viewers commented upon the human face of politicians which came over in the programmes, especially the partnership of Mr Powell and Mr Foot, whom they had always considered to be at opposite ends of the political spectrum, but who in this programme were working together.

One correspondent wondered how MPs divided their time between the House, their constituencies and their outside obligations, whilst another was impressed by the total commitment of the Members to their Parliamentary duties. Another suggestion made was that there should be a research establishment which MPs could consult, or that they should have permanent research/investigating assistants. This point was also covered by the idea that there should be freer traffic for all MPs with the higher echelons of the Civil Service, whose talents appear at present to be regularly available only to Ministers. One viewer felt that MPs were politicians first and thinkers second; another felt that an MP should be the voice of the silent majority. For another correspondent the programmes gave a new image of politicians, which he felt could well be further projected by the parties in their political broadcasts. Finally, on the subject of MPs; for one viewer it gave him a much greater respect for them; for another it just increased his impression that they behaved like schoolboys.

2. Civil Servants

Many people were concerned about the amount of power that Civil Servants appeared to wield and their sense of superiority.

3. Parliamentary organisation

It appears from many of the letters received, that the electorate would very much like to see Parliamentary proceedings televised, either wholly or in part, as the programmes, they wrote, gave an excellent insight into the working of Parliament. Various suggestions were put forward about the use of committees.

One correspondent suggested a series of questions that he would like to put to a Select Committee about their functions. On the reform of Parliament, it was suggested that the House of Lords should be re-organised, and another suggestion was that there should be an elected Upper House, consisting of experts from all walks of life, who could be consulted by the MPs and known as the 'House of Experts'.

One viewer suggested that investigations (à la Watergate) would be of immense educational value. A revision of public accounting was proposed, as was the weekly publication of arrangements for all Parliamentary business, a month in advance, in newspapers apart from *The Times*. One other suggestion was that there should be more MPs.

4. Party politics

As a result of the recent upsurge of the Liberal Party, there were several letters about the non-inclusion of minority parties in the programme. Party politics being used to obstruct legislation and the tediousness of political bias were points also raised. The fact that toeing the Party line seemed more important than individual persuasions also caused comment, although one viewer thought that the Party machine was a valuable aid to the politician and another correspondent suggested that in the modern world of electronics the discipline of computer analysis should be used for solving problems, ignoring Party prejudice. Coalition politics were also suggested as an alternative and better method of running the country.

5. Electors

As electors, most correspondents felt that they had very little say in the Government of the country. One pointed out that as a result of the programme, he was left with the impression that politicians thought that politics were too important to be left to the electorate, but another declared that the programmes had persuaded him to vote. The method of selection of MPs by the constituencies was commented upon by one viewer although another viewer wrote that this hardly mattered as people voted for the Party and not the candidate.

There were several letters from younger viewers, one of them stating that the programme was boring and difficult to understand. Others said that they had found it very helpful especially for their studies. There were also enquiries as to whether the series could be repeated, preferably at an earlier hour, and whether a series of programmes for schools could be made out of them.

It was obvious from some letters that the programme aroused feelings of cynicism. One correspondent, however, felt that the winter months could well be spent watching a series of debates based on the format of the programme.

from Scott Targett MBE, St Albans, Herts

Dear Sirs,

A fascinating, interesting and enjoyable three nights. But why oh why – so late?

Monday – A trifle slow; the most outstanding personality in my opinion was Elizabeth Llewellyn-Smith – she seemed to grasp the purpose and implications of the proposed Bill. Sally Oppenheim MP also knew what she wanted. but Geoffrey Howe MP gave the impression that he had other and, to him, more important things on his mind. The work in the Department came over well.

Tuesday – The outstanding contributions were from the professional Civil Servants, especially Sir William Armstrong and

Sir David Pitblado. One realised that this country has the best Civil Service in the world. I agreed with Sir William's submission that the Executive and the House of Commons are losing out to the Civil Servants. This may not be a tragedy if the Civil Servants always are of the calibre of Sir William. One remembers the great influence of Sir Edward Bridges (late Lord Bridges) when Head of the Civil Service.

Wednesday – Excellent contributions from John Mackintosh who conveyed the impression that he really believed in the motion. Richard Crossman, as always wordy, and less convincing. Enoch Powell and Michael Foot (what a fascinating partnership) both admirable. Enoch Powell a master of logical, clear, concise, statement; both he and Michael Foot passionately believe in the effective worthwhileness of Parliament. God deliver us from the experts. I agree with them.

Brian Walden MP made a first class contribution – he should go far. Reginald Maudling and Edward du Cann were much less convincing. A splendid series – excellently presented – the commentator had exactly the right approach.   ✤

from Ian R McLaren, Hull

Sirs,

Thank you for producing such an excellent series of programmes, showing the present realities (and no less important the personalities) in Parliamentary politics; and for the invitation to respond to the questions raised by the series.

The excellent debate at the end of the three 'all-night sittings' should be a lesson to all current affairs producers – the question was clearly put, the speeches of the highest calibre, and interest held through two hours without the tone becoming angry.

Coming to the matter of the debate, the two sides of the question were equally strongly defended, and it does seem as though a real problem exists; I agree with the reformers that legislation and Government action get away with too little deep investigation, which allows the Executive to have too much scope to operate in, without the oversight of Parliament; but I also agree with the 'orators' that to provide the manpower for investigatory committees would weaken debate on the Floor of the House (and probably lead to overwork by the Members leading to inattention to other duties, including attending debates and to their constituents' problems). However, I believe that there is an answer, and it was suggested to me by the juxtaposition of Messrs Foot and Powell, agreed in debate as they were over the Parliament (Number 2) Bill: and due to their action at that time, the House of Lords still awaits reform – and is it not the *Senate* investigating committee that is studying the 'Watergate Affair'?

I suggest that in order to have meaningful investigations one should use investigators who are experts in the subjects being investigated – so that expert groups of all kinds should be represented in the House of Peers; I suggest the following pattern of membership. In a House of about six to seven hundred peers, most working only part time, of the present membership, the life peers and the law Lords should continue to be members, and a group of about 50 elected from among the hereditary peers to represent their number (and according to Viscount Massereene and Ferrard, in his book 'The Lords' (Table A) only 300 of the categories outlined above are regular attenders at present). A further 300 or so peers would be elected or selected by the members of professional bodies, trade unions, employers' organisations, amenity and pressure groups, churches, charities and other groups of experts, on a basis to be decided largely by the group concerned (i.e. the appointment could be for any period between one year and life). The remaining 200 peers would be directly elected by popular franchise, but I foresee that they should be eligible as candidates only if they have special qualifications (such as in Eire). They would be elected 100 at each General Election (so that each serves for two Parliaments) by proportional representation. Apart from the work done at the moment by the Upper House, the reconstituted body would provide the membership for Select, Legislative and Standing Committees, committees of enquiry, Royal Commissions and tribunals.

The form of business would be different for the legislative and Select Committees – legislative committees would study Bills sent from the Floor of either House, and report on them; the Select Committees would study a particular area or problem, and suggest to the Houses of Parliament the types of legislation or amendments to procedure that are required. In the case of the legislative committee, it should take a Bill, and the amendments proposed by the Members of each House, immediately after the Second Reading of the Bill in the House in which it was initiated, reporting back to that House so that the Committee Stage could be taken in the normal way. In order to safeguard both sides, various rules would have to be laid down, so that legislation proposed by the committees could get a First Reading debate within a reasonable time; and so that Bills did not 'disappear upstairs' for an unreasonable length of time. Many other such changes would be necessary.

Such a reform I hope would strengthen Parliament – more time would be left for purely political argument in the Commons, a new role would be given to the Lords, both Parliament and the Executive would have new and powerful sources of information and Parliament could feel that they had more information about the actions and intentions of the Executive. I hope that this document gives those who read it some new ideas, and that it can prove a basis for discussion of this problem.

For the record, I am a post-graduate student at the University of Hull, and a member of the Conservative Party ✤

from Graham Facks-Martin, Launceston, Cornwall

Dear Sirs,

First may I congratulate those responsible for producing one of the most intelligent programmes on politics that I have seen on television.

Before I express my own views, as requested, I had better declare my own interest. I have been actively concerned in constituency party politics for some twenty years. I have served as a councillor in local government for some six years and I have twice unsuccessfully attempted to be placed on my party's list of Approved Candidates for Parliamentary Elections.

What is wrong with Parliament today? First and foremost the view expressed by Michael Foot in the debate – that the most important thing to preserve in Parliament is the party battle, the confrontation between left and right – the obstruction of legislation pure and simple. This, in my view, is *absolutely wrong* and I believe the vast majority of the public have only contempt for the party political slanging match that passes, so often, for political debate. Certainly in the last century the party system was too weak and it was very difficult if not impossible for the parties to present a policy and get it enacted, but the pendulum has swung too far the other way and the able young MP who has ambitions – and there is nothing wrong in that – pays too much attention to the whips and the party view, especially when his party is in Government. The solution is in the hands of the Members themselves. But too few of them seem to have the courage to exercise their own judgement especially where it would be most appropriate, in the detailed consideration of legislation.

Secondly the massive weight of Government legislation and the extensive involvement of Government in practically every facet of our lives needs full-time Members who are properly equipped and informed. All Members should have at their disposal, paid for out of taxation, modern office facilities, secretaries and greater assistance in obtaining information both by the provision of research assistants and by the amendment of the Official Secrets Act. And, of course, they should be able to use the information they obtain by serving on legislative Select Committees. The more extensive use of these committees might sometimes further delay the passing of necessary legislation, but they might also mean the improvement of a great deal of legislation that is passed; a good example that was not mentioned would be the Industrial Relations Act, an Act that needs very considerable amendment to render it workable and relevant, which is I think widely accepted, in private if not in public (I support the Act!). The view expressed by Messrs Powell, Foot and others, that the most important duty of Parliament is to operate on the major issues and debate them is in my view quite mistaken. The electorate at a General Election gives a Government a mandate, one side or the other, to enact a programme the major parts of which are generally well recognised. Governments very rarely indeed give way on matters about which they feel strongly however strongly they are opposed – one might say the more strongly the opposition opposes the more determined the Government is to put the legislation on the Statute Book! If *both* parties in opposition could, after determined protest on the Floor of the House accept the fact that the Government is *going* to have its own way, however much they may detest what is proposed, and get down to a sensible and constructive consideration of the small points the better.

The difference between the major parties is much less clear-cut than it was 20 years ago. It is quite possible, indeed I believe oftens happens, to agree with a particular policy of one of the other parties and disagree with one policy of one's own party – is there anything wrong in this? And if the distinctions become blurred and the party differences less clear-cut and eventually perhaps electors consider to a greater extent than they do the candidates as well as the party labels they carry and there is sometimes a movement towards coalition on certain issues – might we get better Government? – we might!

In my own view, to be really arrogant, there is enormous ignorance and lack of application among the amateurs, be they councillors or MPs, and a different breed of professional would certainly evolve in time with a new approach – the professionals, local government officers or Civil Servants do in my view exercise a great deal of power, much more than the public realises – perhaps your programme opened a few eyes – and until the elected representatives work as hard and are as well informed as the Civil Servants this will continue. Many Civil Servants have, in private, a very low opinion of a great many elected representatives, I believe justified.

The most hopeful development for the future is that the general public are becoming much better informed and better educated than they were – even if there is a great deal further to go and in time they may expect and demand a different approach. I hope so.

Thanking you for this opportunity and congratulations again.
✤

from N Haynes, Warstock, Birmingham

Sir,

I listened to this debate with great interest and if Parliament itself performed like this then televising of Parliament would be a great success. Incidentally, the curtailing of speeches made the debate more incisive.

I was impressed by the courtesy of the speakers and found, for the first time, politicians have an acceptable human face. If I had to cast a vote it would go to Mr Crossman and his colleagues. Mr Crossman's closing speech was a model of clarity and effectiveness.

If, as Mr Crossman said, the effect of these committees would be to leave more time for debating crucial issues then we would have a lively House of Commons which would give to Michael Foot the cut and thrust of rival politicians.

Finally, with the increasing complexity of modern living, the House of Commons does need reforming and if at the same time the MPs could regain a modicum of respect from the GBP this would be a revolution indeed. ✤

from Ewan Davies, Cardiff

Dear Sirs,

I watched the programme *State of the Nation* on Tuesday and Wednesday evening last, and was fascinated by it.

I am writing in response to your invitation for comment 'for' or 'against' the Resolution moved by Mr Anthony Crosland.

On balance, I am in favour of Mr Crosland and his colleagues. Certain telling points were made by them notably the point by Mr du Cann that tax legislation was so complex that it was necessarily best referred to a Select Legislative Committee. I also agree with the exhortation that MPs get out and about, and be seen to be out and about, enquiring and finding out how legislation is affecting the citizen; and I think a natural requirement to further this end is the investigatory Select Committee. Again, most telling, were the figures produced by Mr Mackintosh of the persons in the Chamber on Tuesday night, when only four committees were sitting.

The fear by those opposing the motion that the creation of further committees would strip the Chamber of its prime function was not, I feel, justified. Debates in the Chamber have declined not due to the existence of committees, nor is the decline likely to be increased by the setting up of further committees. Badly informed debate does lead to political ping-pong. Let the committees be set up; let them do their work; and then let the issues return to the Floor of the House for more informed debates.

Further, what an excellent public relations exercise your programme was! Politicians, like lawyers, are unfortunately regarded by the vast majority of the population as deceitful crooks.

The programme indicated what first class brains were available to represent the voter. Was the programme not a complete justification for the introduction of television into the Chamber? It has been said that television would lead to even more political ping-pong, but I consider that it would bring the working spirit and sincerity of the politicians home to the voter in a most telling way, as demonstrated over the last few nights.

Reading Hansard may have been a feasible method of communication in more leisurely times, but now that every other institution is examined (if not put on trial) by television, why should the most important institution of all, be neglected or spared?

I would therefore agree that many MPs are not sufficiently informed to carry out their tasks as ably as they might; that further Select Committees would be a considerable tool in aid to the MP; that on Report Stage to the Floor of the House the debates would be much more informed and interesting, and lead to much higher attendance figures; and if the end product was then televised to the nation, we might see that we were not in such a bad 'state' after all!   ✣

from Mrs J Wharton, Sunderland, Co Durham

Dear Sir,

In your programme *The State of the Nation* the 'mix and match' presentation of MPs was a deception to which I take exception. A precedent for unipolitics to be presented on television is being established. The BBC have twice used this method of presentation. Who gives television producers the freedom to give the nation this false image of British politics? The essence of Parliament and the election of MPs has for hundreds o years been one of a rigid party system. The parties are lined up on opposite sides of the House. It is an exceptionally brave or foolish MP who crosses the Floor to vote against the collective wisdom of his party.

It is dangerous to present MPs out of the context of their party setting. The impression is fostered that there is nothing to choose between one MP and another; they are merely part of the power machine conniving together to legislate for some vague common purpose not specified to the electorate.

Who then do we vote for if an MP can argue and vote any way at any time and is open to influence from all-comers? Are we to be persuaded that we have no identifiable protagonists fighting to preserve whatever we think are our rights and interests in the political arena? ✤

from Peter M Westlake, Catsfield, Sussex

Dear Sir,

I am not normally in a position to be able to watch television, but was fortunate enough to be able to watch the debate you presented on *The State of the Nation* last night. I understand that there were two previous programmes, which I missed, and I apologise if anything suggested in this letter has already been covered.

The motions of the debate were variations on the necessity and method of acquiring information from the Executive by Members of Parliament. To comment, first, on the debate, I must agree with the member who complained about the 'hyperbole of the motions'. There are very few occasions in life when the solution to a problem lies solely between two alternatives and the suspicion arises that debates based on such polarisation are exercises for pleasure rather than serious attempts to achieve satisfactory solutions. I bring this point up since it is a common reaction which detracts from the reputation of the House.

Because of this, it was difficult to evaluate each argument properly since it was apparent that both sides were forced into exaggerated postures. However, it became clear that the problem was, as Michael Foot said, 'a question of balance' between Select Committees and the Floor of the House itself. Enoch Powell arguing that it would be a disaster to democracy if the Commons were to lose its power of disconcerting the

Executive (agreed) and claiming that the Select Committee would, if used more extensively, reduce the authority of the House. This is naturally a hypothetical argument since the position doesn't yet exist and therefore cannot be proven. However, it appears to be a strong fear among people of considerable knowledge and intelligence. Therefore, as an outsider, one is forced to accept the possibility that this may be true.

The argument for Select Committees, legislative Select Committees at least, is extremely strong. They are said to provide facilities for extended cross-examination of Ministers and of Civil Servants which I do doubt would extract significantly more information than the normal question time in the House. However, no-one disputes that this may well be true. The dispute is that it were better to suffer from lack of knowledge and to keep the authority of the House, than to be expert in a field and lose the power of decisive action.

There is a simple solution that would (I have unfortunately only the information that was presented last night to work on) satisfy each side of the debate. In other words, to have Select Investigatory Committees and yet maintain, without question, the authority of the House. As I understand it, a Select Committee of this kind is comprised of chosen Members, who investigate proposed legislation by cross-examination of witnesses. Cross-examination in a court of law is undertaken by prosecuting counsel. The prosecuting counsel does not then make a decision on the facts. That is left to a jury. Now it appears that Members are expected to be prosecutor, judge and jury on a committee plus undertaking their other functions as MPs. This strikes me as being absurd and unnecessary.

It is unquestionable that an MP has sufficient work for him to do in the House and in his constituency. I would like to draw your attention to a phrase that occurs in all other walks of life – 'delegation of responsibility'. Many people detest it. They feel unhappy when they themselves cannot do everything. However, necessity is just that. Here is a classic case where it is essential to delegate. If each Member of Parliament had a special investigatory assistant whose duty it was to attend such committees and act on behalf of his MP there would be no conflict between House and committee work. Remembering that such committees are purely investigatory and not decision-making the position is analogous to magistrate and constable.

It has been apparent for my lifetime that the complexity of modern government has increased beyond the capacity of normal procedures and for any extra demands to be placed on Members would not improve the situation since it would inevitably lead to deficiencies elsewhere. To sum up, a special assistant would act, if you like, as a detective for his MP passing on condensed reports to him and keeping him fully informed in his constituency or about happenings in Europe should he not be tied up on a committee. I feel sure that this is by no means a new idea, but since it was not brought up in the debate I felt I must re-contribute it and show that it has at least some support outside of Parliament. ⚜

from Jenni Merrall, Byfleet, Surrey

Dear Sir,

I am seventeen, and I listened to all three of your programmes. I found it very boring and difficult to understand. I'm sure that most people (like me) found that it dragged on a bit. It would have been better if it had been simplified and shorter.

After about half an hour I couldn't keep my eyes open because of the tedious way things were put. Finally I must say if I hadn't have read the newspapers to find what the programmes were about I wouldn't have known at all, because I couldn't see the point of any of it.

You may say that as I'm only young I wouldn't understand, but this programme should have been aimed at all ages, not just the older people who might have understood. ⚜

from R Fraser, Glasgow

Dear Sirs,

Congratulations on your *State of the Nation* series, which was fascinating.

Starting as an impartial observer, it soon became obvious to me that the present powers of the Commons were inadequate to keep a check on the Government departments.

In the final debate, I gained the impression that Mr Powell and

Mr Foot really believed in an elitist approach. Their view seemed to be that politics was too important and involved to be left to the electorate but should be the preserve of experienced parliamentarians. That is reminiscent of the attitude of the opponents of the Reform Bill in the run up to 1832.

As a general proposition, surely the more information that is available the greater the chance of reaching the right decisions.

One criticism, however – why was there no representative of a minority group invited to take part in the debate? You could have chosen from Liberals, Democratic Labour, Scottish Nationalists or one of the Ulster minorities. That would have given a more balanced panel of speakers.   ♣

from H Birtles, East Sheen, London

Dear Sirs,

May I offer congratulations on your three programmes. They have been one of the best things ever done on TV and I hope the forerunner of a new pattern of informed programmes. The public is indebted to your staff and to those who took part.

I hope too that these programmes will be a step towards breaking down opposition by Parliament (and local councils) to the televising of selected proceedings. Despite the high-minded reasons usually advanced, I am convinced that the real reason is the often low standard of debate which would disgust the public if they knew and saw what went on. What Mr Maudling so aptly described as yah-boo! tactics.

On the motions debated in the series, my view is that legislative Select Committees would help substantially to raise standards. Whatever may be the nominal position, much legislation and subsequent executive action, is instigated by departments. Even the best Ministers are manipulated at times in what departments may consider to be the best interests of all. Sometimes these interests may be influenced knowingly or otherwise, by empire building within departments. This can occur just as easily in Whitehall as elsewhere, in fact perhaps more easily. A more rigorous examination by Select Committees of what goes on in Whitehall could produce valuable results. Most Ministers' basic instincts and interests are to defend their Civil Servants and vice-versa. This is not necessarily synonymous with the public interest. ❧

from R W Ferrand, East Grinstead, Sussex

Dear Sirs,

I want to protest most strongly that you omitted to include any Liberals in your otherwise excellent series on Parliament, *The State of the Nation.*

How you can justify this omission when there are now 10 Liberal Members of Parliament and about 3 million people voted for Liberal candidates in the last General Election and even bigger numbers in recent by-elections and county and district elections beats me.[1] ❧

from W E Walters, The Institution of Engineering Designers, London

Sir,

Debating the motion 'that MPs are too ignorant to do their job properly', those taking part demonstrated convincingly that not one of them is an ignoramus, meaning an ignorant person. At the same time they disagreed on what the job of an MP actually is or is not. Can anybody do his job properly without knowing exactly what it is? ❧

from Victor Bridges, Belfast

Dear Sir,

This was the finest TV documentary that I have seen. I hope it will be shown again.

My principal objection to the working of Parliament is that it assumes that the citizen is not interested in legislation and ought not therefore to be permitted to take part in the democratic process except for the purpose of casting a vote every

[1]See footnote on page 224 for the producer's reply.

five years. It further assumes that Members of Parliament are the only repositories of political wisdom.

The only advance warning to the citizen – unless he makes very special efforts – of proposed legislation is (a) the Queen's Speech, which gives a brief outline only of the principal measures to come before Parliament in the session ahead; and (b) the Parliamentary Diary published, I think, in two daily newspapers, giving the titles of next week's business.

The citizen has virtually no advance warning of proposed legislation and is therefore precluded from expressing his views to his MP.

Lists ought to be published weekly showing the arrangements for parliamentary business for four weeks ahead. These lists should be published in the London, Belfast and (Edinburgh) Gazettes and circulated to the press and public libraries.

The price of Hansard and other parliamentary papers is out of reach of the ordinary citizen. A more widespread distribution of Hansard and parliamentary papers in public libraries is clearly desirable.   ❧

from R A Hetherton, Acton, London

Dear Sirs,

As someone who will be reaching retiring age shortly and who has never cared a damn whether Parliament functioned or not, and even less so *how* it functioned, I have to congratulate you sincerely on achieving from now on electorate participation from one of the (almost) non-voters of this country.

Your quite lengthy commercial on behalf of Parliamentary Democracy was most interesting and perhaps historically valuable in that it showed up the advantages of our system of doing things as against a one-party dictatorship where the 'consumers' simply have to take their rations of whatever they are given. If there was one lasting impression that I had from my four to five hours of compulsive viewing, it was that of high-powered salesmanship on behalf of a political product in competition with the spectre of a prison in the background where MPs might not even be able to talk among themselves any more – as I thought they always had done.

Any ham acting had clearly been cut to a minimum, and everybody was photogenic, competent, intelligent, and apparently well-meaning. I for one am sold on it. ❧

from Elizabeth Bartlett, Stockport, Cheshire

Dear Sir,

As a student who previously had no knowledge of, nor indeed interest in the workings of Parliament, I was drawn to your series of three programmes out of a lazy wish (it being the end of term) to obtain a few easily digestible facts which might educate me a little. I am writing to assure you that I was astonished and thrilled by the series. I have never gone to bed after a television programme so entirely satisfied yet so intellectually stimulated. As a very inexpert judge I heartily congratulate and thank you.

Feeling I should do something in return and prompted by Mike Scott I am writing to record my probably naive reactions. Mr Scott asked us to state with which side of the debate we agreed. If this is all that is needed let me say quite simply (to save you reading further if necessary!) I agree entirely with the proposers of the final motion on Wednesday night.

It seemed to me during the course of the three programmes that grave problems, which have arisen comparatively recently, face Parliament today. Problems of which intelligent and responsible men are all too well aware. In spite of the smoothness of the participants' handling of these three slightly artificial situations, and in spite of their remarkable eloquence (words such as pomposity or verbosity seem perhaps unkind when their job after all is to speak and speak well), these problems could not be hidden.

During the four months inside the Ministry where we watched the progress of the Fair Trading Bill, though nothing could be precisely pin-pointed as misuse of the system, one could feel the tacit acceptance of the idea that this was merely an outward display. Amendments discussed and perhaps accepted would be defeated in the Commons before the Bill became law.

The frightening idea that all this is an utter waste of time was strengthened by Mr Whitehead's account of his experience on a Standing Committee. In the face of his evidence even a layman can see there is room for change, if not as radical as would at first seem desirable.

To move to the final night's work, here Parliament seemed to be presented in miniature. But first one wonders how typical in fact this debate was. We learnt from the speakers that Mr Jennings is an exceptional chairman. Indeed he had no need to chair this debate as the speakers seemed informed, experienced and intelligent. One wonders how often a debate of this standard is seen on the Floor of that House of Commons Mr Powell so much reveres.

Which brings me to my strongest reaction which was horror at the blatant sixth-form tactics even these distinguished politicians used. At the importance they attach to *argument*. The deliberate and continual stressing of opposition and the subsequent loss of individual identity in the adoption of extreme positions.

This was an important matter, yet the age-old quibbling about the wording of the motion, the unwillingness of the opposition to agree with the proposers on any point or concede that their speeches contained any degree of sense, in case this acknowledgement weakened their own argument, raged on with all the eagerness, on the part of some, of schoolboys anxious to win the Debating Cup.

Mr Powell, I felt, was the culprit with others too willing to back him up. His attitude in speech content and method of delivery seemed to epitomise the ideal for which he was fighting. The Glory of Debate, and the glory of the Floor of the House. Perhaps too personally the proposers tried to point out his mistake. There is no glory in oratory. No glory in scoring points against the opposition. This is not the searching examination of the Government the country needs. This sort of showmanship has no relevance to the problems of constituent X who perhaps doesn't even know the name of his own MP let alone follows the debates in his Parliament.

Another point which came out was the extreme fear of America, of the expert, of information in general. It did rather seem that some politicians would prefer to muddle blandly along hoping that the actions of the Government will be revealed 'by accident', by the wit of the MPs or by the method of boring 'repetition'. What an endearing and farcical picture they drew for us! Funny, if it were not that the actual governing of this country is at stake; I was lulled at first into accepting what they said, but thank heavens they were matched by men of equal speaking ability, wit, experience, and with the right priorities. The analogy of the 1838 car is so right. To run a highly complex society on the lines and ideals of another century, when efficient alternatives are available at no loss to the electorate or to the powers of Parliament, is pointless.

I was shattered to discover the prejudices which lie behind the most eloquent speeches of some of our most famed politicians but I must once again thank you, this time for showing the nation that there are such men of integrity, realism, skill and experience as Messrs Crossman, Scott, Mackintosh, du Cann and Crosland who have the interests of the nation at heart when they recognise the sorry state of her Parliament.

✤

from Roland Hall, Reader in Philosophy, University of York

Dear Sirs,

Congratulations on an excellent series of programmes! They were all interesting and useful, sometimes exciting. They convinced me that Parliament should be televised, because they showed it was possible to have undistorted televised debate.

But they also persuaded me that the system of government needs reform, which I did not believe before. It was clear that back-benchers with amendments are fobbed off with cynical reassurances when they ought not to be; and the quality of the Civil Service is lower than I had suspected. I had no idea Civil Servants worked so hard on Bills, but their thinking seemed stereotyped and unimaginative. No doubt this is why the Government has had to introduce the think-tank.

What I most enjoyed in the series was the civilised method of debate in the final programme, when MPs *gave way to each other,* without bickering, in order to pursue genuine argument. None of that 'point of order' stuff that so spoils all other debates I have attended. ✤

from Desmond B Dorrian, Saltcoats, Ayrshire

Sir,

What an enlightening series of programmes!

Maude is not really such a cold fish. Foot *is* intelligent. Crossman has authority and du Cann has more than a silver spoon in his mouth. Seeing and hearing MPs out of their normal pigheaded pedantic party roles is a revelation!

This series has certainly restored my faith in our parliamentary system. If Select Committees will show us more of this type of reasoned, able argument I'm all in favour – and the first party to somehow incorporate and project this new image of MPs into their party political broadcasts will gain enormously.
❧

from Frank R Argent, London SE22

Dear Sir,

Having watched with considerable interest the three parts of this absorbing subject, I was left with the feeling that, apart from its undoubted value in showing how things are done, it posed more questions for the general public than it really answered.

For instance, the MPs themselves appeared to be uncertain of their proper role; is it to represent the views expressed by their constituents or merely to tce the party line, or again merely to give parliamentary approval to schemes dreamed up by the Civil Servants? Why, if Parliament is concerned, as it should be, with the well-being of the nation and its future, should it be influenced by pressure groups who, by their very nature, can only represent selfish sectional interests, or is it that the major political parties are themselves no more than pressure groups of a deeper and more significant kind?

One thing is obvious: to keep employed in their chosen profession, they need our votes, and it would be interesting to discover just how much this need influences their parliamentary behaviour.

I happen to be one of those who no longer vote at elections, simply because I feel that I have no real choice in the Dutch Auction-type way they are conducted, we never get a clear-cut opportunity to register our opinions on major issues, like the Common Market (which I agree with as a measure of defensive strategy), capital punishment, or the obvious failure of our penal system.

The shortage of houses, is an instance of a hardy perennial, used for the last fifty years as a vote-catcher by simply promising to build X number of houses a year, while concealing how many will be demolished for whatever reason, the result being that the shortage persists and prices rocket.

I also happen to be a retired fitter and turner who left school at the age of twelve, so can fairly claim to express grass root opinions to the extent of the discussions I have with others while enjoying a pint in the local.

Having regard to the fact that Parliament, and its procedures, are still held in thrall by the historical precedents of its six or seven hundred years' existence, of course it needs to be remodelled into twentieth century terms, but I doubt very much whether the members of the club are likely to initiate a move in this direction, preferring, as now, to retain their freedom of action, and relying on the votes of a largely politically illiterate electorate to maintain the *status quo*. Meantime we as a nation slip further down the scale of world influence and power.

Ah – well!!   ✤

from Dr Robert L Bradford, Director, Susquehanna at Oxford, Oriel College, Oxford

Gentlemen,

As an American professor of politics currently visiting your country, I took very great interest in your extraordinarily fine series on the decline of Parliament aired over the past three nights. I found myself more in agreement with Messrs Mackintosh, Scott, Crossman and Crosland than with the other side.

Could you tell me if you have any current plans to distribute these films or tapes to commercial or educational agencies in the US. They would be extremely helpful to those of us university professors who try to teach British politics. My own students, for example, would find them engrossing. They are, in short, an excellent teaching aid. I certainly hope you will in future make them available in America.[1]   ✤

from Jean M Lucas, Constituency Agent, Putney Conservative Association

Dear Sirs,

Many congratulations on your absorbing presentation of parliamentary procedures in action, and proposals for their reform. I am glad the programme was timed late enough for those of us engaged in politics to see it, and it proved compulsive viewing for those interested in the country's administration.

For me perhaps the most revealing aspects were the 'timewasting' nature of the work of the Standing Committees because these are run on party lines, and the lack of effect of committee amendments on the Bill. If the average MP engaged on committee work is so ineffective, it is a wonder that anyone is willing to do the job, and it is *no* wonder that the electorate is increasingly disillusioned by, and uninterested in, 'political ping-pong'.

I believe the electorate has a wistful desire for 'coalition' politics and would like to see a measure emerging at the end of the legislative process as a sensible, realistic, foolproof law. We are paying our legislators to legislate, and I believe the electorate wants them to do this rather than to indulge in permanent bickering. This is why the word 'political' is rapidly becoming a dirty word for the man in the street. To achieve a lessening of the battle of politics in committee it would probably be better if those proceedings were in private.

If committee proceedings are more private, then the main debates in the Chamber should be more public. Here the clear-cut party divisions have their rightful place and should be emphasised so that voters know the differences and can feel a closer identity with both the politicians and the decisions made on their behalf. TV coverage of debates, to which your programme incidentally has converted me, would surely

[1] Film or videotape copies of the programme may be bought or hired from The Film Librarian, Granada Television, Manchester M60 9EA.

improve attendance on the Floor of the House, about which concern was rightly expressed.

The ordinary man in the street gets his politics from TV (or radio) anyway, and is it not better to give access to the authentic debate or the edited highlights of it, rather than confine him to pseudo-political entertainment programmes in which sometimes those without political responsibility tend to sneer at, and decry the efforts of those who have it. TV participation is only an extension in principle of the concept of the public gallery.

The proceedings of the party conferences now achieve a pretty wide viewing audience and become more real and meaningful without coming to any harm. I think we urgently need to make Parliament more meaningful to the electorate if we are to have a good poll of enlightened voters at the next General Election. The present mood of 'a plague on both your Houses', shown by a swing to the Liberals at by-elections, is unhealthy and unenlightened.

The programmes made out a good case for reform of parliamentary procedures, and while this is my personal opinion, I also know from my professional experience, that many electors in the constituencies feel it is already overdue. ⚜

from Roger Elliot, London SW7

Gentlemen,

What emerged most forcibly from last night's debate was the ability of experienced speakers to conduct a rational, keenly argued discussion without the presence of a TV interviewer.

The debate showed how politicians could reason rather than make party points; could combine humour with passion; and could provide an enthralling two-hour programme purely through talk.

I should like to see a series of such debates, say at monthly intervals, through the coming winter. They would serve to focus attention on Westminster attitudes as well as give superb entertainment. The topics to be discussed need to combine some philosophy with factual policies, and the more they cross party boundaries the better.

This programme raised my respect for MPs more than any other public discussion I can remember. I want more of them.
⚜

from Robert O Whitaker, Bedford

Dear Sirs,

I have always taken a completely cynical view of MPs and, strangely your programme of 25 July *The State of the Nation* when a debate was shown, merely served to reinforce even more strongly that cynicism. Here we were presented with an assortment of MPs of notoriously divergent party loyalties arguing for the most part on the essentiality of maintaining the cut and thrust of party political argument, and at one and the same time, by their very presence, contradicting this point by virtue of their standing shoulder to shoulder with hitherto supposed enemies.

I don't find this at all cheering – to my mind quite simply a Tory is a Tory is a Tory and a Socialist is a Socialist is a Socialist. The precise difference in their ideologies renders it quite impossible to me that they could at any time agree if only purely on grounds of party dogma.

At the same time this does not mean I approve of such a system – our history, and that of all nations in the world, has been be-devilled by the curse of dogmatism, the only ones to benefit having always been the power hungry individual.

Yes – we do need a new kind of MP – yes – we do need to sweep away the cloth cap and the top hat images adhered to so lovingly by Mr Foot and Mr Powell – let's get rid of Tories and Socialists – let's have good government instead for *all* the people, not just favoured sections of the community as dictated by whatever government is in power today. What we want and need are people who care about people – not party dogma – the problem is, I believe, due to the fact that MPs like Mr Maude live in the past, steeped in so much tradition that they have forgotten that the world has changed dramatically, is still changing at an alarming rate and will continue to do so.

I had the final impression I was listening to a collection of professional speakers who, given any other subject, would have spoken just as enthusiastically either for or against, whichever was most attractive to them, rather like barristers who can one day be prosecuting, the next day defending, yet able to lunch sociably with their opposing counsel – the ultimate in hypocrisy. I want my MP to mean what he says and really, really believe it – I don't think the average MP today does – any label will do so long as he can be a professional MP.

❧

from H B Mackinnon, Birmingham

Dear Sirs,

In response to your suggestion at the end of the series may I please make the following few observations?

Enthralled by all three programmes may I first offer very sincere congratulations on such a magnificent effort. A devoted BBC viewer, for once I felt that the 'other channel' was one up.

The first programme, one felt, was easily the most interesting with a decline through the second one to the last. This was due mainly to the pretty obvious superiority of the Civil Servants, both apparently in knowledge and in ability to argue and reason.

The politicians on the last night were not helped by the somewhat hyperbolic phrasing of the motions before them. However they did little to enhance their reputations. There were exceptions, notably Mr Crossman and Mr du Cann, but the usual 'yes it is – no it isn't' type of argument was really too apparent. One could see why their standing in the country is not as good as it could be. Why do they have the feeling that under all circumstances they must oppose irrespective of the merits or demerits of the proposition?

Both in the presentation and fact the supporters of more Select Committees had the edge. The decisive argument in favour of such control was not too well put. Every managing director knows that he has to solve the dilemma of conflicting advice from experts. His solution, surely, is to confront and cross-examine them directly. How the Commons used as a debating chamber with no such direct confrontation can be of use, with the important exception of non-technical matters, it is hard to see.

In conclusion may one suggest that the series did reinforce the oft held belief that television reveals a person's real character. One was fascinated to see the complete arrogance of Mr Powell and his apparent inability to see, or one felt, even to believe the possibility, that he could be in error.

Similarly the eagerness of Michael Foot to seize only upon those points which fitted his own pre-conceived ideas was plain to see.

Thank you again very much indeed. That very tender flower that we call Democracy was well served.   ❧

from Mrs A Chessell, Lyme Regis, Dorset

Some reform is necessary so that time allotted for debates is not wasted by the schoolboy antics and jests of MPs. This is witnessed by members in the public gallery and brings contempt – one is ashamed to witness the amazement felt by overseas visitors at such actions. If our local council behaved thus, the proceedings would be suspended until members remembered their responsibilities to the electorate. Reformers, however, need to guard against excessive probing and searching – witch hunts and inquisitions show unpleasant faces. Moderate reform – yes – Watergate Committee – No!
❧

from Theodora Higgins, Welwyn Garden City

Dear Sirs,

First, I plead with you to show this series again, and if possible at an earlier hour. It could easily be broken into halves, before and after the 10 pm news. It was by far the best programme I ever saw, politically (though I was unable to watch all of it because my husband insisted on the Show Jumping and something else trivial). Your series, to my mind, ranks with Sir Kenneth Clarke's *Civilisation* for its level of wide-ranging intelligence, easy presentation, and not talking down to the audience. All qualities, as rare as they were stimulating. I felt better for hearing you all, though wishing you were more numerous in Parliament.

Since I was deprived of hearing the whole of each night, my opinion is of doubtful value and may even be wrong, but I have a few things to say:

About the Civil Service and the Fair Trading Bill: I was left with an extremely bad taste and it still bothers me. The attitude of most of the speakers, and especially all of the Civil

Servants, was so aloof as to make me feel either they or I did not live in the present world. I felt they were not on the side of the problem they were dealing with. The liquidisers they bought never broke down and their retailer shrugged off responsibility. They never ordered one colour and had another delivered, of stove, carpet, or anything. They lived in a privileged world . . . where customers' complaints are (sometimes) taken seriously. They know enough law to protect themselves from anything that happens to lesser people, and worse, they seemed to think that 'we' get what we deserve. One man said as much, in effect. I always had a cynical suspicion that this attitude existed and hoped to be proven wrong. I went to bed feeling bereft and as though nobody but Sally Oppenheim cared. The Civil Servants also seemed more anxious to smooth over her possible complaints than to tackle consumers' problems. My husband, a real old Waldron Smithers type, was hurt even more. He honestly believed his party's speeches, through the years, and is now disillusioned and says he won't vote for anybody.

The second night, on money, was better in that the speakers on the whole were more involved in their subject, and the level of argument was high. But I got the impression, from what I heard, and it was not all, that nobody really cared deeply when things went mildly wrong. Please don't think I'm a crusader or expect fervour or that you find easy solutions. But over the years I've seen so many highly touted plans go wrong, right back from the groundnuts scheme . . . that I feel it only right for Members and Ministers to take extra care to prevent similar things from happening again.

This brings me to the last session, the question of special committees. You all spoke well (I missed three, and regret it) and with conviction. Bless you all for no political bias. If you knew how tedious that is generally, and what inherent vote-catching power there is in straight unostentatious remarks, you would treat each other in public, the way I suspect you do in private. The best of you do that already, but I won't be specific because I admire you all. About the committees though, I was convinced by the speakers in favour of them. The Canadian parliament has introduced them and none of their members wish to go back to the old ways now.

I'd just like to give my reason for this. I have the impression that debates in the House are important for the individuals concerned, and generate much heat – though I often wonder how real that is, and if it isn't like the pretty flickerings in the electric fire logs – just for show. But in the end you all vote according to your own side, and the issue is what it was always going to be – decided previously in the Cabinet, or by the Minister and his Civil Servants. (Perhaps even vice-versa in that last phrase.) So I've become disillusioned with debates because so rarely do they end in anything which even *I* could not predict. I would hope that if Select Committees were staffed by specialists and had the respect which knowledge always should command among intelligent people, that in time the proven worth of the committees would filter through.

It is because you are all, every single one, such obviously intelligent men, that an appeal to your reason could be profitably made. Of course, it may be, you are not able to use your intelligence the way you prefer, and have to be politicians first, and thinkers second. If this is the case, it is sad for the country, and for you in your jobs, and for us as citizens.

On a purely personal note, it was a joy to listen to you all, an intellectual treat, and I thank you for the time you gave. If you have any influence with ITV, do try to get the whole thing shown again.   ✤

from Jon Wonham, Morpeth, Northumberland

Dear Sir,

re: Are MPs too ignorant to do their job? – a response to this final request for viewer participation.

1. During this debate it became obvious that each speaker had a different idea about what the function of an MP should be.

2. It is crucial that there should be agreement on this matter before deciding whether, in general, MPs are too ignorant to do their job.

3. Personally, I think more recognition should be given to the fact that the country is really being run by professional Civil Servants, who are also constantly drawing on the advice and expertise of specialists and consultants in various fields. MPs may be reluctant to admit this!

4. Parliamentarians complain about the little opportunity they have to affect the progress of legislation through the

House of Commons, i.e. how few amendments are accepted, etc, in spite of the present number of Standing and Select Committees.

5. But, according to a recent article by Barbara Castle in a colour supplement, speaking as an ex-Cabinet Minister, she was often up against tremendous intransigence on the part of her Permanent Secretary to implement her sincerely held political views while in office, and had to accept compromises and watered-down versions on the advice of Civil Servants.

6. Is it surprising then, that run-of-the-mill MPs feel ineffectual when even Ministers are curtailed by the Mandarins of Whitehall?

7. It seems that the administrative Civil Servants have (perhaps rightly) adopted the view that they know better than the politicians. The Minister has to get the legislation, as drafted by the Civil Servants, through Parliament.

8. It would greatly hinder the efficient running of the Civil Service if Civil Servants were subjected to cross-examination by 'expert' MPs as suggested by Mr Crossman. It is better that the Minister should be cross-examined, MPs should acknowledge that on technical matters, by the very nature of their occupation, they are probably less well-informed than the Civil Servants. It is inevitable, therefore, that about 99.9% of the content of Bills has to be accepted without amendment.

9. My conclusion is that MPs are best qualified to debate matters of principle than to become excessively involved in committee work. They should spend more time in their constituencies and in the country at large assessing the situation. The main role of Parliament should be enacted on the Floor of the House of Commons.   ✤

from Helen M. Brown, Edinburgh

Dear Sirs,

Your programmes were excellent, if a little late at night to catch any but the faithful.

They were stimulating, immensely informative and clarified much of the mystery of the everyday working of the Select Committees, and the manoeuvrings of the interest groups both within parties and also inter-party. Most importantly the programme gave a real insight for the general public of the intricacies and burdensome detail of the government machine. It displayed admirably the till now, for me at least, strange interaction between Ministers, Opposition and the Civil Servants themselves. It also humanised and flattered the MPs. The debate which wound up the programme was fascinating and extremely entertaining. It led me, for one, to support Dick Crossman and his colleagues on their motion for the removal of much of the technical argument to committee rooms to leave the House more time for the more controversial debates. Parliament certainly does need reforming, but many of us would never have known how drastic and how important those reforms must be if it was not for six hours of really good television.

I do not particularly support access television, perhaps for the wrong reasons, but your programme has thrown massive weight behind the argument for televising Parliament. Congratulations.   ✤

from Mrs Mary R Dain, King's Norton, Birmingham

Dear Sirs,

May I send to all concerned my warmest congratulations on your production of *The State of the Nation*. I cannot pay you any higher tribute than to say that I agree with every word of Peter Lennon's review in this week's *Sunday Times*, unless, perhaps, his final sentence. Surely our MPs have already enough on their plates without being additionally 'handicapped' by television?

It seemed to me that the politicians came out of this searching but fair examination remarkably well. What came over for me was their total commitment both to their job and to the Parliament they serve, the incredible amount of work a great many of them must put in, and their sheer professionalism. A better understanding of their task by the general public would, I should think, do nothing but good, while more exposure and hence more criticism might, perhaps, discourage the excessive, futile and often deliberately obstructive scoring of party political points on every possible occasion which does, perhaps, do more than anything to exasperate the more thoughtful voter.

This admirable experiment does seem a triumphant vindication of the case for televising at least some aspects of the work of Parliament and to provide at least a partial answer to some of Milton Shulman's strictures. To do so more fully, however, programmes of similar quality, if not of such depth, would have to be available to a wider public at an earlier hour!

On your specific question as to how one would vote on the final debate, I find it difficult to answer – but, I think, should in the end come down on the side of Richard Crossman's team, if only for the reason that the sheer volume of work does seem to be getting out of hand. Anything that could lead to greater efficiency and the lessening of party bickering on the Floor of the House about trivialities would seem desirable and his words and experience did carry conviction. One does regret the fact that so many excellent Private Members' Bills never see the light of day and that it was left to the House of Lords to spot the offending 'retrospective clauses' in the recent Immigration Bill. More time for Commons debates on the broader issues and for the detailed examination of Bills by a legislative Select Committee might avoid such happenings. If there are not enough Members for such work, perhaps we should have more Members of Parliament? Certainly some areas seem to need more representation. But one does not want to introduce too many red herrings!

Altogether it was a most stimulating and illuminating experience and a very timely one. For those of us who sometimes despair of ever regaining an informed and responsible electorate and can well understand the attitude of Tom Stacey your trilogy came as a most welcome shot in the arm.

I hope it receives the reaction it deserves and shall await developments with interest. ❧

from Dr D W Budworth, London, W4 1DP

Dear Sirs,

At the end of the programme on Wednesday, 25 July, you invited comments from the general public. On the understanding that the invitation covers comments on the issues raised by the programme, I am writing this letter.

First, I think it was very good to see such a considerable expenditure of effort, money, and broadcasting time devoted by Granada and the ITV network to the subject of the state of Parliamentary democracy, even if commercial considerations meant that the three parts of the programme had to be transmitted at an hour when I, at least, am not at my most receptive to matters of this importance.

In making more detailed observations, I should perhaps say that, as a CBI official, I have a somewhat nearer view of Parliament and Government than most citizens, although I have been less closely involved than those of my colleagues who appeared in the programme. In particular, I have followed the work of the Select Committee on Science and Technology fairly closely for the last two years and have appeared before it as the junior member of a CBI group. The opinions expressed in this letter are, of course, my own, and not those of the CBI.

It seems to me that the crux of the matter of Parliamentary control of HMG was correctly identified by Michael Foot when he said in the programme that the reform party (to give them a convenient label) were essentially advocating a more bi-partisan, coalition approach to government by their advocacy of more use of Select Committees, both investigatory and legislative. I think he is quite correct in his diagnosis, but I am strongly in favour of such a development – indeed, I would put the aim of producing more universally-accepted policies first, and the means of achieving it second – whereas Mr Foot wishes to preserve the party struggle. Anthony Lejeune's article in *TV Times* is surely right in saying that as long as the Commons continues to divide at least for voting purposes, along strictly party lines then its prestige will continue to decline.

More importantly, it seems to me that the country will be badly governed as long as this behaviour continues, because of the relaxation of the control of the Executive which results from it. As was pointed out by Sir William Armstrong, it often happens that legislation rushed through by a government in full control of the Commons needs to be amended within a short time, when its deficiencies appear. At a time when the direct influence of HMG over the day-to-day life of the country is increasing, the tendency to change policy, not only when the party in power changes, but even within one government, is an increasingly important factor in the poor economic progress of the country.

A more informed Parliament composed of responsible Members would be much less inclined to fall in with the convenience of the government of the day, and Select Committees seem to be the best way of producing the information. If, however, Parliament is to become sufficiently well-informed to debate on equal terms with Ministers and with the outside pressure groups of which it is increasingly jealous, it must take a leaf out of their book and not merely provide itself with Select Committees, of which it may well have enough already, but must give those Committees adequate staff. This is the main burden of my letter: Select Committees can do much good in their present form, but they will not be really effective without adequate staff. I am not suggesting that they all need the Comptroller and Auditor-General and his 600 staff, but they must have enough people to brief them on the relevant literature, the past history, and the current thinking in informed circles, so that their political contribution can be set in an effective framework.   ❖

Appendix 1

A note on Part 1 by Roger Graef

The chief significance of *A Law in the Making – four months inside a Ministry* was that it was made at all; it was the first time in history that cameras were permitted to film the internal workings of the Civil Service and Ministers at work on legislation – without being staged (or re-enacted) for the viewers. It is only a partial record, of merely the Committee Stage of a Bill (the Fair Trading Bill). We were not permitted to film the proceedings of the Committee itself, or of the Chairman selecting amendments or the Clerk receiving them. We were tightly bound inside the Palace of Westminster; filming only in interview rooms booked in advance by an MP, or in MPs' offices. It was only permissible to film in the Chamber and corridors when empty (not even a reporter may be filmed there) and before 10 am. So, we missed much of the goings-on, the informal chats in the lobby or corridors, as well as the debates themselves. This is a meaningful omission, for it has been pointed out that our film gives a picture of the legislative process that seems to take no account of the actual arguments put forward in the debates.

Though we could hardly have done otherwise, it is a good point, I think. But the Civil Servants and Ministers clearly use arguments of principle in making most of their decisions about amendments – though the question of how they deal with them becomes a matter of tactics. Politics is just that – a mix of principle and tactics, and I feel we were able to show that mix more honestly than either a summarised report or a studio discussion or even glimpses of the debates by themselves would do.

As already described it took many months of negotiations to gain approval, first in principle to allow Civil Servants to be filmed – and then in particular to find a Minister and a specific Bill which would be acceptable to all the parties concerned – the Government, the Civil Service and us with our needs as producers of television.

The rules we adopted for making the film were as follows:
(1) Having agreed on the Bill, to focus on a short list of sub-

jects – two or three Clauses and film only those discussions relevant to them. The choice was worked out in consultation with the Minister and Civil Servants but the final choice was made by us, not them. We needed a matter which would be clear enough to the audience without elaborate explanation. (2) We required access to all meetings at which these subjects might come up – no matter how informal. In fact, we missed certain of these because the mechanics of informing us of the meetings rested in their hands, not ours, and if it was only forgetfulness that interfered we missed a step. Also, we did not have free access to the Minister – we only filmed him at the briefing meetings he called himself – so his telephone calls and informal meetings were not covered. But the Civil Servants' were, and so we have a good account of their contribution to this stage of the Bill. As the guidelines were already established at Second Reading, the bulk of the work was left to them, so as an account of the decision-making process it seems to us a fair one. The Minister tended to check and approve or disapprove work done by the Civil Servants, rather than doing it himself. (3) We used no lights, conducted no interviews, and interfered as little as possible with the proceedings themselves (other than asking MPs to meet in the few places we could film). Our attempt was to become part of the furniture, which is rather inaccurately described as a 'fly on the wall'. In fact we used the absolute minimum of equipment, and kept all unnecessary team members out of the room. Often cameraman Charles Stewart and sound recordist Iain Bruce were filming on their own – we tried hard, as a matter of principle, never to outnumber the participants. We would never suggest that our film is 'reality' as would happen without cameras – merely that the participants were, on the whole, pleasantly surprised at their ability to carry on despite our presence. One key Civil Servant attributed this more than anything else to our decision to film throughout the course of the arguments on our chosen Clauses rather than to appear briefly and switch on only at the dramatic moments. Once accepted, there we stayed, and continued to film – thus we became part of the circumstances surrounding those Clauses.

In the end it took us from January to May 1973 to keep track of the discussions around our subject: we had happened on two Clauses that involved endless circling around the basic principles of the Bill. To compress the fifty hours of film of these discussions into ninety minutes and still be faithful to the events, involved Film Editor Terence Twigg in a delicate process of extraction – leaving out anything that might be irrelevant, and retaining enough repetition to be characteristic of the circuitous route the decisions had taken. It was a formal decision by all of us to resist the temptation to compress and clarify the material still further – it would have made a more entertaining film, but one untrue to the events, and one which would have presented a false picture of the process of law-making that we had been able to witness.

Appendix 2

An extract from an article by Dr Mallory Wober of the Independent Broadcasting Authority's research staff

Figures provided by JICTAR show that the Monday programme was seen by 1,240,000 adults, Tuesday's by 2,000,000 adults, and Wednesday's debate by 1,210,000 adults.

We know something also, of the make-up of the audience. The social class of individuals is categorised from 'AB' (upper and upper middle classes) to 'DE' at the opposite end of the scale. One might expect that a demanding set of programmes like *The State of the Nation*, in which there is little 'entertainment' and in which much of the significance and meaning is implied rather than brought out and underlined by the producers, would appeal to the ABs. The DE groups might lose patience with such programmes. But the data do not support such ideas. The general public contains some 12% who occupy the AB social class range, and between 8 and 12% of this group watched the programmes on different nights. There are 33% of DEs in the general population; but between 40 and 44% of the audience on different nights was made up of DE viewers. The DEs generally are more diligent viewers, so we may expect a greater part of the TV audience to be DE, than is implied by their proportion in the public as a whole. Nevertheless, the programmes clearly did not scare away DE viewers, and the proportion of these in the audience on the three days was fairly constant.

The age of viewers also related to their interest in these programmes. Though there are 17% of young adults between 16 and 24 in the population at large, slightly less of the audience (12–13%) were from this age bracket. Other age brackets up to 54 were represented in the audience very much in the same proportion as they exist in the public at large. But though only 29% in the general population are aged 55 and over, the first night had an audience with 37% in this age range. This proportion was maintained on Thursday; but on Wednesday, 29%, exactly as in the general population, of the viewers were from this oldest category. The three programmes therefore reached a very representative cross-section of the general population; even though overall figures varied somewhat, with more people watching on Tuesday, the proportions of different ages and social classes did not vary much. There are two slight exceptions to this: an initial 'bulge' of older viewers had smoothed out by the third episode; and it appears that among young adults it was more likely that men were watching, while among the oldest adults (as in the general population) a greater proportion of viewers were women.